The Christian Camp Counselor

Becoming A Camp Counselor
After God's Own Heart

BY JIM BADKE

QwanoesPublishing
Box 250 Crofton, BC
Canada V0R 1R0

Qwanoes Publishing is the publishing arm of Camp Qwanoes, a non-profit society operated by member Fellowship Baptist churches in British Columbia, Canada. Qwanoes is a Coastal Salish Indian name meaning "new birth." Copies of this book and other materials may be obtained by contacting the publisher:

Box 250, Crofton, BC, V0R 1R0
Phone: (250) 246-3014 • Fax: (250) 246-3227
E-mail: resources@qwanoes.bc.ca

Anecdotes and case studies presented in this book are composites of actual cases. Names and other details have been changed to protect identities. Male gender pronouns are occasionally used to denote both male and female for the sake of clarity.

Scripture is taken from the *Holy Bible, New International Version®*. NIV®. Copyright © 1973, 1978, 1984 by International Bible Society. Used by permission of Zondervan Publishing House. All rights reserved.

Where marked (NCV), Scriptures quoted from The Youth Bible, New Century Version, copyright © 1991 by Word Publishing, Dallas, Texas 75039. Used by permission.

Scripture quotations marked (NLT) are taken from the *Holy Bible*, New Living Translation, copyright © 1996. Used by permission of Tyndale House Publishers, Inc., Wheaton, Illinois 60189. All rights reserved.

Canadian Cataloguing in Publication Data

Badke, Jim, 1958-
    The Christian camp counselor

Includes bibliographical references.
ISBN 0-9683123-0-6

1. Camp counselors. 2. Church camps. 3. Counseling--Religious aspects--Christianity. I. Title.
BV1585.B32 1998   259'.2 C98-911031-1

Photography, Design & Editor: Scott Bayley
Printed and bound in Canada by Hignell Printing Limited, Winnipeg

To the two finest
"come alongside"
counselors I know:

my mom and dad,
Bert and Anne Badke

ACKNOWLEDGMENTS

My thanks to those who encouraged and edited me through this project: my wife Sarah, Jack Purdie, Bill Badke, Katrina Lockwood, Scott Werdal, Ken Bayley, Scott & Julie Bayley, Phil Castle, Amber Verreault, George Bertness, Brian Joyce, Melissa Holland, Steve Herbert, Jen Witbeck and the Qwanoes CIT's of 1997 and 1998. Your example and input have been the mold that shaped this book.

Thanks also to the several camp veterans who read the draft and offered their analysis and suggestions: H. Norman Wright, Rob Tiessen, Heather Kobielush, David Morrison, Link Wallace, Mary Kay Meeker, Roger Johnson and Dick Angelo. Thanks also to the many other camp directors who responded to our readership survey. Your suggestions and enthusiastic support have been greatly appreciated.

Jim Badke

CONTENTS

SUGGESTIONS ON HOW TO USE THIS BOOK................................7

PART ONE: PREPARING FOR CAMP LEADERSHIP
1. Servant Leadership:
   Following Jesus the Counselor................12
2. Sanctification:
   Made Ready For God's Use................20
3. God's Word:
   Why & How To Read, Study & Live By It................26
4. Prayer:
   God At Work................36
5. Compassion:
   Seeing Every Camper Through Jesus' Eyes................45
6. Responsibility:
   Making Wise Decisions................52

PART TWO: THE CAMP ORGANIZATION
7. The Spiritual Environment:
   The Basis & Purpose of Christian Camping................59
8. Entering the Spiritual Environment:
   Getting Started in Christian Camping................69
9. The Counselor:
   Creating The Spiritual Environment................87
10. The Camper:
    Understanding Age Patterns................116

PART THREE: COUNSELING SKILLS
11. Building Relationships:
    Individual & Group Dynamics................152
12. Helping Individuals:
    Becoming A Caring Listener................166
13. Discipline:
    Principles Of Correcting Behavior................179
14. Leading Bible Discussions:
    Helping Campers Discover Truth................192
15. Communicating Your Faith:
    Leading a Camper To Christ................212
16. Discipleship & Follow-Up:
    Direction For The Christian Camper................229

RESOURCE SECTION:

A. A Story:
    Christ At Home In My Heart............................241
B. Resources for Listening
    Intelligently to Campers' Problems..............246
C. How to Deal with Some
    Specific Discipline Issues............................255
D. Role Plays and Scenarios to
    Help You with Discipline Issues...............266
E. Rainy Day Ideas to
    Keep Your Campers Happy........................271
F. A Workshop to Help You
    Prepare Your Own Bible Discussions...........276
G. Ideas for Creatively Starting and
    Applying Bible Discussions.......................286
H. How to Prepare Your
    Personal Testimony...................................289
I. Ideas for Staying in
    Touch with Your Campers..........................297
J. A Resource List for
    Counselors...303

CAMP PREP BOXES:

#1 Undergo Heart Surgery 25
#2 Develop a Prayer Habit...............................44
#3 Practice Wise Decision-Making 57
#4 Get Yourself Grounded.................................68
#5 Do Your Homework.....................................86
#6 Know Your Job Description 115
#7 Develop Your Age Awareness.......................150
#8 Become Quick to Listen..............................178
#9 Do Some Role-Playing................................191
#10 Make-Your-Own Cabin Devotions.................211
#11 Be Prepared to Share Your Faith 228
#12 Plan Your Long-Term Commitment to Campers.........238

SUGGESTIONS ON HOW TO USE THIS BOOK

The goal of this project is to provide a training resource for camp counselors that is as comprehensive as possible. As a result, the book has turned out a bit lengthy. However, I trust that this will not deter you from considering the many uses of this book, whether you are a prospective counselor or a veteran camp director.

1. If you are a future camp counselor, reading this book will be a great introduction.

It may seem a lot to read, but when you consider the monumental task you are taking on as a camp counselor, this is the kind of preparation you need. Hopefully your camp will round out your preparation with some hands-on training when you arrive there.

2. If you are a camp director, send a copy of this book to new counselors well before summer.

Ask them to read this text and do the **CAMP PREP** suggestions throughout as part of their pre-camp preparation. They can keep the book over the summer and return it to the camp before they leave, or purchase it. Or your camp may consider giving the book to them as an investment in their future.

3. Assign specific chapters of this book to your staff during your staff training time.

You have much more content to get across to your staff than they can absorb in pre-season staff training sessions. Have them read applicable chapters in this book each day in preparation for discussion during your training times, and allow them time in the schedule to find a quiet place to read.

4. Use this manual as the basis of your Counselor-in-Training program.

This book was first developed out of the CIT program of Camp Qwanoes on Vancouver Island in British Columbia. During the first two weeks of the program, CIT's are assigned one to two chapters to read each day as a supplement to training sessions and hands-on instruction and experiences.

This enables the instructors to get across the content they feel is necessary, yet they avoid burdening the training sessions with lecture. Over the years, we have found that trainees are able to absorb the material much better when they not only read or hear it, but also have the opportunity to interact with one another on each topic. The material can be creatively discussed and tried during the training, and the details are left to reading.

5. Give this book to your head counselors as a resource.

The book is formatted to make it easy to find resources and solutions for everyday counselor concerns and problems.

6. Many chapters of this book are adaptable to ministries outside the camp.

There is valuable information and training material here for the Sunday school teacher, kids club worker, Bible study leader and vacation Bible school or daycamp organizer.

ABOUT THE ICONS

Icons are a fun way of getting your attention, pointing out important stuff and showing you where to look for further help:

 "Pay Attention;" there is something here you better not miss.

 "Tricks of the Trade" from veteran counselors, scattered throughout the book.

 Important scripture references.

I THESSALONIANS 2:8

 Find more detail on whatever is being discussed

CHAPTER 14

 It is time to think about "What Would Jesus Do?" in this situation.

INTRODUCTION

The last day of the last camp in the summer is an incredible day. Counselors give tearful good-byes to their campers, while trying at the same time to fit in a meaningful last few words to one another. One hour, hundreds of campers and staff fill the air with shouts, laughter and camera flashes. The next hour, they are all gone.

Those of us who remain often sit on a bank overlooking the camp, not saying much, just staring at the empty field and trees and water, and wondering if the summer really happened or if it was just a pleasant (and exhausting) dream. We wonder if the work of God throughout that summer will take root in the hearts of those he touched, and if it will grow there to produce godly men and women.

In the days to come, we will talk about the summer and complete many evaluations, trying to decide what has happened and how effective it all was. We will avoid comparing this summer to previous ones, because we know from experience that every summer is different.

Why different? The camp property and full-time staff are essentially the same each year, but every summer the counseling, program and support staff are a different combination of personalities. As they combine to form the staff team, a dynamic develops that uniquely shapes the summer.

It is this dynamic—or "dynamo", if you want—that God chooses as his machinery to create change and spiritual progress in the lives of campers. While they and the staff eat, play, laugh, learn and live together in the special environment called "camp," God is at work in an incredible way.

Observing this thing happen every summer, I have learned that as we select staff to come and serve at camp, we are not just looking for a collection of activity skills, administrational ability and counseling experience. We are looking for a certain kind of people. They may be from any race or country or family background, but if they are to form an effective staff team, they must be people after God's own heart.

Not perfect. King David was a man after God's heart, and he was far from perfect. However, there is a reason that God loved this man so much, and why he entrusted the kingdom to him. David's heart had become like God's heart, a little bit anyway. David wanted to love God more than anything on earth, and returned to his arms every time he failed to love God fully. So God entrusted to him his most prized possession: his people.

God could use a person like that. I want you to know from the start that this book is about becoming that kind of person. Plus some counseling skills are offered to make the summer easier. I know you are reading this book because you want to counsel at camp, or you teach counselors at camp, or your camp leader or pastor made you read it. If you have no desire to chase after the heart of God this summer, please close the book, give it back and consider another way to spend your summer.

My prayer, of course, is that you will read this book. I pray that God will move you to become more of a person after his own heart. My hope is that he will be willing to entrust to you his most precious possessions—his campers—and that the experience will be as life-changing for them as it will be for you.

PART ONE:
PREPARING FOR CAMP LEADERSHIP

"I want to see every camper through Jesus' eyes."

1. Servant Leadership: Following Jesus the Counselor

I remember arriving at camp with big expectations and all the enthusiasm of being ten years old. At the registration table they told me that I would be with all my friends, and that my counselor's name was Bob. Bob who? I didn't know any Bob—he wasn't here last summer. I was not impressed. I dragged my bag over to the cabin, determined not to like this new guy.

My determination was short lived. Bob was cool. I guess he was in his late teens or early twenties, short, strong, full of energy. I very soon came to realize that this was not just another guy who was there to make sure we went to sleep on time, and who would get mad at us if we didn't.

Bob genuinely cared about us. He did stuff with us that no other cabin did—like the night we went on a secret mission and had chips, pop and devotions out on the dock. He made every one of us feel worth his while and important. When we talked he paid attention and listened, and he looked right at us. If we were sitting around telling dumb jokes, he laughed with us until we were all rolling off our bunks. When he talked about Jesus, it was as if he was talking about a real guy he knew personally and who mattered to him in everyday life.

I decided that when I got old enough I wanted to be just like Bob. Probably one of the reasons you want to be a camp counselor is that you want to be like someone in your past—maybe a counselor, or some other Christian worker whose example made you sit up and take notice. That's a good reason.

But there is another counselor—The Counselor—whose example is the one your favorite counselor or teacher or youth worker followed. If you want to become like the Counselor Bob of your past, you will need to become like this other Counselor. They called him Jesus.

WHAT IS A CAMP COUNSELOR?

The term "counselor" is used most often in our society to describe a professional—often a doctor—to whom people come with their emotional and psychological needs for professional help. This is *not* what is meant by a "camp counselor" in this book, nor should a camp counselor think that this will be his or her role at camp. Traditionally, the leaders of a small group of children or youth at a camp have been called "counselors." Some camps have moved away from that term because they don't want anyone to assume that the students who lead their cabin groups are professionals; however, "counselor" is still a good word to describe the position of the small group camp leader.

The word "counselor" is found several times in the Bible. Isaiah prophesied that the Messiah would be called, "The Wonderful Counselor."[1] Jesus described the Holy Spirit as "another Counselor" like himself who would remain with his disciples forever.[2] If you were an ancient Greek you would know that the word for "counselor" is *parakletos*, which means, "one who comes alongside." The Holy Spirit comes alongside to daily guide us, comfort us, teach us from God's word, warn us and correct us. This is exactly what Jesus did with his disciples for the three years he was with them. He was their Counselor.

So, if you want an excellent example of a counselor, you should take a good look at Jesus. Read through any one of the gospels and take note of how Jesus spent his time with his disciples. He used everyday situations and each passing bird and twig to teach them the things of God. He let them watch as he prayed, as he healed and as he preached, until they too began to preach and heal and pray like him.

Jesus loved his "campers." He was so patient with them, and yet did not hesitate to put them in their places or even scold them when needed. He allowed those who should have been his servants to be his friends instead, and proved his friendship when he laid down his life for them, taking away their sins. In everything he did with his disciples, Jesus was saying, "This is the kind of leader I want you to be."

JESUS THE SERVANT-LEADER

However, this style of leadership was not what Jesus' disciples were expecting in their Messiah. They were awaiting a warrior-king, who would wipe out the Romans and set up his own government. They thought they would become little rulers under him. The disciples even started a game among themselves called, "Who's the Greatest of Us All"? As they walked from town to town, their conversation often revolved around the question of which of them would have the highest positions in the kingdom of God.

Peter was the most headstrong of the group—perhaps he started the argument. But James and John were the fast movers who came up with a strategy to get into first place. They had their mom go and ask Jesus to make them his right- and left-hand men. They seriously did.

I bet Jesus sighed. Maybe even rolled his eyes. And then, the Bible says,

> *Jesus called them together and said, "You know that those who are regarded as rulers of the Gentiles lord it over them, and their high officials exercise authority over them. Not so with you. Instead, whoever wants to become great among you must be your servant, and whoever wants to be first must be slave of all. For even the Son of Man did not come to be served, but to serve, and to give his life as a ransom for many."*

MARK 10:42-45

You can guess that made them squirm a bit. Slave of all? They wanted nothing less than to be princes in Christ's kingdom! Jesus taught and lived a different kind of leadership than all other examples they saw around them. His motive in coming to earth was not to *be served* or to have his own needs met by his followers. He came to *serve,* and pour himself out to satisfy their needs. He was that kind of counselor, and he expected his disciples to be like him.

WHY DO YOU WANT TO BE A CAMP COUNSELOR?

What is your *motive* in coming to camp as a counselor? Are you doing it to satisfy your own thirst for fun and adventure? Is it for approval from God or from people? Or to meet some special guy or girl? Or even to seek revenge from the time you were a camper? Or are you coming to *serve* the needs of the kids God entrusts to you? Motive matters to God.

One of the great examples of Jesus' servant attitude was when he washed his disciple's feet, a performance not even expected of a slave in those days:

> *When he had finished washing their feet, he put on his clothes and returned to his place. "Do you understand what I have done for you?" he asked them. "You call me 'Teacher' and 'Lord,' and rightly so, for that is what I am. Now that I, your Lord and Teacher, have washed your feet, you also should wash one another's feet. I have set you an example that you should do as I have done for you. I tell you the truth, no servant is greater than his master, nor is a messenger greater than the one who sent him. Now that you know these things, you will be blessed if you do them."*

SEE JOHN 13:1-17

When would they start to understand? On the night before his death on the cross, Jesus needed an object lesson they wouldn't forget. Ever have someone wash your feet? It is hard to say which is more humbling—being the washer or the washee. You tend to remember it. Jesus wanted them to understand that choosing to humble yourself as a servant will not remove from your authority or your credibility with people. It just causes them to love you more.

Jesus was undeniably the greatest leader who ever walked the face of the earth. Why did his unique style of leadership work? Why would people want to follow a servant? When Jesus demonstrated how much he loved them, the people came to love him in return. Napoleon is said to have admitted on his deathbed, "I have tried to conquer the world by force, and have failed. Jesus conquers by love, and he will succeed."

God's plan from the very beginning was to have people who obeyed him because they wanted to, not because they had to, and out of love for him and not fear. God loved the world so much he gave his Son, and we responded and believed in him. We follow Jesus not because he forces us to, but because we love him in return. To obey him is a joy and pleasure.

My experience is that people will generally love and follow us when we serve them as Jesus did. In the movie, "Mr. Holland's Opus," Richard Dreyfuss plays a songwriter who has to return to teaching just to pay the bills. At first he hates it, and his students hate him. Then he begins to care for his students and enter into each individual's life. He challenges them to be more than they are, and teaches them to love music. As a result, they begin to love him and respect him. The closing scene is a huge gathering in which all those whose lives he touched come to pay him honor.

Jesus is the teacher we *want* to work for, the hero whose example we *desire* to follow. We want to be just like him. If you want to be an effective leader and counselor, be like Jesus. To serve and care for your campers in this way will make a huge difference in everything you do as a counselor. A servant attitude will affect how you discipline campers, your method of doing cabin devotions and your commitment to doing follow-up after camp.

What are your reasons for wanting to come to camp as a counselor? What style of leadership will you choose? If you are coming to have your needs met, to be the boss, to know that when you say jump your campers will ask how high, think again. Think of Jesus. He is the kind of Counselor you want to be.

WHAT WILL BEING A SERVANT MEAN IN THE COUNSELING SITUATION?

Let's break it down a bit and get practical. What will it mean to follow Jesus' style of leadership in the various situations you will face as a counselor? Read the following words penned by the Apostle Paul and think of how you as a camp counselor would apply them:

> *Do nothing out of selfish ambition or vain conceit, but in humility consider others better than yourselves. Each of you should look not only to your own interests, but also to the interests of others.*

> *Your attitude should be the same as that of Christ Jesus:*
>   *Who, being in very nature God,*
>   *did not consider equality with God*
>   *something to be grasped,*
>   *but made himself nothing,*
>   *taking the very nature of a servant,*
>   *being made in human likeness.*
>   *And being found in appearance as a man,*
>   *he humbled himself and became obedient to death —*
>   *even death on a cross.*
>   *Therefore God exalted him...*

PHILIPPIANS 2:3-11

1. Look out for your campers' needs before your own.

You look at your glow watch and shake it, but it still reads the same: three in the morning. What woke you up? Then you hear it again—one of your campers up in his bunk is making sniffling noises, accented by the occasional quiet sob. Maybe he is homesick. Probably he wet the bed. It would be so easy to roll over and go back to sleep and pretend you never heard him. So easy, and really you do need to sleep. The campers kept you up an hour past lights out, and you have a right to get some rest. How can you be expected to...

But then you sigh, pull back the covers, get up and deal with it—calmly, gently, feeling compassion for this little creature. It *is* dark in here, and a little spooky. There are noises in the night. And a wet sleeping bag is the worst. An hour later you finally crawl back into bed, glad you took the time to get up and bring help and comfort.

Are you crazy? Should this be expected of any sane person? Maybe not, but if you follow Jesus' style of counseling, this is what you will do. Take on the attitude of Jesus, and you will find yourself looking out for the needs and interests of your campers *ahead* of your own needs and interests. Very extreme idea.

So what about your own personal needs? Ignore them? No, but when it comes to a choice between meeting your own needs or the need of someone under your care, Paul says: *his* need before your own. Examples in the camp environment abound. There is time left for one person to waterski, and you give your turn to a camper. The cook miscounted and your table is one bun short, and you don't get one. That gorgeous counselor wanted to talk with you during free time, but you end up chatting and playing ping pong with a camper who hasn't said two words to you all week. It could really make you feel gypped.

Except for two things: First, because you decided to follow Jesus, you made a *choice* to look out for your campers' interests ahead of your own. Love is your motivation, and it is the greatest motivation in the world. Second, you know that when you pour yourself out to meet the needs of others, God himself will fill up the needy places in your life. It's a promise: "Give and it will be given to you. A good measure, pressed down, shaken together and running over, will be poured into your lap. For with the measure you use, it will be measured to you."[3] You can never out-give God.

2. Place yourself in a position of humility.

Have you ever felt humiliated? I will always remember (though it is forgiven) when my family and I were at the relatives' for Christmas dinner. There were the usual traditions: wolfing down a huge turkey dinner; getting sick on homemade fudge and mandarin oranges; cheating at Rook; that sort of thing. Then out came the home movies (this was before video cameras), and before I knew what was happening, my cousins were rolling around the floor, laughing at the screen. I could have died—it was me as a baby in the bathtub. Though it was unintended, I felt utterly humiliated.

Humiliation is awful, and it is not something God wants for you or expects from you. But Jesus knew about *humility*. Don't let those famous paintings of his crucifixion fool you—Jesus probably hung on that cross with nothing on. The Bible says they even gambled for his underwear! The difference between my humiliation and the humiliation Jesus experienced is this: Jesus was not *being* humiliated; he was *placing himself* in a position of humility. He could have come down from that cross at any time, but he stayed up there out of obedience to his Father and out of love for you and me.

Think about it: with whom did Jesus spend most of his time? People who were as popular as he was? No, he gathered to himself a group of uneducated fishermen, a national traitor, a revolutionary and a few other nobodies. He hung around with the "creepy" people—prostitutes and other local nasties—to the point that he annoyed most respectable people.

At camp, you may be tempted to hang out with the "cool" kids, the ones with the right clothes, the athletes, or maybe the ones who are very much like you. You might have a natural revulsion to the ones who came to camp dirty and smelly and who just get smellier all week, or the ones who for whatever reasons are just not comfortable to be around. But those are the kids Jesus would hang out with, if he were in your shoes.

How did Jesus spend his time with people? He healed them, physically and spiritually, because they were sick. Most of us do not enjoy being around sick people—whether in the medical or moral sense—but Jesus said it is the sick who need a doctor. You will find it a temptation to spend more time and energy on "well" campers than on the "sick" ones. Kids without many personal problems are simply easier to handle. But it was people with problems who received major attention from Dr. Jesus.

Increasingly, kids arriving at camp are from difficult home situations, and some of these are not the nicest kids to be around. Some of the kids from well-off homes can be just as obnoxious, or worse. Will you give them the time they need? Or will you pay more attention to the nice kids, or the "cool" ones, or the intelligent or the good-looking ones? Taking on the servant attitude of Jesus means avoiding favoritism and prejudice. It means giving attention where attention is needed, even if it is not as fun or glamorous as you expected camp counseling to be.

A servant does some pretty humble stuff. Like Jesus washing His disciples' feet. Like a counselor hanging out a camper's wet sleeping bag at 2:00 a.m. Like spending time with that especially unlovable kid. What are you prepared to do for your campers? Your small acts of kindness can make a huge impression on them. The unlovely camper will place more value on your attention than you can imagine. You might find that it is the camper whom no one liked and who got into fights all the time, who later calls to talk about the great time he had, and to ask if he can be in your cabin again next summer.

3. Be ready to sacrifice.

What will you need to sacrifice for your campers? Some days you might think it is your very sanity! They will get on your nerves, stretch your patience, take you to the limit of your temper. They might damage or mess up or steal your stuff, even though the reason you moved your bags into the cabin was to identify with them as part of the group.

But remember that whatever sacrifice you make is a small price to pay for the results: Incredible relationships. Profound memories. Deep conversations. Campers brought from darkness to light. Treasure in heaven. Paul said of his ministry, "I consider that our present sufferings are not worth comparing with the glory that will be revealed in us." [4] In other words, it will be worth the sacrifice.

Follow Jesus and you will find that to be true. He who had all the glory of being God the Son let it out of his grasp and came to earth as a servant to meet our need for a Teacher and Savior. He made the supreme sacrifice so our sins could be removed and we could become the children of God. So God honored and exalted him. It was worth it all.

Again and again I see staff applications coming to camp that say something like this: *"I want to become a counselor because the counselors I had when I was a camper made such a big impression on me. I want to pass that on to other campers."* I am in camp ministry because of people like Counselor Bob. You are reading this book because of the example of some great leader or counselor in your life.

Those were the counselors who were servants like Jesus. When you become more like them, and more like Jesus, it is then that your campers will be drawn to the Savior.

---

[1] Isaiah 9:6
[2] John 14:16
[3] Luke 6:38
[4] Romans 8:18

2.   Sanctified: Made Ready For God's Use

Reach down into the depths of your soul and admit it: there is not much more fun than going to the garbage dump. For those of you in the city who think that garbage gets eaten by big trucks, there is still such a thing as a small-town dump. It is the place where local residents go regularly to see the bears and hope to find one man's junk that can become another man's treasure.

It was at such a dump that my brother found exactly one half of a wooden rocking chair. He brought it home and it stayed out in a shed for several years before I re-discovered it. The whole top half was missing except for a few spindles. It had several multi-colored coats of paint, and in places you could see them all. It still smelled like the dump, and probably should have stayed there and become the dump. But I became determined to bring it back to its original purpose.

At this moment it is sitting in my living room, happy as could be. It has no paint on it—just a clear finish to show off its natural maple beauty. It doesn't smell like the dump. Next time you come over to my house, you will have to sit in it and marvel at how well its maker understood the human body in a sitting position. It is that comfortable. And it is ready for you to use and enjoy.

"SANCTIFIED" IS A GOOD WORD

Maybe you are thinking, "Okay, I just want to find out about how to be a camp counselor. When are we going to get to stuff like leading cabin devotions and breaking up fights in the camp store line-up?" My question to you is this: are you sure you are *ready* to be a camp counselor? It is much more than a question of your willingness to serve at camp, or whether you know what to do in any and every camp situation (we will get to those issues later). It is more a question of whether you are spiritually *fit* enough to be placed by God in the critical role of being a camp counselor.

We have already looked at some of the things Jesus said and did the night before he went to the cross. It was a night of making sure his disciples were ready for what lay ahead—the spreading of the gospel and establishment of churches all over the world. Much of what he said that night is very applicable to you as you prepare to come to camp to be a counselor. Take a look, for example, at what Jesus prayed that night for his disciples:

> *My prayer is not that you take them out of the world but that you protect them from the evil one. They are not of the world, even as I am not of it. Sanctify them by the truth; your word is truth. As you sent me into the world, I have sent them into the world. For them I sanctify myself, that they too may be truly sanctified.*

JOHN 17:15-19

Well, here's a word you didn't use on the school campus this year: "sanctify." Funny word. What does it mean? When I took a piece of junk and restored it to its original purpose of being a rocking chair, in a sense I "sanctified" it. I cleaned it up, did some repairs and rebuilding, and made it suitable for the use of my family. In old times, sanctification meant taking some commonplace thing normally used for ordinary or even bad purposes and making it clean and ready for sacred purposes. An example would be the gold in the temple, which God's people gained from plundering the nations around them. Some of that gold once took the form of idols; now it would be used in the worship of the one true God. You can bet it was washed up, melted down, refined all over again, and cast into some new shape and form before it ever entered the temple of the living God.

So, what would it mean to sanctify *people*? Remember the story of Jesus washing his disciples' feet? Peter got a little embarrassed at the indignity of what Jesus was doing and declared, "You will never wash my feet." Jesus told him that his relationship with him was on the line, and Peter said, "Okay then, give me a whole bath." How patient Jesus had to be with this man! He explained that Peter already had taken a "bath" when he had gone completely under in the deep ocean of God's forgiveness. What did he still need? His feet washed, and regularly, please! In other words, he needed to go to Jesus often for spiritual cleansing, as he muddied his spiritual feet in the world.

HOW TO CLEAN BEHIND YOUR EARS

How do you take a spiritual bath? How do you get your feet washed? Jesus said that his disciples would be sanctified by the *truth*, the word of God. How can a person take a bath in the *Bible*?

1. The truth about Jesus.

People take a spiritual *bath* when they hear and respond to the truth of the gospel (or "good news") of Jesus Christ, by trusting in him and turning away from their sins. God takes away all of their sins at that very moment, and they stand before him entirely clean. I am not assuming that because you are reading this book or because your parents have dragged you off to church all your life that you have had a spiritual bath. If you have never yet discovered *personal* faith and forgiveness, or if you are not sure, my prayer is that before you read many more chapters you will meet Jesus Christ. Today is the day to turn away from sin and trust in Jesus to forgive your sins and give you eternal life.[5] Without that kind of bath, this book will be of little use to you, because you have nothing to offer of any eternal value to campers at a Christian camp. But God's invitation still stands, for as long as he gives you breath.

2. The truth about you and me.

We who are believers in Jesus still need to have a regular spiritual foot washing, called "confession." As we pick up dirt and sin from the world, God's truth revealed in the Bible will show it for what it really is: dirt and sin. We need to go and confess it to God daily. John writes, "If we confess our sins, he is faithful and just and will forgive our sins, and purify us from all unrighteousness." What does he mean by "confess"? To confess your daily sins to God is to simply go and tell on yourself.

I JOHN 1:9

You remember what that's like. You borrowed dad's adjustable wrench to work on your bike, but left it out on the back lawn. Then after two weeks of nagging, you finally mow the grass—and run over the wrench, which is now both rusty and chewed up, to say nothing of the mower blade. You are tempted to put the wrench back in dad's tool kit and hope he doesn't notice, but he will notice. He probably has already noticed and just hasn't said anything, which is why you feel so bad about the whole business. So you go to him and tell on yourself.

Think about what kind of "confession" your dad wants from you, and it will tell you something about what God wants from you when you confess your sin to him. Your dad doesn't want you to blame it on the rain, or your kid brother, or the camouflaging effects of tall grass. He wants you to admit that you were at fault, without any stammered rationalizing. He also wants you to see that your actions were wrong and below his expectations of you. And he wants you to change your behavior. Real confession always involves repentance—a change of heart and a change of action.

You need to go to God *regularly* to confess your sins, just as you regularly wash your feet at camp (okay, maybe you do it to improve your sandal tan). One year my youth group went to a little village in Mexico and picked up the litter off the streets. No, I mean *litter*. About twenty or thirty years worth. No one had picked it up in all that time and it didn't go away by itself. It just accumulated. The same thing is true of sin. When we don't confess it, sin accumulates and begins to choke our relationship with God. Have you had your feet washed today?

READY FOR GOD'S USE

Now maybe you are wondering what this has to do with camp. Let me say this: you could know everything there is to know about being a counselor and yet be entirely ineffective, simply because sin clutters your heart like a neglected broom closet. This is the place to begin. Before filling your mind with stuff about camp counseling, empty your heart before God. Make it a habit to confess your sins to him daily. Do it well before campers begin to pour out of cars and buses at your physical feet, so that your spiritual "feet" will be clean and not a spiritual plug-your-nose zone. God will not use filthy instruments to do his work, but he is more than willing to make us clean and ready to serve him.

Otherwise, it is very possible that when you go to unpack your bags at camp, you will be shocked to discover stuff there that you thought you had left at home, things that would totally embarrass you if anyone saw them. Not the Archie comics or the junk food, but the ragged baggage of your heart and lifestyle: evil thoughts; bitterness and blame; lust and envy; doubts and rebellion; prejudice or feelings of worthlessness; maybe even thoughts of suicide; eating disorders that make you run down to the bathroom and puke up everything you eat; music about sex and violence and the occult. Things like that just won't stay home—they come with you everywhere.

It doesn't take drug addiction or sleeping around to make a believer spiritually defeated. One of Satan's best (or worst) strategies is to lead us down a path of small defeats—in our devotions, our prayer life, our witnessing, maybe a few habits like immoral thoughts, a problem with gossip, or a few people we have never forgiven. Before we know it we are trapped in a cycle of inconsistency and guilt. I've been there before, and I know—it is like being aware that you are drowning, and if you could just get your head above water for a minute you would do something about it. Maybe tomorrow. Or on the weekend. Glub, glub, glub.

My grandest hope for you as you prepare to be a camp counselor is that you will become sanctified. Maybe you are wondering why we are focusing so much on the Bible instead of "How To Teach Canoeing To Campers." It is because most of us need our feet washed first, if we are not in need of a whole bath, and the Bible is the place to begin.

Today is the day to do something about the sin in your life that will hold you back from being the counselor God wants you to be. I'm not talking about perfection here, but the start of a process of being cleaned up for God's use. Then you won't bring tons of garbage with you to camp that will get in the way of God's purposes. The **CAMP PREP** box below is a suggested way of getting started, and I pray it will be a turning point for you in the direction of becoming more like Jesus, the Counselor.

> *"May God himself, the God of peace, sanctify you through and through. May your whole spirit, soul and body be kept blameless at the coming of our Lord Jesus Christ. The one who calls you is faithful and he will do it."*

I THESS. 5:23-24

---

[5]See II Corinthians 5:17 to 6:2. For more help on this, see Chapter 15, "Communicating Your Faith: *Leading a Camper To Christ*," and be sure to talk with your youth leader or pastor

CAMP PREP #1:
UNDERGO HEART SURGERY

Suggestions on how to prepare for your counseling experience.

Today, or sometime soon, find a quiet place and let God search your heart as you pray, for 45 minutes.

• *Ask God to make this a time when he has your full attention.* Pray that he will block out interruptions, especially the accusing and defeating thoughts from our enemy, the devil.

• *Let God write up the agenda for your meeting.* Usually when we go to prayer, we go with our shopping list of topics we want to talk about with God. This time when you pray, let *God* bring up the subjects for prayer as he probes your heart and life.

• *Take your Bible with you and find a place where you are all alone.* Make it a place where you won't be distracted by anyone else. Go to him in humility, putting aside your pride; give up rebellion in every area of your life. You will sometimes be surprised at the things that come up, things which God brings to your attention that you hadn't even realized were a problem. Or he might tackle a well-established habit that you thought would be with you for the rest of your life.

• *Ask God to show you what needs forgiving in your life and who needs to be forgiven by you.* Ask God to bring to mind unconfessed sin and any bitterness toward other people. Confess these things to him and commit yourself to letting him cleanse and change you. My guess is that 45 minutes won't seem like nearly enough!

• *Before you go, take time to read the short story in Resource Section "A" entitled, "Christ at Home in my Heart."* Invite Jesus to have a look around in your heart, his home, and make changes there as he sees fit.

3.   God's Word:
Why & How To Read, Study
& Live By It

Imagine yourself at the lunch table at camp, and the day's mail is being handed out. At long last, they call your name—there is a letter for you. They make a big fuss over it because it has hearts and embarrassing phrases all over and it smells of a familiar perfume (or cologne). You have to do some silly thing like spell your name with your bum to get your hands on it, but finally you sit down, and the letter is yours.

What do you do? (a) Take it with you everywhere until the envelope looks worn and ragged, but never open it, or (b) Tear it open and inhale it at the first private moment? I hardly need to ask. Someone whom you love has written to you. It is hard to keep your priorities straight while your campers argue about who is going to scrape the plates. The only thing you really want to do in all the earth is read that letter.

Do you love God? If you have a problem with reading God's word perhaps it partly has to do with a lack of motivation to read it. The strongest motivation in the world is love. So if God's word is going to be a priority in your life, it will not be because of habit or discipline or stick-to-it-iveness. It will be out of a passion to know and love the God who authored it and sent it to you. Love him, and you will love what he wrote to you.

THE *WHY* OF READING THE WORD OF GOD

What are your *reasons* for reading God's word? What moves you to get out of bed in the morning in time to open up your Bible? If you have no reasons to read it, you won't, or at least not for long. Or if your reasons are negative (such as guilt or a sense of duty), reading God's word will certainly not be enjoyable or meaningful. What do you want to receive from this Book of books? Check out these reasons for reading it regularly:

1. Wisdom.

Having wisdom is more than having knowledge about something. You could read God's word just for knowledge, but what on earth for? Do you really care about the laws and history of a tiny Middle Eastern civilization that existed several thousand years ago? If the Bible was about the laws and history of Lower Slabovia, or a biography of Socrates, or the collected letters of Copernicus, would you read it every morning before you went off to school or work? Would you join a study group once week to gain a better understanding of it? Would you regularly attend the local museum to hear the curator discourse upon it? How very silly. Of course you wouldn't, not even if you were a history major.

Why then do Christians so often go to the Bible simply to learn the facts? If you (like me) have gone to Sunday school from the time you were minus nine months old, you know the stories of Noah and Moses and Jonah and Jesus and Peter and Paul better than Snow White and the Seven Dwarfs. But if you only *know* them, they are not much more use to you than fairy tales.

Knowledge is a good thing, but what you need from God's word is *wisdom*. The kind of wisdom spoken of in the Bible is usually more than an ability to know what to do. It is through God's word that a person becomes "wise for salvation through faith in Christ Jesus,"[6] which is why it is so important to use God's word in our evangelism of unbelievers. Wisdom in the biblical sense is usually *moral*; that is, it has to do with making decisions about right and wrong. The basic test of wisdom is love: does this action demonstrate love for God and other people, or selfishness, pride and greed?[7] "The fear of the Lord is the beginning of wisdom," says Solomon,[8] because to revere and honor and obey God is the beginning of morality.

The teaching of the Bible is a good deal more than common sense. Read God's word because it offers *spiritual wisdom* for daily life and decision-making. Have you ever read the story of David, when he was running away from Saul? He crawled into a cave because Saul and his troops were too close for comfort, and who walks in behind him to go to the potty but Saul himself, his mortal enemy! Common sense would say, "Here's your chance—hit him with a rock! Use your spear! Do him in!" So what was it that told David to risk his life, secretly cut off a corner of Saul's robe and wave it at him from the top of the hill so he could prove that he forgave Saul and didn't want him as an enemy? Not common sense, but his long-term practice of hiding God's word in his heart, so he might not sin against him.

I SAMUEL 24

Most people in our nation make their choices in what is nearly a moral vacuum—anything goes. That is not wise, as many find out too late. You have the opportunity to fill yourself up with moral wisdom, from a Book written by our Maker. It will begin to change your perspective on everything, as you learn to see everything from God's very objective point of view. Look regularly into this book, and it will begin to affect every decision you make, and will keep you in line with the will of God. Good reason to read it. Better than winning "sword drills" and answering Bible trivia questions.

2. Reflection.

Another good reason to read God's word. "Anyone," says James, "who listens to the word but does not do what it says is like a man who looks at his face in a mirror and, after looking at himself, goes away and immediately forgets what he looks like." You can relate. How many times have you crawled to the bathroom in the morning, **JAMES 1:23-24** stared at your bed-head hair and puffy face in the mirror, turned around and walked off to school or work that way? Exactly zero times. One look tells you what to *do*, and twenty minutes later you have it all fixed and then—and only then—you venture out into the world.

Think about this: when you look into the mirror of God's word, who should you expect to see? Were you thinking it would be God? Big surprise: James says you will see *yourself*. That makes sense, doesn't it? God's word shows us who we are, and what is right and what is ugly in our lives. When Isaiah saw God in the temple, high and lifted up, and the angels chanting, "Holy, holy, holy," the first thing that came out of his mouth was proof that when he saw God, he became very aware of himself. "Woe to me!" he cried out. "I am ruined! For I am a man of unclean lips, and I live among a people of unclean lips!"[9]

The same thing should happen when we read God's word. We should become aware of ourselves, as if we were looking in a mirror that tells no lies and offers no flattery. The Bible shows us for who we really are. It would be crazy for us to go away and do nothing about what we see. Read God's word to see *yourself*, so that you will know what needs fixing and what deserves admiration.

3. Surgery.

The Bible is twice called a sword, a nasty instrument meant for one thing—to cut people. A guy with a sword is a guy in charge.[10] The letter of Paul to the Ephesians tells us to wield this sword against our enemy, who is not flesh and blood.[11] Think of how Jesus brandished this sword against Satan out in the desert.[12] Jesus, who could have called on all the authority of the universe, put himself under the authority of the Bible and quoted it to his enemy as his only defense against temptation. This is one mighty weapon he has placed in your hands! Don't forget to pull it out of its sheath the next time you face temptation.

There is one other reference to the Bible as a sword, but this time we are on the pointy end. We are the victims of this sharp and flashing weapon, as God's word does open-heart surgery on us:

> *For the word of God is living and active. Sharper than any double-edged sword, it penetrates even to dividing soul and spirit, joints and marrow; it judges the thoughts and attitudes of the heart. Nothing in all creation is hidden from God's sight. Everything is uncovered and laid bare before the eyes of him to whom we must give account.*

HEBREWS 4:12-13

Do you like going to see the doctor? I tend to get nervous. People have been diagnosed as having high blood pressure when it was just their hearts' response to being in the doctor's office. That's me. I have been to doctors enough to know it is not much fun. When we let the truth of the word of God examine our hearts, it is like when the nurse says, "Go behind that screen, remove all your clothes and put on this skimpy little robe." It is like God opening us up and doing exploratory surgery. Not exactly enjoyable, but a little discomfort is better than dying of some unsuspected disease. His truth shows up the lies in our lives.

How do we submit to this kind of examination by God's word? It will take more than speed reading. We need to look intently into the word of God, study it, come to an understanding of what God is saying, and make a decision about how it applies to us personally. Why go to Dr. God if we are going to disregard his diagnosis and refuse to submit to his recommended treatments? By submitting to his examination, we put ourselves under his authority.

> *Search me, O God, and know my heart;*
> *test me and know my anxious thoughts.*
> *See if there is any offensive way in me,*
> *and lead me in the way everlasting.*

PSALM 139:23-24

WHAT DO YOU DO WITH A SET OF INSTRUCTIONS?

Because it looks as if it should be fun, you buy one of those little plastic model airplanes. Two hours later, after nearly gluing yourself permanently to the table and producing something that looks more like a bird's nest, you finally decide to look at the instructions. If you had done that in the first place, chances are it would have looked a little more like the picture on the box (well, maybe not, since the picture on the box is a re-touched photo of a *real* airplane).

What do you need to do with a set of instructions? No matter if it is model plane plans or the Bible, here are three things you need to do if the instructions will be of any use to you:

1. Read it, and come to understand what it *says*.

This is where you blew it with the model plane. Okay, maybe you briefly glanced at the plans, but because you *assumed* you knew what was in them, you missed some important stuff. You need to read carefully, because if you read it wrong you're in trouble. Each time you go to God's word, try to read it as if it were the first time. Often the Holy Spirit will cause something to stand out to you that you had never noticed before. Pay attention. Don't assume you know everything there is to know about the passage.

2. Think about it, study it, and come to conclusions about what it *means*.

This is also very important, because to skip over this thinking part can cause you to miss the *intention* of the author. Besides, in the case of the model airplane the author may have had English as his third language. What does he *mean* by "Please insert part A while section D"? Or, what did the writer James *mean* when he said to consider our problems as "pure joy?"

3. *Do* something about it.

This is so obvious it seems dumb to say it. Why would anyone read and try to understand model plane instructions without the intention of making a model plane?

But isn't that what we are often guilty of when we read the Bible? We read the instructions thinking we already know what they say, we fail to give thought about what they mean, and then we do it our way without ever intending to consider what we read. When you think about it, there may be a reason that we sometimes mess up in life. When all else fails, follow the instructions!

SOME IDEAS TO GET YOU GOING (OR GOING AGAIN)

Are your personal devotions (that is, your daily time of reading the Bible and praying) the best part of your day? Or have they become sporadic, dry as dust, or simply non-existent? Before you go to camp to counsel others in their spiritual disciplines, get yours in order. Try the following to give your devotions a kick-start:

1. Choose a book of the Bible to begin reading, and beg, borrow or buy a bookmark to stick in it. I know because I have been there. You get all excited about reading your Bible one day and you open it up at random to Hezekiah and read a bit, and then you put it down and two weeks later you say to yourself, "Now where was I reading again? Oh well, here's the book of Mordecai—man, how do people read this thing every day?!?" It is just too discouraging!

First, choose a book of the Bible that will be especially useful to you (by the way, neither the book of Hezekiah nor Mordecai is among them). Then once you start reading a book of the Bible, use that wonderful invention called a "bookmark" to keep track of where you are.

- *Genesis to Esther.* God's Law and the History of his people. Lots to learn about how God deals with those who obey and those who don't.

- *Job to Song of Solomon.* The Poetic books, but not just for people who like poetry. Here you will find ways of expressing how you feel, and wisdom for making decisions.

- *Isaiah to Malachi.* The Prophetic books. Much of it is God's warning to his people who were disobeying him, but there is lots here about the coming of Jesus, and more to learn about how God disciplines us to keep us in line.

- *Matthew to John.* The Gospels, the story and teaching of Jesus from four different viewpoints. A great way to get to know Jesus better and to allow him to teach, challenge and move you.

- *Acts.* The History of the early church. This is God the Holy Spirit at work, and there is a good deal to learn from the example of apostles like Peter and Paul.

- *Romans to Philemon.* The Letters of Paul to churches and various people. Probably just about everything Paul would teach to a new church or a new Christian is found here in detail.

- *Hebrews to Jude.* The Letters of other people like Peter and James and John. These letters will discuss most of the issues you face day by day.

- *Revelation.* Another Prophetic book, much of it about things that are still to come. But there are also wonderful descriptions of God and heaven that will fascinate you. Read it for what you can understand, and don't worry about the things you can't understand. Someday you will.

2. Decide how much you can read each day.

It is okay to read a paragraph or a chapter or ten chapters. Make sure you read enough that God has opportunity to speak to your heart through the passage. The writer James said to "look intently" into the Bible, and to make decisions about what you have read and learned[13]. So don't try to fly through the Bible as if you are reading a Sci-Fi or romance novel.

3. Before you read, pray.

The Author of the Bible lives inside you! Ask him to open it up to you and bring to your attention the things he wants you to see. Ask for understanding, and the grace to obey what you discover to be God's will. Don't assume you can tackle the Bible like any ordinary book. Not even a degree in literature will help you with your devotions as much as a moment of prayer.

4. As you read, write.

Whether you decide to write notes and underline verses in your Bible, or take notes in a journal, it helps to get down in hard copy what you are learning and the decisions you are making about it all. Even if you never look again at what you have written, getting things down on paper will help you remember it during the day.

5. Memorize.

Get into the habit of memorizing the verses through which God speaks to you. Then they will be there when you need them. Remember the example of Jesus and how he drew the sword of God's word every time Satan tempted him. Out in the middle of the desert, where did Jesus keep his "sword"? His hip pocket? The Son of God took the time to memorize verses from the word of God!

6. Meditate.

Ya sure—sit cross-legged and chant stuff? No way! Meditation is often mentioned in the Bible, but never as the Eastern religions teach it (thinking about nothing or chanting a mantra). The Hebrew word for "meditate" comes from the idea of a cow chewing its cud. You know, the cow eats grass and swallows it. Then later in the day when it has a spare moment, the cow brings it up again and chews on it some more. It does this four times before the food is finally digested! Yum! So after you take your daily bread from the Bible, bring it up again during the day and think about it. Meditation leads to application. As we reflect on what we have read, we begin to put it to practice. Don't read and run! Take the word of God with you.

7. Study with a group.

"Let the word of Christ dwell in you richly as you teach and admonish one another with all wisdom."[14] When do you have opportunity to teach "one another" on a regular basis? Not likely in the Sunday morning service, but when you and other Christians meet as a small group to interact and discuss God's word together. If you are not part of one already, I would strongly urge you to join or create a small group Bible study or care group to keep you accountable for your spiritual growth.

8. What about devotional books?

Okay, many devotional books are good and helpful.[15] Some of them are even quite entertaining. But at this stage in your life, you would do well to have the devotional thing as dessert, *after* being fed by your daily reading and study and application of some book of the Bible. You're not getting any younger, and you need more than "milk and cookies" these days. Make good use of devotionals, but not as a substitute for the "roast beef" (or "veggie stir fry" for you 'tarians) of God's word.

9. Keep at it until you develop a hunger for the word of God.

When you have consistently made an effort to pick up God's word each day, you will develop an appetite for it. Then you will begin to *hunger* for God's word when you happen to miss it, and will be motivated to pick it up again.

10. Share what you learn with people around you.

Teachers always learn the most. When you have learned something from the word of God and are practicing what you have learned, share it with your friends! Not only will they benefit, but you will discover that as you discuss things with others, you learn even more. But remember that those who teach will be held more responsible.[16]

SPIRITUAL NOURISHMENT AT CAMP

I strongly recommend that you not wait until you get to camp to begin a daily habit of reading and digesting God's word. But at camp, the motivation and opportunity for personal and group study is much broader. You will find a greater need to go to God's word because you are constantly "giving out" spiritually to others, and will need replenishment. Your campers and the whole experience will raise questions for which you need answers.

Many counselors like to meet regularly with another counselor for prayer and study. This will help you stay accountable (for example, when you know someone is expecting you at the picnic table at 7:00 a.m., it helps you roll out of bed faster). You can teach one another from the word of God, and support one another in prayer. Unless you both have the same time off together, the only likely time to meet is first thing in the morning before the campers get up. But the benefits will be worth it, spiritually and even physically. Many counselors have told me that it was their devotions with another counselor that kept them going all summer.

Most Christian camps have regular staff meetings which include Bible study and prayer. Don't sleep through these, any more than you would sleep through lunch! You will need this spiritual nourishment as you expend spiritual energy day by day. Use your time off wisely, and include times of being alone with God and your Bible. When the campers gather for praise and worship, keep your heart and mind in gear, not just going through the motions but using the event as a key opportunity to enter into worship.

There are good reasons to drink deeply from the word of God. If you are rightly motivated and thorough in your reading, study and application of his word to everyday life, God's word will become to you your daily sub sandwich. You will never get enough. And you will day by day be sanctified—made ready for God's use—by the truth of his word, just as Jesus prayed would happen.

---

[6]II Timothy 3:14-15

[7]James 3:13-17

[8]Proverbs 9:10

[9]Isaiah 6:5

[10]Romans 13:3-4

[11]Ephesians 6:11-17

[12]See Matthew 4:1-11

[13]James 1:22-25

[14]Colossians 3:16

[15]Examples include "Our Daily Bread" and "Campus Journal" by RBC Ministries (1-800-598-7221), "Every Day With Jesus" and "YP's" by CWR (available from CMC at 1-800-325-1297) and "Youthwalk" by Walk Through The Bible (1-800-877-5259)

[16]James 3:1

4.   Prayer: God At Work

I groaned (inwardly, of course) as my youth group bowed their heads. Pray out loud in a circle? No, anything but that! As the prayer rounded the corner toward me I started to sweat, and by the time Debbie Jackson started her usual "Thank you, God, for a good time tonight...," I was shaking.

Actually my prayer started out pretty good. I thanked God for my youth pastor and for the bagels... Bagels? We didn't have any bagels! I froze. Everybody was waiting for me to say something else, anything else, and the tension in the circle was like the final inning of the World Series. Tom Martens was poking me in the ribs. But I couldn't squeeze out another word. I sat there, paralyzed and wondering who would rescue me from my utter humiliation this time.

Maybe someone once took the time to teach you how to pray. You are most fortunate. Prayer is like shaving—it's something we are expected to know how to do, but few of us are shown how. There are so many questions you have as a kid: Do I have to close my eyes when I pray? How does God hear all our prayers at the same time? What if I forget to say, "In Jesus' name"? And what on earth does "Amen" mean anyway?

LORD, TEACH US HOW TO PRAY

What would *you* do if you were sitting up on a hillside, listening to Jesus praying to his Father right there in front of you? One of his disciples had the right idea when he waited for Jesus to finish and then said, "Lord, teach us to pray." I mean, who better to ask than God himself about how to talk with God? What Jesus taught them on that occasion is recorded in the gospels. Here are a few things Jesus taught his disciples about going to God in prayer:

1. Pray boldly.

Jesus told a story. A guy gets some friends dropping in late at night, goes to the cupboard, and what do you know? No food! To avoid total disgrace (in that culture hospitality was a matter of family honor), he sneaks out the back door and goes to the neighbor. No good. Lights are all out, everyone is asleep. But this man isn't bashful. He starts banging on the door until his neighbor wakes up.

LUKE 11:5-8

The neighbor is not impressed. Says his security system is all turned on and besides, the kids have crawled into bed with him (ya, my kids do that too), so get lost. But the man on the street is *really* not bashful. He doesn't let up until the neighbor goes down and gives him the food. Jesus says that the reason the man finally gets what he asks for is because of his *boldness*.

There's a good one for you—have you ever thought of being *bold* with God?

Lord, I crawled
across the barrenness
to you
with my empty cup,

uncertain
but asking
any small drop
of refreshment.

If only
I had known you better
I'd have come
running with a bucket.[17]

Sometimes we ask God for too little, or for things that would probably happen anyway. The standard youth group prayer I have heard over the years is, "Thank you that we could all be here tonight. I hope that those not with us can join us next time. Please give us all a safe trip home." Somehow, I rather doubt that prayer has had much effect on either attendance at youth meetings or the safety record of teenage drivers. Not because it is wrong to pray this way, but it is something like asking a multi-billionaire for a quarter. Almost an insult.

It is good to pray about every little thing, but don't stop there. Go to God boldly. Ask him for big things that only he could do, and that will bring him obvious glory when he answers. Like asking that the worst camper in your cabin will accept Christ as Savior and Lord, or that the weather will improve in time for the outdoor concert. Go without hesitation or doubt. "In him [that is, in Jesus] and through faith in him we may approach God with freedom and confidence."[18] That's what God wants.

2. Ask first.

It seems simple, but I think sometimes we don't have because we don't ask. Jesus said, "Ask and it will be given to you; seek and you will find; knock, and the door will be opened to you. For everyone who asks receives, he who seeks finds, and to him who knocks, the door will be opened."

LUKE 11:9-10

Why does God want us to ask anyway, since he knows what we need? In reality God knows what we lack much better than we do. Why does he want us to go through the motion of asking him? Think about it this way: do you remember needing some tool like a hammer, or some item of food like last night's leftover chicken, and you took it without asking mom or dad? Why did they get so choked about it? They would have given it to you anyway. But they wanted you to ask first, because it was *their stuff*.

When we go to God in prayer, we are like a kid who wants to use his dad's hammer. We are dealing with God's stuff, and he wants us to ask first, not after we have tried helping ourselves. It is important to realize that every good and perfect gift comes from him,[19] if we will just ask first.

3. Ask specifically.

Compare these two prayers, and think about which one would more likely move God to respond: "Please save lots of kids this summer at camp," or "Please make it possible for me to sit with Johnny during free time so I can tell him about Jesus. And I pray he will be ready to listen and respond with faith."

Take a look at the first prayer. God could answer if you prayed that way, but you must admit it took little thought on your part, minimal sincerity, and minuscule faith. The second prayer, being more specific, took more of all three (especially faith) which is what God is looking for when we pray. Don't be satisfied with, "Please bless all the missionaries all over the world." You don't really mean it (or you would pray for all of them by name), and God knows you don't mean it.

Pray specifically. Of course, it is not for you to give God detailed instructions on what you want him to do. His ways are higher than our ways. We also need to think about our motives when we pray, and decide if we are asking about our *needs* or just our *wants*. But pray for people (such as your campers) by name, and show by your prayer that you are earnestly seeking some specific thing from God. When we ask God for good things, that is what he gives us.[20]

4. Avoid whatever "crowds" you when you pray.

Have you noticed from the gospels how often Jesus went away to lonely, secluded places to pray?[21] Or how he prayed at some pretty unusual times, like all night?[22] It seems he did it to avoid the crowds who followed him everywhere seeking his teaching and healing and attention. He sounds like a camp counselor headed for the staff lounge.

If time and people and a busy schedule crowd out your prayer life, get deliberate. Find a place or time you can pray undisturbed, even if it is in the car on the way to work, or an hour earlier than you are accustomed to getting up, or down at the far end of the dock. To Jesus, prayer was that kind of priority. Prayer should probably cost you something in terms of time you could spend on something else. But the very fact that it costs us something adds to the evidence that we are going to God with earnest and sincere faith.

Take note, however, that Jesus didn't always pray where no one could find him. He often prayed in the presence of his disciples, as in the example above. His example motivated the disciples to pray like him, and instructed them how to do it. Sometimes you should pray and read your Bible where your campers can see you and learn from your example.

By the way, have you noticed that Jesus seemed to usually pray out loud, even when he was on his own? This is a good practice to get into. Praying out loud can really keep a person's mind in gear, and it is the best way to overcome wandering thoughts when you pray. Being a conservative kind of person, I tend to *whisper* my prayers unless I am certain there is no one around within a hundred miles. I hope you are less inhibited than me. But even whispering is easier than trying to pray in one's mind for anything longer than a few minutes. I dare you to try it out!

5. Pray when tempted.

The gospels show that Jesus had two defenses against temptation. The first was the truth of God's word, and the second was prayer. On the night before his death, in the Garden of Gesthemene, Jesus was tempted to not go through with the experience of the cross. He even asked that some other way would be found so that he wouldn't have to go through the awfulness of what he was about to face. The struggle was so great that Jesus sweat drops of blood. But in the end he asked that his Father's will, not his own, would be done.[23]

And where were his disciples? Instead of struggling with him in prayer, they were asleep. In all their sorrow and confusion about the strange things

Jesus was saying, they couldn't keep their eyes open while Jesus knelt nearby fighting angels from hell. "Watch and pray," he said to them repeatedly, "so you will not fall into temptation." Good advice. What do you do when you are tempted so badly it is like a battle? Follow Jesus' example: get on your knees and pray.

6. Pray so God will do his work.

When Jesus was doing his ministry and the lame were made to walk and the blind to see, and bread and fish were multiplied and the storm was made still—who was doing it? Was it Jesus himself, or God the Father?

> *Don't you believe that I am in the Father, and that the Father is in me? The words I say to you are not just my own. Rather, it is the Father, living in me, who is doing his work.... I tell you the truth, anyone who has faith in me will do what I have been doing. He will do even greater things than these, because I am going to the Father. You may ask me for anything in my name, and I will do it."*

JOHN 14:10-14

Jesus by his own decision laid down his own power and authority when he came to earth. He was one of us—perfect, still the Son of God—but living as a man. He didn't try on his own to do the work God had for him. Instead he prayed constantly, and obeyed and trusted in his Father. He prayed so that God his Father would do his work through him. That's why he spent so much time in prayer and made it so great a priority.

He said that we would do even greater things than he did after he was gone—not meaning any one of us individually, but that collectively the kingdom of God would be expanded immensely through the work of Jesus' followers. Notice that he promised this would happen by the same kind of arrangement he had with his Father; we would pray in his name, and *he* would do it. How silly it would be to try to do God's work for him! We pray, we obey, and Jesus does his work through us.

Jesus said essentially the same thing a few minutes later, with a warning attached: "I am the vine; you are the branches. If a man remains in me and I in him, he will bear much fruit; apart from me you can do nothing... You did not choose me but I chose you and appointed you to go and bear much fruit—fruit that will last. Then the Father will give you whatever you ask in my name." There is a danger that by failing to ask God, and by trying to bear fruit on our own as we serve him,

JOHN 15:5,16

that we could end up doing a lot of "nothing," bearing fruit that won't last. Apart from Jesus, the True Vine, all we can produce is artificial plastic grapes that in the end will feed no one. We need him, and so we need to talk with him about our ministry—all the time.

Part of your responsibility as a Christian camp counselor is to pray daily for your campers boldly, specifically, and by name. Do this, and you will see God begin to work in your campers' lives in astounding ways. Don't hesitate to ask other staff to join you in praying for someone. Some camps ask that you form your own "prayer team" at home before you come to camp, a team of people who commit themselves to pray for you daily as long as you are at camp. Imagine hundreds of godly people praying daily that God would be at work through the ministry of you and your camp! God will be pleased to answer.

PRAYING WITH CAMPERS

Do you have difficulty praying out loud in a group? If so, you are not alone. However, as a counselor it is essential that your campers hear you pray. Just as Jesus' example motivated his disciples to learn to pray, the best way to get your campers talking with God is to pray out loud yourself in their presence.

Before you close this book and say, "Well, in that case I guess counseling is not for me," take up this challenge: every opportunity you get between now and when you start counseling, pray out loud in a group. I mean it. The first few times will be tough. What happens if you suddenly freeze as I did and don't know what to say next? Say "Amen"! Start with just a sentence of prayer—no one will laugh at you. By the time you have done it several times, you will wonder why you were so reluctant to pray out loud all this time.

Are you ready to pray out loud with your campers? Will you be able to teach them how to pray by the example of your out-loud prayers? Here are a few ideas for teaching your campers to pray:

1. Be a *simple* example.

Could you imagine sitting behind a bush on the mountainside, listening in to Jesus praying to his Father? Mind-boggling! You probably wouldn't even be able to follow what Jesus was saying because it would be so deep and profound. But when it came time to teach his disciples, how did Jesus pray? It was all about "Our Father in heaven" and "give us this day our daily bread." Not the way he probably prayed on his own. When you pray with your campers, do as Jesus did. Pray in such a way that they will be able to follow your example. It may mean adjusting the way you normally pray, but it seems that is what Jesus did.

When you pray out loud, do you suddenly adopt a different tone of voice and a new vocabulary? Listen to yourself sometime. Yes, you do want to show reverence for God when you talk with him, but often our prayers become nothing more than a long string of phrases we have repeated a thousand times before. That is not reverence; it is brainlessness, and it is not the example you want your campers to follow. Be real. Be yourself, and be conversational. Talk with Jesus as to an older brother whom you love and respect, because that is who he is. Lots of words are not as important as the sincerity of your heart.

2. Explain why we pray *together*.

God is happy when two or three or more people come together to agree about something in prayer. Jesus promised that where his people gather, he will be there with them.[24]

3. Try "popcorn prayer."

Prayer can be intimidating for campers, especially those from non-church homes. Start them off with one-word prayers. You begin by praying, "Father, thank you for..." and then they take turns filling in one-word or single-phrase prayers, expressing thanks for "sunshine" or "my friends" or "forgiveness". Or you could start it with, "God, you are...," and they fill in words and phrases that describe what they think of God.

4. Encourage them to pray in their own words.

Just a sentence or two. Each time, make up a list of things you will pray about as a cabin, and have everyone keep their eyes on the list while they pray.

5. Help them develop the habit of praying about everything.

Do it by praying about everything![25] Show them your example by taking the daily small problems and worries of you and your cabin to the Lord in prayer. If possible, don't even put it off until evening devotions. When something comes up, form a cabin huddle and pray about it together right then and there.

6. Make a cabin prayer list.

Put it up on the wall of the cabin so that anyone can add requests to it whenever they want, and anonymously if they want.

7. Have them write down a prayer.

They could read it out loud during your cabin prayer time.

8. Use prayer questions.

Ask your campers, "If you could ask God one question, what would it be?" Or "If you could ask God for one thing what would it be?" Their answers to the question are a form of prayer. This can help campers make the transition from curiosity about God to actually seeking him.

By the way, is it okay for unbelieving campers to pray during your cabin prayer times? If they are willing to pray, you should let them. But remember that their prayers are by way of introduction to their Maker, and that it is only through faith in Jesus that they can approach God in prayer. Don't let them go home with the impression that they have an audience with God on their own merit. None of us do.

9. Teach them different kinds of prayer.

Don't forget to teach them *gratitude*, because a thankful heart is of great worth in God's sight, and prepares us to ask for things with the right attitude. Show them that *praising* God is simply saying back to him who he is. There are many great examples in the Psalms. Teach them how to *confess* their sins to God, telling on themselves and turning away from their sins. Give them examples of things they can *request* for themselves and their spiritual walk. Encourage them to *intercede* for one another, their friends and their families. Give them examples of answered prayer in your own life!

WARNING: GOD AT WORK

Expect that when you and your campers begin to pray, significant things will begin to happen. One of the results of faithful prayer will be abundant opportunity to serve God and see him at work through you. He will open doors for you to share your faith and disciple your campers. Very often God employs us to answer the very requests we have brought to him. May your adventure of prayer draw you closer to God and allow you to experience his power:

> *"We proclaim him, admonishing and teaching everyone with all wisdom, so that we may present everyone perfect in Christ. To this end I labor, struggling with all his energy, which so powerfully works in me."*

COLOSSIANS 1:28-29

[17]Nancy Spielberg, *Decision Magazine*, Billy Graham Assoc., November 1974
[18]Ephesians 3:12
[19]James 1:16-18
[20]Luke 11:11-13
[21]Luke 5:15-16
[22]Luke 6:12
[23]Luke 22:39-46
[24]Matthew 18:19-20
[25]Philippians 4:6,7

CAMP PREP #2:
DEVELOP A PRAYER HABIT

Suggestions on how to prepare for your counseling experience.

Not enough time to pray? Many godly men and women of the past discovered that they did not have enough time *not* to pray! If you have not already done so, develop a habit of praying regularly and about everything, so that you will not find yourself struggling to do for God what only he can do:

• Start a prayer journal, keeping track of the requests you bring to God and how he answers. Include people, ministries, decisions, problems and new discoveries that you are taking to God in prayer.

• If you have any difficulty or hesitation about praying out loud, get deliberate about overcoming this fear. Begin praying out loud in a private place when you have your own prayer time. Make it a point to pray out loud at every opportunity, such as Bible studies, youth group, mealtimes and (gulp!) church services. You will only become more comfortable with praying out loud as you practice it regularly.

5. Compassion: Seeing Every Camper Through Jesus' Eyes

You may be getting the impression from all this that being a camp counselor is a tough job. If so, you are coming along nicely, and I admire your sense of perception. Being the Messiah was infinitely tougher, and it seems that sometimes Jesus felt a bit like you will one day soon: "I just gotta get away from these people for a while." Let's tune in to a scene from Jesus' life in which he seemed to feel that way, and see how he reacted.

Jesus had sent out his disciples to multiply his ministry. They had gone two by two out to the surrounding countryside, preaching the gospel of Jesus, healing the sick and casting out demons. After a time they all came back full of excitement about what happened. They had to fight their way through the crowds around Jesus so they could report to him. Oh ya, the crowds; they had forgotten the masses of people that appeared everywhere Jesus went. Jesus was still there, handling them all on his own.

Pressed by the crowd of sick, curious and desperate people around him, and with his disciples clamoring for his attention, Jesus suddenly had enough. The Bible says that so many people were coming and going they did not even have a chance to eat. So Jesus told his disciples to come away with him for a break. They got into a boat, left the masses on the shore, and headed for some secret cove where they could get a bite to eat and maybe a snooze.

> *"So they went away by themselves to a solitary place. But many who saw them leaving recognized them and ran on foot from all the towns and got there ahead of them. When Jesus landed and saw a large crowd, he had compassion on them, because they were like sheep without a shepherd. So he began teaching them many things."*

MARK 6:32-34

Totally unfair. Unreasonable. Too much to expect from any sane person. He is going to have a nervous breakdown, if he doesn't get burnt out first. That's the sort of thing I guess was going through his disciples' minds. Enough is enough, and this is too much.

So why did Jesus give in? Why didn't he just calmly explain to the crowds that this was an area reserved for staff, and it was time for their break? See you tomorrow afternoon, same time, same place. Don't call us, we'll call you. He didn't say those things because he looked at the people with *compassion*.

Jesus had eyes of compassion. He could have looked upon the crowds as an interruption; instead he looked on them as sheep in need of a shepherd's love and care. When we see people the way Jesus did, it will change our perspective. Rearrange our priorities. Hopefully also alter our actions. Make it your goal to see each camper through Jesus' eyes.

You can't imagine how tiring one week of camp counseling will be! There will be times when you will have every right to get a bit of rest, and if you can, take it! But if God gives you the opportunity to stretch a little more... that is part of becoming a servant-leader like Jesus. When you have nothing left to give, compassion will teach you to pray and trust like never before.

Compassion is an *emotion* in response to seeing a need. You see starving kids in a picture, or hear some heart-wrenching news story, and you feel compassionate. The word for compassion in the New Testament means "to be moved in your gut." But if it stops there, it is incomplete. Compassion moves your insides, but it must always be followed by *initiative*, which moves your hands and feet. Though he had every right to rest, Jesus passed it up and got back to work because he was moved by compassion and then moved by initiative. It didn't come easily for him. Here are areas of your life to develop to make sure compassion moves you to initiative and action on behalf of your campers:

COMPASSION SKILLS

1. Become more observant.

Someone has said, "We really don't need to worry about what others think of us, because they so seldom do." Unfortunately it's true. We think of ourselves much more often than we think of the needs of the people around us, even those who are our friends.

Paul said this: "Each of you should look not only to your own interests, but also to the interests of others."[26] Jesus is offered as the ultimate example of what he meant. He lived in a sea of needs, and constantly people were coming to him. If he had looked out for his own interests he would have taken a limited number of appointments in some comfy office with air-conditioning. But his own comfort and peace of mind were the last things on his mind. Jesus was always out on the street, spending his days with people who needed him. He poured out his life for them, while he himself had no place to lay his head.

I had a friend who was observant of others' needs like that. He was a busy guy, but somehow he discovered that I usually forgot to pack a lunch for work. So occasionally he would come down to the office and share his sandwiches with me, or even take me out to lunch. He did it because he noticed a need. He took the time to be *observant*.

Next time you are in a mall or other place where you can just sit and watch people, develop your skills of observation. What seems to matter to these people? What are they looking for? What do their faces tell you about them? As a person passes by and you see the many needs and hurts in their eyes, pray for them. Try it in church sometime, or when you are in the car with some friends, or sitting at the table with your family. See them with *Jesus'* eyes.

2. Allow yourself to be moved.

Remember the story of the Good Samaritan? Three people came to the scene of a crime, and all three saw the same thing with their eyes—a guy beaten up and bloody, maybe even dead. The priest and the Levite walked right on by without helping the man. Maybe they were afraid they would be next, or maybe they just couldn't be bothered. Finally, a Samaritan came by, stopped and helped the poor fellow. What he saw *moved* him to action.

LUKE 10:25-37

Being moved by the needs we observe in other people takes the right kind of motivation. Our motives are so important to God that without the right ones our actions count for nothing.[27] Genuine love and care for campers will enable you to overcome your fears and apprehensions about getting involved in their needs.

Sometimes it is not hard. When those big tears well up in campers' eyes on the last day of camp, compassion flows and natural inhibitions drop. Everybody hugs, even the boys. But sometimes love will be a little more gutsy, like when you sit down with the camper whose every sentence is filled with obscenities and profanity, help him realize his problem and offer to work toward solutions. Love isn't always fun, but it will always show you the right thing to do.

What will motivate you to keep on meeting needs when the going gets tough, or when there are other things you would rather do? What will keep you going when counseling isn't fun anymore? Do you *love* your campers, or are you motivated by the feeling of authority, the coolness of being one of the counselors, or the way your campers are so impressed by you? Let *love* move you, because love never fails.

3. Be thoughtful.

One of the traits I look for most in people is *thoughtfulness*. When Abraham sent his servant to find a wife for his son Isaac, the servant asked God for a sign to indicate the right woman. "May it be that when I say to a girl, 'Please let down your jar so I may have a drink,' and she says, 'Drink, and I'll water your camels too,' let her be the one..."

GENESIS 24

Kind of a long shot. Once a person gets a jar full of water up on her shoulder, it is not likely she will lower it again to give a drink to some passing stranger. And who is going to offer to bring water for your camels—do you know how much a camel drinks after a trip through the desert? Neither do I, but you can bet it was a lot of trips to the well. God was looking for someone who was thoughtful, and Rebekah had that great quality (notice, by the way, that a thoughtful person makes an excellent wife or husband).

What makes thoughtful people tick? Is thoughtfulness a gift, or do they work at it? It seems to me that thoughtful people put time and *thought* into questions like, "What would it be like to be the cook here? What would that camper want someone to do for him right now? If this was my last day at camp, what would I be hoping someone would do for me?" Jesus described thoughtfulness when he said, "Do for others what you would have them do for you."[28]

When you observe someone in need, make a decision to act on that need as soon as possible. Decide when you will do it and how. Don't procrastinate or you will likely never do it. "Do not withhold good from those who deserve it, when it is in your power to act. Do not say to your neighbor, 'Come back later; I'll give it tomorrow'—when you now have it with you."[29] Put your compassion into action.

INITIATIVE SKILLS

Initiative is seeing a need and jumping in to do something about it without having to be led or told to do it by someone else. Does it take you a long time to make up your mind about what kind of ice cream to get, or which video to rent? When you take on a new job, do you have to ask many questions about what to do, or can you decide on your own what is the right thing to do? Initiative is an important part of compassion, because it is not enough to simply be moved in your heart toward someone; you also need to move your hands and feet. Initiative is what will get you going. Here are some things that *initiative* is made out of:

1. Confidence.

Is it okay for a Christian to be *self*-confident? Wouldn't that be pride and a lack of dependence on the Lord? God said through Jeremiah, "Cursed is the one who trusts in man" and described such a person as a bush trying to thrive in a desert. Then he said, "But blessed is the man who trusts in the Lord, whose confidence is in him." The

JEREMIAH 17:5-8

person whose confidence is in God is described as a tree growing beside a stream, with limitless resources—not his own resources, but the Lord's.

This is the kind of confidence the Christian leader needs: confidence in the person that God has made him; and trust that God will supply the resources needed to do his will. When Jesus chose a man named Simon to be one of his disciples, he looked at him and saw what this man would *become*: Peter, Rocky, the one who would become a foundation stone for the church.[30] As "Simon" put his faith in Jesus he discovered that he became more and more the "Peter" that God intended him to be. Have you ever thought about what name Jesus might give to you?

Confidence in the person God is making you will enable you to step out and meet needs as you see them, without hesitation. You will know that even if you feel less than competent for the task, God has chosen you and can be trusted to supply what you need to do his will. So, you have been asked to give your testimony in front of the whole camp tomorrow morning? Do you really think God would allow you to get in this situation if he didn't think you could handle it? Have confidence that he is *making* you into the person for the job.

Are you someone who has always lacked self-confidence? Do you sometimes kick yourself for missing opportunities to serve or to say the right thing because you lacked confidence? There can be advantages to this problem. You may have greater sensitivity to people's needs, and might understand their weaknesses better than the over-confident person. You may also be more ready to depend on God rather than yourself.

But what would help you *build* confidence as a servant-leader? Start taking reasonable risks, and trust God. Start with smaller risks, like going up to that new person in the crowd and introducing yourself. Then move on to bigger risks, like saying yes to that volunteer position you have been declining. Each time, trust God that since he has put the opportunity in front of you, he will also give you what you need to manage it, or the wisdom to know when to pass it on to someone else. "My grace is sufficient for you," said God to the Apostle Paul, "for my power is made perfect in weakness."[31]

2. Faith and readiness to obey.

Why did Eve listen to that snake and cause so much trouble for us? Okay, okay, Adam was there too and fell for it just as hard! Satan convinced them that it was not *good* of God to tell them not to eat the fruit, and that God did not have their best interests at heart. The same doubt will get you into trouble as a leader and counselor. When God puts something on your heart—something that needs a response—believe that he is *good* and that he has your best interest in mind. To hesitate is to show lack of faith. You can do no better thing than to obey him, without delay.

Are you one of those people who is the first to volunteer, even when you don't know what you are volunteering for? Or are you one of those who looks around expectantly at the rest of the crowd, wondering who is going to stick up his hand? What makes you hold back your hand from being the first up? Fear? Deference? Start making it a habit to get your hand up first. Even if it means doing a few unpleasant jobs as a result, people will begin to appreciate your willingness and look to you for leadership. It will also give you more confidence next time you have opportunity to take the initiative.

Anticipate what is happening next so you can be ready to offer leadership. For example, the crew chief is explaining some maintenance project to the staff. Be thinking ahead to what the steps will be, what equipment is needed, and who could do what, so that you can be ready to help organize the group as soon as he is done with his instructions.[32]

3. Recognition by others in your group.

Next time you are with a group of a dozen or more friends, try this out. Tell a story in unison with everyone trying to say the same words at the same time, without any pre-planning. It is pretty funny to listen to people trying to listen to one another and speak at the same time. Watch and listen carefully: who is the person to whom everyone looks for direction for your story?

The person who gives your unison story direction (by speaking first or speaking loudly) is recognized by your group as the true leader. If you were to remove that person, someone would likely take his place. That person is the one taking the initiative, and he is doing it because he has become a leader in the eyes of those around him. There is probably some group that looks to you for leadership right now. Maybe it is not the student body of your school, or even your 8:00 a.m. Biology class. However, it could be the group you lead at kids club, or your particular circle of friends, or (in the near future) your cabin of campers.

Recognition like that demands responsibility, as will be discussed in the next chapter. It also expects that you will take the initiative and make the first move. If people are looking for direction from you, trust God, pray hard, and give it to them. Don't hold back, or get frustrated that everyone expects you to make up their minds for them. They have recognized your leadership, and you must provide it. Initiative is the suitable sequel to compassion. Let yourself be moved, and then move!

THROUGH JESUS' EYES

The job of a camp counselor is tough, but here is the key: you will keep going if you follow Jesus' example of compassion for your campers. See them through his eyes, and those long camp days will not seem long enough. It is not just boundless energy you need for this work; it is a bottomless heart. Ask God to fill you with compassion for your campers. He will enable you to act in such a way that could not be fueled by your own limited patience and endurance. He will give you the grace to bear lasting fruit in your life and in the lives of your campers. It can be quite surprising to watch yourself under the influence and power of God!

---

[26]Philippians 2:4

[27]I Corinthians 13:1-3

[28]Matthew 7:12

[29]Proverbs 3:27

[30]Check out Matthew 16:17-18 and Ephesians 2:19-20

[31]II Corinthians 12:9

[32]For a good example of this, see Nehemiah 1 and 2. Nehemiah was ready with his plans for rebuilding Jerusalem long before the king popped the question to him

6.   Responsibility: Making Wise Decisions

King David made a rash decision. Against his better judgment and all advice, David decided to count the men in his army. As soon as it was done, David's guilt tormented him and he admitted his sin to the Lord. He had trusted in the size of his army rather than the size of his God.

However, the decision was made. The damage was done. It wasn't long before a prophet came to him with the bad news. Even though David had confessed his wrong, there would still be consequences. God offered him his choice of punishment for the sin: three years of famine; three months of fleeing from enemies; or three days of plague passing over the land. What would you have chosen? All three options sound bad. David decided to place himself in the hands of God, and chose the plague.

II SAMUEL 24

An angel crossed the land with the plague and tens of thousands of people fell like dominoes and died. Finally God himself couldn't stand it anymore and ordered the angel to stop before the gates of Jerusalem. When David saw the angel, he cried out the same thing you are probably thinking: "I am the one who has sinned and done wrong. These are but sheep. What have they done?"[33]

It is a good question. Why did the people of Israel have to suffer for David's dumb decision? Why not give the plague only to David? Was God looking for some tricky way of getting back at David, like the mobster who kidnaps the children of the guy who has done him no good? I don't think so.

David was responsible for the people given to him, just as you will be responsible for a group of campers when you are a counselor. How far-reaching were the effects of David's decisions? Not only was David himself effected, but also the people in his care. His decisions as king could do them great good, but could also do them great harm—even though they themselves were innocent.

Why didn't God intervene and rescue the people from King David's bad decisions? God had handed over the responsibility for these people to David. Because he has given you the responsibility for the campers in your care, you also can do them great good—or great harm—by the daily decisions you make as a counselor. It may be that no one will rescue them from your bad decisions. Maybe not even God.

In a way being a counselor is like being a king. Though you are accountable to a director or possibly a head counselor, you still have much freedom to do with your campers what you like. Nobody is watching your actions 24/7, except God. Your work at camp may be satisfactory to the director, but what really counts is whether it is pleasing to God. He knows the motives behind your daily decisions, and knows if pride or selfishness or the desire to impress people is clouding your choices.

The comforting part is that we, like David, can place ourselves in God's merciful hands. He may not let us off the hook for our bad decisions, but he is very good at turning a bad situation into something good. The place where the plague halted later became the site of Solomon's temple. David was right to entrust himself into the hands of God; as a result, God granted him greater wisdom for future decisions.

MAKING WISE DECISIONS

As a counselor you will need wisdom in making decisions for other people. As discussed previously, wisdom in the Bible denotes much more than the usual dictionary definition of "making correct use of knowledge." Wisdom in the Scriptures is usually moral, a decision of right over wrong. It begins with a proper fear of God, because when we know God and desire to please him more than anything else, we will learn to make not just right choices, but righteous ones. How do people *learn* to make wise decisions?

1. Prayer.

Pray *first*, not as a last resort. "If any of you lacks wisdom," says James, "he should ask God..."[34] When you don't know what is the right thing to do, before you try anything else ask God. When you ask God for wisdom, expect him to provide you with wisdom beyond your own understanding of the situation. Otherwise, James continues, you will be one mixed-up person, trying to figure everything out by yourself and wondering why God isn't helping you. Pray, and then trust him to answer! He wants to give wisdom to you, and generously.

2. Principles and values.

Abraham and his nephew Lot were standing on a hill looking over the land of Israel. God had given all of it to Abraham, but he said to his nephew, "Go ahead, take first pick. Where do you want to live?" Lot chose what was then the fertile Jordan Valley, while Abraham chose the dry dusty fields of Canaan. What made them choose so

GENESIS 13,18,19

differently? Abraham made decisions based on his faith in God, and so his actions reflected God's generous character. Lot operated by greed and foolishness; he chose to live next door to party animals and nearly got roasted together with them.

Every decision you make is based on previous decisions you have made. The most important of these "pre-decisions" are about what you believe is *true* (your "principles") and about what you hold as *important* (your "values"). If these are out of line, you will consistently make decisions that are also out of line. For example, if all the fun activities at camp are more important to you than the well-being of campers, you will start exchanging the time and attention your campers deserve for time spent on activities. If you have too much concern for what others think of you, you will base your decisions on things that satisfy your own need for approval, rather than satisfying the needs of your campers.

Our best source for good principles and values is of course God's word. If we read our Bibles regularly and are open and submissive to the Holy Spirit, we should not have difficulty choosing the good and recognizing and rejecting the bad. King David said from experience, "Your word is a lamp to my feet and a light for my path."[35]

At this time in your life it would be good to make some pre-decisions about your values and principles, especially in areas of life where God's word is not so explicit. For example, how important is it to you to follow the laws of the land, like traffic laws about speeding and coming to a full stop at stop signs? In a guy-girl relationship, what are your standards about respect and intimacy? How committed will you be to staying in touch with your campers after they go home? What are your top priorities in the use of your free time? Making decisions about these things *now* will help you make wiser decisions later in the heat of the moment, when you don't have much time or opportunity to think it through.

3. Objectivity.

Become as *objective* about your decisions as you can be. When you base your decisions on how you *feel* about a situation, you are being *sub*jective, not objective, and you will likely not make a good decision. Becoming objective means looking at your decision from the bigger picture and from every angle. Being objective is like watching a parade from a rooftop above the street, rather than on ground level peering between two big people. You need to see the end from the beginning.

A good way to gain objectivity about a particular decision is to write down all the options you have to choose from, even the options you don't like very much. For example, let's say you were trying to decide which topic to use for your cabin devotions that evening. Start by brainstorming and writing down every relevant topic that comes to mind. The "writing down" part is important, because seeing it on paper helps you become more objective.

Then, for each option, work out the possible consequences. Try to think of what would happen if you chose that option. For example, think through the advantages and disadvantages of tackling one particular cabin devotion topic. As you take time to go through this mental process, you will become more objective, and will probably choose a topic more quickly than if you just worried about it all day.

Remember, though, that God's wisdom is higher than ours.[36] Sometimes he will make it clear that he wants us to do something that doesn't make sense to us (like Abraham leaving his family and traveling to a place he didn't know, which would later be called Israel). In that case it is God's responsibility to show us clearly what he wants us to do.

4. Advice.

Getting advice from people is another way of gaining objectivity, because people looking at your situation from the outside can often see things you missed. However, be careful where you go for advice. When Solomon's son Rehoboam sought advice on how to rule, the elders recommended that he lighten the heavy yoke his father had placed on the people. His friends recommended the opposite, advising him to tell the people, "My father scourged you with whips; I will scourge you with scorpions." It sounded cool, but following their inexperienced advice split the kingdom and drove the people to idolatry.

I KINGS 12:1-19

When you need advice, make sure you go to several people with experience who have a good track record. Don't go to people who have no more experience than you, or who have a reputation of bad decisions. Don't expect (or allow) an advice-giver to make a decision for you. Weigh the advice given to you from several sources, and make the decision yourself.

5. Experience.

Wisdom is something we should seek. "Wisdom is supreme; therefore, get wisdom. Though it cost you all you have, get understanding."[37] Wisdom is worth getting, which means you should pay attention to the people whom you respect and take note of what they say and do. Learn from their experience and example.

Don't miss out on learning from your own experience, too! It is not fun to mess up and get laughed at, scolded, reprimanded or embarrassed. However, if you are a seeker of wisdom, you will take correction and turn it into greater wisdom. As the wise man Solomon said, "Do not rebuke a mocker or he will hate you; rebuke a wise man and he will love you. Instruct a wise man and he will be wiser still; teach a righteous man and he will add to his learning."[38] Store up for yourself a wealth of wisdom from your daily experiences. Hold on to the lessons God teaches you in life.

6. Decisiveness.

Make your decision and stick to it. You are likely to have doubts and disappointments and problems no matter what options you choose. So hang in there unless it becomes obvious to you and everyone else that you have made a mistake, and God is saying loud and clear, "Get out of there!" Everyone will benefit more if you stick to your decision and work through the problems than if you get into a pattern of starting something and quitting as soon as the going gets tough.

At the same time, if you have clearly made a mistake, it is never too late to start over. It is also never too late to apologize to those effected by your decision, though the sooner you do it, the easier it will be. People respect leaders who can admit mistakes and who make the effort to correct them.

TAKING UP THE RESPONSIBILITY

A leader is a decision-maker who makes decisions on behalf of other people. Speaking as a parent, I can say that it is a very weighty responsibility to be entrusted with someone else's children or youth. Be serious about prayer, be sensitive and thoughtful in your love, be decisive and objective in your decision-making. Do your campers good, not evil. "See that you do not look down on these little ones. For I tell you that their angels always see the face of my Father in heaven... Your Father in heaven is not willing that any of these little ones should be lost." [39]

A COUNSELOR'S PRAYER FOR WISDOM (with apologies to King Solomon):

> *"Lord my God, now you have made me, your servant, a counselor at camp. But I am like a kid myself; I don't know how to do what must be done. I, your servant, am here among your chosen campers, who seem to be too many to count. I ask*

that you would give me an obedient heart so I can counsel my campers in the right way and so I will know the difference between right and wrong. Otherwise, it is impossible to counsel this great cabin of yours." [40]

---

[33] II Samuel 24:17
[34] James 1:5-7
[35] Psalm 119:105
[36] Isaiah 55:8-9
[37] Proverbs 4:7
[38] Proverbs 9:8-9
[39] See Matthew 18:1-14.
[40] Based on I Kings 3:7-9, NCV

CAMP PREP #3:
PRACTICE WISE DECISION-MAKING
Suggestions on how to prepare for your counseling experience.

As a younger person, it is likely you have one big decision or another looming on the horizon, waiting for you to make it. Choose a decision and apply the above principles of decision-making to it, both for your benefit and as an opportunity to practice methods of making wise choices:

• Pray *first*. Keep in mind James 1:5-8.

• Seek objectivity. Write down all your options, and the pros and cons and consequences of each one.

• Seek advice from reliable sources. Weigh their wisdom carefully, comparing it to what you know of the wisdom of God's word.

• Make your decision firmly and confidently, and begin putting it into action. Trust God to be at work toward your best interests, because you love him and are called by him.

PART TWO:
THE CAMP ORGANIZATION

"Camp is God's idea"

7. The Spiritual Environment: The Basis and Purpose of Christian Camping

Okay, we are going to talk about history here, but I promise not to bore you with lots of dates and names of people and places to memorize. It really is important to know where the tradition we call "camping" comes from if you are going to find your place in it in the near future. The people who are best connected with the present are those who have the best understanding of the past.

CAMP IS GOD'S IDEA

A survey of biblical history shows that God often took his people out of their usual contexts and placed them in a special setting to accomplish a specific purpose. In other words, he had them go to "camp." Out in the wilderness, away from the usual routine and pressures of urban life, God had a better audience with his people and they tended to respond to him in ways they may not have responded back at home. In this special spiritual environment, God met with his people, provided for their needs, and accomplished a specific purpose that could not be done any other way. The examples go back to the very beginning:

1. The Garden of Eden.
God made a big, wide world, but Adam and Eve he placed in a particular garden. There he walked with them in the cool of the day. He gave them ample food within arm's reach (and no dishes to wash). Most importantly, he set into motion his great plan of redemption by giving to mankind a test of obedience. It was a sad day when they blew the test and the first two people were sent home from "camp"!

2. Abraham.
God called Abraham out of the city of Ur and directed him to the barrenness of Canaan. How many of the wonderful experiences of God's provision would Abraham and his family have experienced had they stayed back home? Would Abraham have become "God's friend" without those close encounters face to face with his Maker in the wilderness? There God

established a people of his own, the Hebrew race, out of whom would come the Savior.

3. The Children of Israel.

Abraham's descendants, the children of Israel, left their homes in Egypt and spent years and years wandering in the wilderness. God provided them manna from heaven and water from the rock. He met with them, confronting them with their sin and their need for him. He achieved his purpose of giving his Law in a way they would not forget. God said that if his people were obedient, this is what he would do: "I will put my dwelling place among you, and I will not abhor you. I will walk among you and be your God, and you will be my people."

LEVITICUS 26:11

The phrase, "I will put my dwelling place among you" literally means, "I will set up my tent among you." Every time the Israelites set up tents and camped out during their journey in the wilderness, by God's command a tent was also set up for him. One of my best memories as a youth was going camping with my father, just the two of us. Camping was more my thing than his, and so I remember how excited I was to have him share the experience with me. Imagine having your Father God camping with you!

This unique experience was so important that God instituted a one week wilderness reunion, called the "Feast of Tabernacles."[41] For one week of each year, the Israelites left their homes and lived in tents. They celebrated before the Lord and remembered their forefathers who camped out in the wilderness with God. Imagine that! God had his people go to camp one week a year!

4. John the Baptist.

The examples carry on into the New Testament. When John the Baptist began preaching and preparing the people to meet Jesus, he didn't go to the streets of Jerusalem. Instead, "the whole Judean countryside and all the people of Jerusalem went out to him. Confessing their sins, they were baptized by him in the Jordan River."[42]

Now think for a moment about what that meant. The Jordan was a full day's journey from Jerusalem, the closest main city. To get to it, people would have to travel the infamous and dangerous road that was the setting of Jesus' story of the Good Samaritan. People would have to travel in caravans to the Jordan River and set up their tents on its banks. The people of God were once again called out of the city to go camping with him. Out there, God's call to repentance would be much more effective than if he tried to reach them at home.

5. Jesus and his disciples.

When Jesus came, he gathered a band of disciples and acted as their counselor as they traveled the Judean countryside. When John describes the ministry of Jesus, he says, "The Word became flesh and made his dwelling [literally, *set up his tent*] among us." This time it was God's Son who was camping with his people! Jesus provided for them in miraculous ways, and spoke words of hope to the outcasts and common people. He accomplished his purpose of dying for our sins and being raised again so we could have eternal life.

JOHN 1:14

6. Heaven.

Camp is not heaven, but there are more "hints of glory" there than in many other earthly settings, and that is perhaps why it has such a profound affect on people. John in the book of Revelation sees Jesus on his throne in heaven saying something that by now should sound familiar: "Now the dwelling of God [again, literally *tenting-place of God*] is with men, and he will live with them." Guess what? One day, God will again camp with his people. Heaven *is* going to be like camp, only unimaginably more wonderful, and never-ending! God will provide for us glory upon glory, he will meet with us face to face, and will forever accomplish his purpose of having a people who love him, to the glory of his name. This is the camping experience we long for!

REVELATION 21:3

Camp is God's idea. Today's Christian camp is one of those spiritual environments where God often works in people's hearts and lives more effectively than in their usual environment. Historically, the "camp" setting has been where people have made their most profound and life-changing decisions about commitment to God and faith in the Lord Jesus Christ.

Notice, though, that throughout history camp has always been a temporary setting for a specific purpose. Your campers who get dragged off to church every Sunday might say to you, "Why can't church be like camp?" Well, it isn't. Most Sunday mornings don't have the same dynamic and life-arresting qualities found in a week or even weekend of camp, and shouldn't be expected to. Camp for most people is just one week a year. The church is for the other 51 weeks, and the church is also God's idea. It is where the real stuff of living the Christian life takes place.

THE TRADITION OF CHRISTIAN CAMPING

In modern Christian camping, two traditions merge. The first tradition comes out of the revival tent meetings of the 19th century in North America. Early in the 1800's, rural families would gather from miles around to spend several days camped around a central tent or barn or meeting hall. Food was abundant, and the fellowship was wonderful. All day long, speakers preached the gospel; hundreds and thousands responded to their calls to repentance. God's power was evident in a spectacular way as his people left their homes and gathered in these unique rural settings. This tradition provided most Christian camps today with innovations such as "chapel" and "altar calls" and much praise and worship music as part of their programs.

The other tradition comes from the days of the pioneers of North America and the other "new worlds." The wilderness survival skills learned from First Nations peoples and used by woodsmen of the past were no longer needed on a practical basis, so "camping" became a way of preserving these arts and passing them down to future generations. Early camps of this type were not much different from school, except that the disciplines exercised to mold young minds and wills were of the outdoor kind.

In the early 1900's, this form of outdoor education began to merge with the spiritual focus of tent-meetings, so that today most Christian camps also incorporate traditional skills such as canoeing, archery, campfires, horsemanship, crafts and wide games. Along the way many camps have developed new activities that might include anything from skateboard ramps to waterskiing to high ropes courses.

Towards the middle of the century, many camps chose to become "decentralized." This meant that rather than remaining an institution that forced children to adapt to a rigorous program, camps became more focused on the needs of the individual camper. This is true of most Christian camps: counselors take responsibility for the care of a small group of campers who do most of their daily activities together. The advantages are obvious, and will be discussed in more detail in other chapters.

Other innovations enjoyed by some Christian camps include wilderness camping and adventure learning. These camps specialize in (or have as an alternative) a program involving experiences such as backpacking, canoe tripping, river rafting, rock climbing, challenge courses, winter camping and other rigorous activities. These give the camper an experience that has a high *perceived* risk but minimal *real* risk, and there is much emphasis on safety training. The effectiveness of this style of "stress camping" for formulating character and relationships, and for producing an environment conducive to behavior change, is well documented.

GAIN A RESPECT FOR YOUR CAMP

Almost every camp in the world is the best camp in the world, in the eyes of those who go there. It doesn't seem to matter if it consists of a ring of tents in a farmer's field or a hundred-acre high-tech conference center. When people have spent time at a camp, their experiences tend to produce a deep sense of loyalty to that camp. Bring together a few people from different camps, and you will quickly see this is true. In no time they will be saying, "You do *what* at your camp? Let me tell you how *we* do it." It's inevitable.

It is not a bad thing to gain experience at a variety of camps. I have done this myself, once working at four different camps in as many summers. However, I groan inside when a new staff member constantly pesters the rest of us with, "This is how we did it last summer at Camp Perfect-in-Every-Way." I find that if he persists, he soon loses the respect of all the rest of the staff, no matter how good the ideas he brings forward.

Take the time to understand and gain a healthy respect for your camp. It is not "perfect-in-every-way," or they would not have accepted *you* on staff! Some of their expectations and ways of doing things you will quickly come to appreciate; some you may not. But unless you take up a position on the camp board, you are not the one with the responsibility to alter the course of its operation. Your job is to understand and work toward the philosophy and objectives of your camp. If you seriously cannot agree with these, it is time to find another camp that suits you better—if such a camp exists.

When you have shown yourself to be a willing member of the staff team, working with everyone toward one purpose, *then* you will gain the credibility to have your ideas heard and have your creativity appreciated. By serving wholeheartedly in the framework already established at your camp, you will become one of the movers and shakers who make the positive changes in the future.

THE ADVANTAGES OF CAMP TO THE CAMPER

There is a phrase used at some point in every camp staff training session: "Camp is for the camper!" Everything we do as camp staff is to be done with the campers' advantage in view, whether it is a direct benefit like time spent with campers instead of other staff, or an indirect benefit like getting sufficient rest and time in prayer and Bible study so we can be prepared to serve them. Here are some of the things camp can do for a camper:

1. A change of scene.

Campers have come away from their usual contexts into an atmosphere that is conducive to change, renewal, good attitudes, fun and release. Camps usually have a unique setting which offers wilderness or country living. A camp should be a place with unique qualities: there should be opportunity for quietness; and a relaxed but energetic pace. The camp property should be a space with lots and lots of room, but with definite boundaries. It needs to be a specific area one can get to know quickly.

2. A condensed experience.

All day, every day, you do things that you would normally do over a much longer period of time. Where but at a Christian camp do you have a sleep-over every night, eat out at every meal, go to church every day, do recreational activities and sports and games constantly, and build close relationships with dozens of new people? The result is that considerable learning, spiritual growth and attitude and behavior change can be accomplished in a relatively short time. Some of the most significant life decisions take place in the setting of a camp. Memories of the experience linger for months or years, creating opportunity for continuing change when the camper gets home.

3. A relationship opportunity.

Camp allows new and (hopefully) positive relationships to develop so that the faith and values of the counselor can be communicated to the camper. For one week you eat, sleep, sing, laugh, cry and play with the same people. Being a condensed experience, people tend to get to know one another very well very fast. The tears on the last day are quite real. But you will be surprised at how many details about your campers you still don't know at the end of the week.

4. New skills and experiences.

Kids do things at camp they have never tried before, and sometimes never imagined before. Did you know before arriving at camp that if you try to hold 7-Up and a chewed-up piece of banana in your mouth at the same time you will explode? Where else do most kids get the opportunity to ski behind a boat, make a new craft and sleep out under the stars all on the same day? For many kids, camp is the place where they learn important life skills like overcoming shyness and resolving conflict.

5. A Christian community.

Unlike the outside world, the Christian camp is uniquely spiritual in its values and principles. For many non-church campers this is a foreign world, where expectations and practices are quite different from those to which they are accustomed. Camp can be a great introduction to Christianity, because campers not only hear about faith in Christ but see it lived as well. Those not from a church background get a concentrated experience of what Christians are like and what they believe. Christian kids can gain more benefit from one week of camp than they would from a year of Sunday school. There is almost no better context in which to be introduced to Christ and to have the opportunity to put one's faith in him, and almost no better place to be challenged to follow Jesus in daily life.

WHAT CAMP CAN DO FOR ITS STAFF

Many of the people who have come through the experience of serving as staff at camp have gone on to become pastors, missionaries and leaders in their churches, and most of these would say that their experiences at camp had much to do with their decisions to enter into full-time ministry. For many, an experience on staff at camp is the point in their lives where they move from faith in God to also serving him. These are some of the reasons staff want to be involved at camp:

1. Opportunity to serve at a relatively young age.

One of the reasons young adults are attracted to camp ministry is the opportunity to take on greater responsibility and serve God in more significant ways than they might be permitted at their age at home. Because it is a closely supervised environment, responsibility can be given to youth and college students who have little experience beyond that which they are gaining on the job. This experience can take them a long way in a short time on the road to becoming confident, competent and godly leaders.

2. Opportunity to work alongside experienced people.

One element of most counselor-in-training programs (and probably the most important one) is the opportunity for youth to counsel in a cabin alongside a senior counselor. Becoming a counselor is like learning to ride a bike: you can't do it simply by reading a book on the subject. A person may know everything about being a counselor, but during her first week in a cabin she will find herself learning it all over again through experience.

A wise camp leadership will extend this type of instruction to other areas of leadership, creating assistant positions to the waterfront director, head counselor, property manager and other management positions. This is not only valuable training, but will also ensure that these positions will always have people in the wings waiting to fill them.

3. Opportunity for support and life-long friendships.

It has long been my practice to go up to a group of staff who are talking together while their campers are who-knows-where and make them feel uncomfortable by my presence. Since returning to the position of camp counselor myself for a week recently, I have become more humble and sensitive toward these staff huddles. I had forgotten what a tough job it is to be a counselor, and how much counselors need the encouragement and support and friendship of one another.

Because camp staff depend on one another so deeply, camp tends to produce lasting relationships among staff. We serve at camp to build relationships with campers in hope that our faith and way of life will be caught by them. A side-product is the relationship developed among staff, and the opportunity they have to mutually encourage and build on one another in their walk with God. Make sure this benefit remains a side-product, though, and that time with staff does not take priority over time with campers.

THE ROLE OF CAMPING IN GOD'S DESIGN AND YOUR PLACE IN IT

Today's Christian camp can be one of those unique environments God uses to accomplish special purposes in people's lives. Two warnings are needed at this point:

1. We should not assume that God will always choose to do his work this way.

This is one of the problems met by many Christian ministries. God uses a method of ministry to achieve some purpose of his, and we get so excited about the results that we act as if it were the *method*, rather than God, that is so effective. We expect great spiritual decisions and life changes to happen among campers again and again, year after year, and end up puzzled when our methods no longer appear to be working. It may be instead that *God* is no longer working—that is, not through that particular method. Christian camping needs to stay humble and flexible to the movement of God. It is *his* work, and for us to attempt to use some camp method to bring about spiritual results is like a child borrowing dad's hammer to fine-tune the shifting system of an expensive mountain bike. We are prone to do damage.

2. We should not assume that God has chosen you or me personally to be involved in this ministry.

Those who want to be involved in Christian camping need to stay humble too, and faithful in their relationship with Christ and persistent in prayer. A spiritual casualty among the staff of a Christian camp—the counselor caught in sexual misconduct, or the program director who lets the program become more important than the camper—will have far-reaching consequences. Not one of us is immune to such tragedy. It is to avoid these problems that the first section of this book is devoted to discussion of becoming a man or woman of God. This is not a ministry to enter without prayer and careful consideration.

GET A VISION

Shortly before I came back to Christian camping full-time after a decade of ministry as a youth pastor, I had a vision. Nothing spooky or ethereal, just this thought that flashed into my mind and stayed with me for days. I imagined a whole generation of youth cascading over some horrible edge, and other youth workers like myself desperately trying to hold back a few. In the middle of that overwhelming flood was an island, a place of refuge, and many young lives were being saved as they clambered on to it for a while. It occurred to me that in all my personal experience of ministry among youth there was currently one name for that island, and it was "camp."

At that moment, as much as the idea scared the life out of me, I realized that I should be on that island. It's funny, but the camp I ended up at *is* on an island. I went rather reluctantly, and it was not the easiest or even most personally rewarding thing I could have done. But for me, at that time, it was exactly the right thing, and God confirmed that fact to me a hundred different ways. Even on those dismal days when I feel like packing up my bags, I know—I am supposed to be here.

Why do you want to go to camp this summer? Do you have a vision from God that is calling you there, and that will keep you there even when it is not fun anymore? It might not be any more than an understanding, as you filled out the staff application form, that you were doing it in obedience to God. You might be going to camp quite willingly and with a sense of anticipation or (like some of us) trepidation. In either case you need to know that you are doing this because it is the right thing. It is what God wants of you. All other reasons are—and should stay—peripheral.

The wonderful thing is that when you give in and say, "Okay God, I'll go," you can know for sure that God will equip you, and probably has been equipping you all along. St. Augustine prayed, "Give me what you command, and command what you will." In other words, when God "commands" you to counsel at camp, it is his business to give you what is needed to make you a counselor. Camp counseling is not something to tackle on your own like a hero out for his own glory; God can do so much more when we take the passenger seat and leave the driving to him. I hope and pray this book will encourage you toward that end.

[41]Leviticus 23:33-43
[42]Mark 1:5

CAMP PREP #4: GET YOURSELF GROUNDED

Suggestions on how to prepare for your counseling experience.

Find out what you can about the *history* of the camp at which you will be serving. Maybe they have something written up already: read it, even if it is less than thrilling literature. Also ask some of the "veterans" about the *traditions* of their camp and get them to tell you their favorite stories and memories. You may learn a few things and gain a better appreciation for the traditions you will come across at camp. You may also gain a few new friends by your show of interest.

ASK YOURSELF WHY

Take a few minutes to think about and write out in point form your *reasons* for wanting to serve at camp this summer. You will probably do this anyway (if you haven't already) as part of the camp staff application you will complete. But it would be wise to think it through now:

- *What is your motivation for serving at camp?*
- *What do you hope to accomplish for God's kingdom this summer?*
- *In what ways do you hope to grow and develop personally?*

8. Entering the Spiritual Environment: Getting Started in Christian Camping

Are you excited about the ministry of Christian camping? Is God placing this opportunity on your heart? Perhaps you already have a camp in mind, or maybe you are not sure where to begin. Here are some practical suggestions on choosing a camp and preparing yourself for a summer of pure adventure and extreme ministry:

HOW TO CHOOSE A CAMP

When choosing a camp at which to serve, probably one of your first considerations will be "Who will I know there?" It is natural to want to serve at a camp where you know someone, or a camp you attended as a camper yourself. There are a few other questions you should ask, related to the philosophy of that camp and its priorities and policies. For example:

1. Is this a Christ-centered camp?

Is the spiritual welfare of the campers central to everything else? Or is this a pleasure resort with Christianity tacked on the side? Is the purpose of the program activities to provide opportunity for God to work in the lives of campers and staff? Or is recreation an end in itself, and receiving the most attention? Is there an urgency to share the gospel, yet the absence of pressure tactics in seeking a response? Do the staff members seem to share the single purpose of knowing Christ and making him known to campers? The grounds and buildings of a Christian camp form one big "chapel," a spiritual environment.

2. Does this camp have a good connection with the church?

A good relationship between camp and church is essential. Make sure that the camp at which you choose to serve is committed to the ministry of the local churches and communities that send campers and staff year by year. The Christian camp should seek to complement and not compete with the local churches. Camp has always been a special but temporary event for specific purposes, not the usual routine of life. For the daily life and health of his children God gave us the church.

One of the ways to connect your camp and church life is to help with the follow-up of campers who have made spiritual decisions and commitments. The farther you travel to serve at a camp, the more difficult it will be for you to be involved in follow-up locally, and this should be considered when you choose a camp. Talk with your pastor about helping him make connections with campers in your area who are in need of a church.

3. Does the camp focus on relationships or program?

Does the camp run a standard program with the expectation that enough campers will respond positively to carry the rest along with them? Or is the program simply a means of developing relationships between campers and staff? Is there a "distance" established between staff and campers that might take away from your opportunity to meet needs? Or are campers and staff drawn together through the activities of the camp? Does the program promote competition and rivalry, or play and cooperation? Is the camp program run mostly by schedule or by interaction with people? There will be a balance between program and relationship, but relationship should be the priority. God chooses to accomplish his work in people's lives through other people. He didn't send a fax; he sent his Son.

4. Is the camp more "centralized" or "de-centralized"?

Depending on the age group, is the camper scheduled into the program by the camp ("centralized" program), or does the camper schedule himself into the program ("decentralized" program)?[43] Does the camp leader plan the camper's day or does the camper plan his day and activities? Is there a focus on large group events (chapel and worship, wide games, team competition), or are all activities done as a cabin group? Is the speaker responsible for all the spiritual teaching of your campers, or will you and other staff share the load? Do the staff work together as team members or more on their own initiative? What is the balance between the large group and the individual at this camp? This will greatly affect your style of ministry there.

5. Is the program more about fun, or about learning?

Some camps are much like outdoor schools, with emphasis on achievement and competition, and activities that allow you to earn certificates and learn new skills. Others emphasize fun and recreation, hanging out and making friends. Which is more important to you? Camps that emphasize skills and achievement may challenge the individual and develop a strong group dynamic. An emphasis on fun may encourage conversation and friendship. Any camp program will contain both elements to some degree; what is the balance at your camp?

6. Is the camp interested in developing you as a leader?

Does the program provide for the training and development of the staff? Will you as a less experienced person have opportunity to work with more experienced people? Is leadership development a high priority to the camp's philosophy, so that they will allow new or relatively young staff to gain experience, even if it means the program is less polished and professional than it could be? Will you be challenged to grow in your faith, and develop new skills and abilities?

TYPICAL CAMP ROLES

Organizational structures and the names of camp staff positions vary greatly, but here are the basic roles you will find in a Christian camp and a description of their responsibilities:

1. Administrative Staff.

The director of the camp is usually accountable to a governing board who make decisions about the policies and major issues of the camp. Depending on the size of the camp, administrative staff might also include secretaries, a bookkeeper, the camp registrar who handles camper registrations, a business or operations manager, and the heads of the various operations of the camp (described below). These are roles with much responsibility, are often salaried positions, and are usually filled by those who have gained some experience and training in camp ministry.

2. Program.

The Program staff are by far the largest group of leaders at a camp and are responsible for the daily running of the camp program. Again, titles vary from camp to camp, but the following are some of the usual positions:

- *Counselors.* This, of course, is what this whole book is about. A counselor is responsible for a small group of campers, usually between six and ten in number. Some camps use alternate terms such as "cabin leader" or "unit leader."

• *Junior Counselors.* Many camps provide two counselors per cabin of campers, especially for the younger ages. Most often, the second of these two counselors will be a "junior counselor," as part of the camp's ongoing counselor training program. This provides a great opportunity for younger counselors to learn from the example of a more experienced counselor, while retaining the opportunity to gain experience at a younger age.

• *Program Director.* This is the person who makes the camp program happen. Some camps have a set program and the program director just needs to keep it all running. At other camps this person will do the planning and organizing of the entire program, from schedule to supplies. At the end of summer, program directors are usually retired to a nursing home or simply shot in the back pasture. Well, maybe not, but it is a demanding position. Usually this person would have one or several assistants, who will also find that their role is no vacation!

• *Head Counselor(s).* Head counselors serve as counselors to the counselors. They are responsible for ensuring that the personal and spiritual needs of the counseling staff are met. Head counselors may be involved in training, scheduling breaks, giving encouragement and counsel, organizing cabin activities and handling difficult camper problems. This position usually requires several years of camp counseling or other ministry experience that will enable the head counselor to act as a resource to other counselors.

• *Activity Leaders.* A smaller camp will depend entirely on its counseling staff to lead, teach and organize the various recreational activities it offers. As a camp grows in size, more of these activities are led by instructors specializing in one or more areas. Previous experience and training are often required.

• *Waterfront Staff.* Most camps have access to a lake, oceanfront or pool. The staff who supervise these areas require special training as certified lifeguards, instructors and first aid responders. Staff in this area might also include boat drivers, ski instructors, sail masters and others with specialized skills.

• *Music Leader.* Traditionally music has been a large part of the program of Christian camps. This leader is responsible for worship, firesides and other meetings that involve the preparation and presentation of times of worship. Many camps have worship bands and drama teams to enhance the worship time, which could be directed or coordinated by this person.

- *Speaker / Camp Pastor.* Another continuing tradition, the camp speaker or pastor regularly speaks to the campers in creative and age-relevant ways, providing not just instruction but also a point of departure for cabin discussions. This spiritual leader may also be responsible for staff devotionals and available for the individual counseling of campers and staff.

- *Counselor-in-Training Director.* The majority of camps have some means of introducing youth to the opportunity of becoming future counselors. The CIT director may be responsible to develop the instructional material for this program, or might use a previously published curriculum.

- *Follow-up Director.* Camps vary in their philosophies and commitments to care for campers and connect them to churches after camp, from no involvement at all to having one or more full-time positions for this purpose. The follow-up director coordinates this ministry of counselors and churches.

3. Maintenance / Housekeeping

Even a small camp has a heavy demand for workers to carry on maintenance, cleaning, repairing and construction projects. Most camps will have a full-time caretaker or property manager, and may have a crew chief or foreman to give instruction and guidance to volunteer staff.

4. Food Service.

Camp without food is like a lake without water. Positions here obviously include cooks and dishwashers and table-setters. Some camps may also have a food purchaser, baker, dining room host and over-all food services manager. Kitchen staff generally have some training or certification in food safety and nutrition; and they know how to make it taste good!

5. Health and safety.

Traditionally, camps have relied on professional nurses as volunteer health workers for a week or more, responsible for everything from bandaging knees to giving hugs to homesick campers, and from cabin clean-up checks to managing major accidents. Some camps prefer paramedics or occupational first aid attendants, and a few have the services of an in-house doctor.

QUALIFICATIONS OF A COUNSELOR

What are the qualifications of the Christian camp leader? Here they are in summary form, and we will discuss many of them in more detail in the chapters that follow.

1. Love for God!

How does a person know he loves God? The Bible tells us that it is by the way we love his children.[44] Love for God means giving to him all that we are and all that we have, trusting him to use it for his glory.

2. Love for Campers!

Not everyone enjoys children and youth, and is suited to leading them. Are you ready to pour your heart, your life and your time into young lives and work toward their best interests? A camp counselor's commitment to his campers should be not only for one week but ideally for a minimum of one year of involvement.[45]

3. Spiritual and Moral Health.

A Christian camp staff member must be a believer, one who is expressing an active faith in God, and who is consistently becoming more like Jesus. Staff must be good role models in terms of their personal habits and lifestyle.

4. A Servant Leader.

A person with a genuine, active servant attitude toward campers will cause them to want to follow him. Camp staff need to be able to work as team players, not out for personal gratification or glory, but able to work and cooperate with the other staff.

5. Dependable.

The camp leadership relies on staff to take initiative, to do what they are asked, and to fulfill responsibilities. They need to be emotionally stable.

6. Flexible.

Camp packs many surprises. The ideal camp worker is one who is ready and willing to do whatever anyone asks of him, even when it is not what he had expected to do. A counselor also needs to be able to adapt his methods and responses to the various personalities he will encounter in the cabin.

7. Physically fit.

Because of the intensity of the camp program, it is imperative that staff be in good physical condition and have a high level of energy. They need to be able to pace themselves, and be a good example to campers in terms of personal habits and cleanliness. However, those who have inherent physical challenges and limitations can usually still act as staff, and may have spiritual resources others lack.

8. Creative.

Staff need to do some preparation for the summer. Counseling requires an ability to see needs and creatively and thoughtfully meet them. Resourcefulness is an important quality, because you will often have no one's resources to fall back on but those God has given you.

9. Evangelistic.

Christian camp workers must have a burden and an ability to share the gospel with campers through the witness of their lives and words, and be willing to pray for them. Balance this burden with tactfulness and an ability to share Christ without manipulation or pressure.

CHAPTER 15

10. Enthusiastic.

Enthusiasm for campers communicates love and genuine interest. Camp people often have a bit of a wild and crazy side to them. Contagious enthusiasm for the camp program is also essential.

11. Ability to Discipline.

Staff need to be able to balance love and care for campers with firmness and control. Counselors need to be aware of the different problems they may come across in the cabin and know how to use "tough love" at times.

CHAPTER 13

12. Ability to Build Relationships.

The unique relationship a counselor needs to build with campers demands a commitment to spend time with them. Warm personality traits and "fruits of the Spirit" such as patience and gentleness are essential. So is a personal experience of the love of God, since "we

CHAPTERS 10-11

love because he first loved us."[46] The counselor needs to have a good understanding of the characteristics of the various age groups he will lead.

13. Ability to Teach.

Every experience in a camper's day is an opportunity to connect him with the Savior. A natural ability or spiritual gift of teaching enables the counselor to maintain interest, and to be used of God to bring about change in campers' lives as he leads Bible discussions and activities. Also important is an ability to teach by example in terms of prayer, kindness and the Christian lifestyle.

SO, ARE YOU QUALIFIED TO BE A CAMP COUNSELOR?

As with any list of qualifications, the one above may seem a little overwhelming. Before you despair of ever being suitable to the task of camp counselor, take heart, and take time to evaluate what skills you have now and what you need to develop.

I resent job advertisements that include the impossible line: "Experienced help only need apply." Where does one get experience doing a job where only experienced people get hired? You need to start somewhere, and with camp counseling you will develop many of the above qualifications along the way. Some of them are essential pre-requisites, such as an active faith in Christ, a moral lifestyle and physical fitness. But even these will develop and mature through the wonderful experience of camp counseling. Here are some ways to get started:

1. Volunteer to serve in your church.

Ask to work or assist with an age group you would like to counsel at camp. This will tell you if you like this age group and whether you are comfortable with them. Stay with it for whatever term you agree to—you will survive—and don't leave your church and the kids hanging if this ministry doesn't suit you. The responsibility alone will be good for you.

2. Counsel at a weekend retreat.

Many camps and most youth groups run weekend youth retreats and will often accept less experienced staff to help out. Retreats are generally intense programs, but you will spend less time working directly with your own "cabin group," so some of the skills are not as vital. A weekend will give you a good taste of camp programming, and you will be amazed what God can do through you in 48 hours!

3. Take a counselor training program and internship.

Most camps offer a Counselor-in-Training program of some kind for high school students. If you are no longer in that category, call the camp and see what other training programs are available. The training could include practical experience, in which you get to counsel real campers alongside a more senior counselor. Counseling is not something you can do because you have read this book; like snowboarding and rock climbing you must try it to learn it. Counseling alongside an experienced person is the best training available.

4. Consider counseling for a week before you counsel for a summer.

Your intentions may be the best in the world, but if you commit yourself to counseling at a camp for a whole summer and find out in the first week that you hate it or cannot handle it, you have done yourself and the camp a great disservice. Pray hard, prepare well, and then commit yourself to one week of counseling. If you survive and see God at work through you, and if others seem to think the role of counselor suits you, then go for it! Once you have committed yourself to a summer of counseling (or any other position), it is important to follow through on your commitment.

APPLYING FOR A CAMP STAFF POSITION

Most camps have an application process for the hiring of paid and volunteer summer staff. In addition to filling out the camp's application form, they may request a resume, references and an interview. You may want to adjust your usual resume to highlight your previous camp and ministry experience with children and youth, since this is what a camp is primarily looking for. Include a cover letter, candidly introducing yourself, outlining your interest and highlighting your reasons for applying for the position. Your references should be adults who know you well, who have had recent interaction with you, and who have been instrumental in your personal development. Good choices include your pastor or youth pastor, small group Bible study leader, school teacher or counselor, college dean or professor, recent employer, and of course the person to whom you were accountable at another camp where you served recently.

If the camp asks for a phone or in-person interview, do some preparation. Consider the kinds of questions they may ask and what qualities, skills and traits they may be looking for in their counselors. Don't be afraid to speak up about your personal characteristics such as reliability, integrity, people skills, ability to take leadership and initiative, love for God and passion for ministry among children and youth. Be sure to back up your claims with relevant examples. The camp leaders place a good deal of weight on these interviews, so do your best to honestly present yourself as someone who will be a great asset to the camp's ministry, by the grace of God in your life. This is also a good opportunity to ask questions about the camp and your potential role there, so think through your questions ahead of time.

Most camps select their staff well before the summer begins, and usually before college students have finished their spring term. Find out when the camp's staff application form is first available, and send it in as early as you can. Camps assume that you may be applying to more than one camp or ministry opportunity, and will want to get back to you quickly. But the process does take time. Contact the camp occasionally while you are waiting, not to demand an answer but to inquire how the process is going and to offer any other information they might require. This will let them know you are still interested, and gives them opportunity to get to know you a bit over the phone.

HOW TO PREPARE BEFORE COUNSELING AT CAMP

So, are you ready to counsel? The following are a few suggestions for getting prepared before you even arrive at camp. Many of these come from the "how-come-nobody-ever-told-me" comments of former rookie counselors, and I hope they will be helpful.

1. What to bring, and not bring.

I am not about to tell you how many T-shirts and underwear to bring. But rather than coveting the ingenuity of other, more experienced counselors, consider including some of these items when you come to camp:

- *A good flashlight and extra batteries.* If the cabins at your camp are without electricity, you will also want to add a good battery-operated lamp (fuel lamps are an obvious hazard). Halogen or fluorescent lamps are the best. Even if the lighting is good at your camp, bring the flashlight—you will use it.

- *The right stuff to wear.* If you are not sure, ask some camp-experienced people about the best clothing and footwear to bring to your camp. Will sandals be enough, or are hiking boots the norm? What is considered modest in swimwear, and do most people bring a wetsuit? Will there be any occasions when the staff are expected to dress up, such as for a banquet? Better to ask than wish all summer that you had brought the right stuff.

• *A Bible suitable to the age group you are counseling.* It is the job of the shepherd to bring the feed to where the sheep can reach it. Here are some English translations you might consider using with campers:

Translation or Version	Level *	Recommendation for Camp Use
New International Readers Version (NIrV)	Grade 3	Primary (age 6-8), junior (age 9-11) and junior high (age 12-14) campers
New Century Version (NCV) or *International Children's Bible* or *Youth Bible*	Grade 4	Primary (age 6-8), junior (age 9-11) and junior high (age 12-14) campers
New Living Translation (NLT)	Grade 6	Junior high (age 12-14), senior high (age 15-18) campers and staff use
New International Version (NIV)	Grade 7	Senior high (age 15-18) campers and staff use
New King James Version (NKJV)	Grade 9	Senior high (age 15-18) campers and staff use
New Revised Standard Version (NRSV)	Grade 10	Staff use
New American Standard Bible (NASB)	Grade 11	Staff use; high degree of word-for-word accuracy
King James Version (KJV)	Grade 12	Staff use
Living Bible (paraphrase) (LB)	Grade 8	Not recommended for camp use
Good News Bible (paraphrase) or *Today's English Version* (TEV)	Grade 9	Not recommended for camp use

* Note: You should use a Bible rated well below the actual grade level of your campers.

• *Study Bible with concordance.* For the sake of your campers use a Bible appropriate to their age level, but for your own personal study and preparation bring a Bible that contains whatever help you need. The NIV Study Bible (Zondervan Publishers) is a standard choice, offering study notes on every page and a good concordance that will help you find what you are looking for in the Bible.

• *Devotional and discussion resources.* Many books and some Bibles contain devotionals appropriate to the age group you will counsel (for example, The Youth Bible by Word, Inc). These can be a good resource, though no substitute for your own preparation. You can also begin creating your own file of devotional ideas. Try pumping some experienced counselors you know for their favorite Bible **CHAPTER 14** discussion ideas, and bring these with you to adapt to your campers' needs.

• *Answer books.* Especially if you are afraid of being asked a question you can't answer, you may want to pick up one of several available "answer books" dealing with Bible and theology topics. A few examples:

   - *A Compact Guide to the Christian Life* (K.C. Hinkley, Navigators Press)
   - *Reasons* and *Answers* (both by Josh McDowell and Don Stewart, Here's Life Publishers)

It is best to admit it when you don't know the answer to a camper's deep question. Better to swallow your pride and ask someone else than to give your best guess, which may be heretical!

• *A note pad and many pens.* I am convinced that camp eats pens. You don't want to constantly bother the camp office for supplies you may need for cabin devotions, exchanging addresses and writing letters, so make sure you bring your own basic supplies. Colored markers and different kinds of paper are a good idea.

• *A battery-operated alarm clock.* A travel clock works great. Don't depend on your campers or the camp rooster to wake you up. Besides, the best time for you to stay consistent with your personal devotions is early in the morning. God will reward your faithfulness with energy beyond your own.

• *A stuffed animal.*[47] Especially with younger children, but surprisingly even with some older ones, a stuffed animal or puppet can be helpful. Sometimes it is not until you bring your "stuffy" out that campers will sheepishly pull theirs out of the suitcase. Something soft and huggable may be used to bring comfort and security to a homesick child. Police and firemen carry teddy bears in their vehicles for children who have been traumatized. An interesting stuffed animal can also serve as a great cabin mascot.

- *Expendables that may be hard to replenish at camp.* If you will be at camp for any extended time, bring extras of things like sunscreen, shampoo, toothpaste, batteries, Kleenex, laundry soap and quarters for the washer (unless provided), bath soap, junk food, etc. Most camps will expect you to bring your own bedding. Bring enough clothes and towels that you won't need to wash clothes more than once a week.

- *Cabin identity stuff.* Bring something that sets your cabin group apart as unique. This can help you produce a good group dynamic. It could be something that you and your campers all wear, or an object such as a stuffed mascot. It should be something cool and trendy, so I will offer no more specifics—you will need to be creative.

- *Move in.* Plan to move enough of your stuff (clothes, sleeping bag, personal things) into the cabin so that the campers feel like you are living there with them. This is your home, and the campers are your guests. If you are actually living out of a storage locker at the camp and not out of the cabin, how will you practice hospitality with your campers?

- *Storage.* If you are counseling all summer, consider using something other than a suitcase to live out of in the cabin. Large, vinyl storage tubs or bins (with covers) work well. Bring items that will make life in your cabin comfortable, but be ready to share any and all "luxuries" with your campers!

- *Don't bring things that are precious to you.* Your gold locket from Grandma, that very expensive sweatshirt and other stuff you would rather die than lose should stay home, or in camp storage.

- *Don't bring things that would distract from the spiritual and social purpose of the camp.* This might include video games, audio equipment (including walkmans), secular music, secular books and magazines. Anything else that could be even remotely distracting, or lead others astray, is inappropriate and should not be brought into the cabin. Check your camp's policies.

2. Spiritual preparation.

The first several chapters of this book examine the spiritual preparation needed for the serious responsibility of counseling other people's children and youth. Take note especially of the **CAMP PREP** boxes included in some of the chapters. Here are a few suggestions by way of summary:

- *Get things right with God.* David prayed this as a counselor overseeing a kingdom: "Search me, O God, and know my heart; test me and know my anxious thoughts. See if there is any offensive way in me, and lead me in the way everlasting." If God has been pressing you with the need to confess some sin or follow PSALM 139:23-24 through in some area of obedience, make sure you deal with it before you come to camp. If that means getting help and counsel from a pastor or professional counselor, don't put it off until you return. Be a clean channel of the grace of God—not perfect, for you are still a jar of clay[48]—but pure and willing to serve him.

- *Get things right with people.* Jesus said, "If you are offering your gift at the altar and there remember that your brother has something against you, leave your gift there in front of the altar. First go and be reconciled to your brother; then, come and offer your gift."[49] What do you as a counselor have to offer to God if you are harboring resentment against someone, or if you have been at fault and haven't made it right with the injured party? Do what you can to be at peace with everyone[50] before offering yourself to bring peace into the lives of campers.

- *Get back into the habit of personal daily devotions.* It is easy to let our daily time with God slide when we are at home. At camp personal devotions are an expected part of one's day. Don't wait until you get there to re-boot your devotions if they have been crashing. Get started now, so God can be at work; mold your life through his word and shape your world through your prayers. Besides, you will otherwise feel quite silly thumbing through the pages of your Bible on that first morning at camp, wondering what to do.

3. Physical preparation.

There is no doubt that camp life is a step above the pace and energy level of most people when they are at home. Just as you might prepare for a backpacking trip or track meet, re-start any physical disciplines you have let slip, and do it well before you arrive at camp.

Get involved in activities that get your heart pumping for 30 minutes, three to four times a week at minimum. Do your best to eat healthily and regularly, and get enough—but not more than enough—rest and sleep. Unnecessary late nights and an undisciplined lifestyle will rob your campers of your care and attention later, when you quickly become exhausted by the camp schedule. More on this in the next chapter.

If you have any physical limitations or handicaps, this should not necessarily deter you from becoming a camp counselor. I have known several physically challenged people who have made excellent counselors, and who have recognized that their physical infirmities are a great means of displaying the grace and glory of God.[51] Talk with the camp leaders well in advance of your arrival there about what you are physically able and not able to do.

HELP YOUR CAMP STAY ON TRACK

If you have chosen your camp because of its philosophy of ministry and its way of doing things, you will of course be concerned that the camp stay spiritually focused and not deviate from its purpose. How can you help ensure that your camp stays on track?

1. Make sure *you* maintain a tight relationship with God.

Jesus used the illustration of a grapevine to illustrate how to stay true to our purpose of "bearing fruit" for him. An individual branch that is not attached to the grapevine is called a "stick"; and it JOHN 15:1-8 can grow nothing. In the same way, we need to be attached to Jesus the True Vine, and realize that apart from him we can do nothing. A grape branch that has some obstruction or disease blocking the path of nutrients from the vine soon withers and stops producing grapes. The same thing happens to our relationship with Jesus when we let sin pile up and scorch our conscience. Especially deadly is the sin of pride and self-dependency.

I must admit that there have been times in my life when I thought I was accomplishing much good for God, but I had let sin and pride get between myself and him. The "good things" I was doing really amounted to nothing. I was like a computer printer that has run out of ink and doesn't realize it. I was busy making the right noises and motions, but producing a blank page in the end. Ministry like that in the closed environment of a camp not only has results that are superficial and temporary, but may deceive and detract others from the purposes of God.

2. Pray for the leaders and governing board of your camp regularly.

I have heard a few people talk scornfully of camp as a "bubble," an unreal fantasy land overprotected from the realities of life in the world. I think camp is *contained* in a bubble, but the name of the bubble itself is "prayer." I am firmly convinced that the many prayers of faithful people are what make camp the temporary sanctuary from the world that it is, protecting it from spiritual forces of evil, major conflict and negativism, and from unnecessary tragedy. Because of this "bubble," God is free to work in the hearts and lives of campers and staff in an extraordinary way so that they will be equipped and ready to re-enter the world.

I remember once in the middle of the summer feeling pretty good about how "my program" was going, and about how I was doing spiritually myself. God quickly introduced me to the concept that the success of "me-and-my-program" was due solely to the prayers of many, many people back home who were remembering the camp at that moment. If it wasn't for the prayers of these faithful saints, I would fall flat on my face, with my program on top of me!

Do you want your camp to stay on track? Devote time in prayer for its leaders on a regular basis. They are as human as you—isn't that a scary thought? But for the grace of God, your camp could end up being the next cover story of the local paper, and another embarrassment to the Christian community. Make camp a subject of prayer in your personal devotions, at your small group Bible study and in your church.

AFTER THE CAMP EXPERIENCE

Sometimes going home from a Christian camp at the end of the week or summer is like stepping out from under an umbrella into the pouring rain. You feel bombarded by many things that you were mostly protected from at camp: sensual billboard ads and TV commercials; people with selfish attitudes and foul mouths; lurid temptations you had practically forgotten about. Suddenly the prayers of your supporters are less, the anxieties of life are greater, and the world presses on you with all its weight.

The first few weeks after camp are a dangerous time for camp staff, and more than one staff member has quickly fallen for some trick of the devil, the lure of the world or a re-kindled desire of the heart. Casualties such as these can cause more damage than the good that was accomplished by their summer of ministry. Ask your prayer supporters to keep remembering you during this time. Maintain the spiritual disciplines that carried you through the summer. But most of all, get quickly re-connected with the church.

The church is God's idea. Camp was also God's idea, but it is the church that Christ loves, as a bridegroom loves his bride. If you are regularly involved in serving at your camp, but not at a church, there is something wrong. The church has a right to benefit from the experience and training you gain at camp because it is the Body of Christ, God's chosen instrument to bring the gospel to the world and build up believers.

Imagine that it is the first Sunday after a summer of serving at camp, and you are pumped to go to church. Mom is amazed to find you awake, showered and breakfasted an hour before it is time to go, and dad is touched by the scene in the living room, where you are doing your personal devotions. Church is now cool. At camp you learned so much about serving God, and now at church you want to *do* something about it. So you walk into church that first Sunday morning and say, "Here am I!"

People are polite, but reserved. Some of them have forgotten that you were away, and a couple ask how your camping "holiday" went. They offer you little credit for the many changes that you know took place in your heart and life over the summer. And next thing you know you are in the church nursery, changing diapers. You feel a bit looked down upon. How do you avoid that feeling?

Here is Paul's advice to young Timothy: "Don't let anyone look down on you because you are young, but set an example for the believers in speech, in life, in love, in faith and in purity." Maybe you really want to work with junior high youth as you did at camp, or operate the sound system or play in the worship team as you know you are able. Maybe your church is first watching to see how you take responsibility for your *own* generation (like your youth or young adult group), and if you will clean up after pizza night.

I TIMOTHY 4:12

Whether it is the nursery or kids club or mowing the church lawn, do it so well and with such drive and commitment that they can't miss your example. People need nurseries. Change diapers and burp babies with a servant's heart, as Jesus would. Be sure to set an example in your daily life and morality as well. Don't give them one reason to look down on you simply because of your age. Jesus said that those who are faithful in a few things will be entrusted with much.[52] Believe him.

WWJD

---

[43] My thanks to Pat Petkau of Camp Forest Springs for clarifying these definitions

[44] I John 5:1

[45] See Chapter 16 for info on the follow-up of campers

[46] I John 4:19

[47] My thanks to Jen Witbeck for this thoughtful insight

[48]II Corinthians 4:7
[49]Matthew 5:23-24
[50]See Romans 12:18
[51]See the Apostle Paul's word on this in II Corinthians 12:7-10
[52]Matthew 25:21-23

CAMP PREP #5: DO YOUR HOMEWORK

Suggestions on how to prepare for your counseling experience.

- If you haven't already done so, make up a resume that will appeal to the needs of a camp for summer staff. Highlight your camp experience, church ministry experience, job and volunteer experience, skills and certification. Write a cover letter that introduces you and your reasons for applying.

- The camp at which you will serve this summer may offer to send you a copy of its Staff Manual before the summer so you will have a better idea of its philosophy, policies and expectations. If not, give them a call and request a copy. It is likely you will have more opportunity to read it over now than when you arrive at camp!

- Using the suggestions in this chapter and (if possible) conversations with past staff of the camp at which you will be serving, make yourself a list of what you will bring this summer, including things to purchase.

- What are the spiritual disciplines (prayer, Bible reading, witness, lifestyle, etc.) in your life that need some attention? List them alongside your "To-Bring List" and make a fresh commitment to them before you arrive at camp.

9.   The Counselor: Creating The Spiritual Environment

Considering that the original and best example of a camp counselor is the Lord Jesus, it is a little amazing that the concept of the "camp counselor" is not original to Christian camps but adopted from the secular camp. This was another case where the church did some crafty appropriation, like Martin Luther borrowing the tunes for his hymns from the taverns and public houses of Germany.

We are about to get quite specific about the role and responsibilities of the camp counselor, but one more general principle will give some framework to these expectations. This one is not borrowed; it is original to the early church and has been an important part of Christian fellowship for centuries.

It is the concept of "hospitality." Camp is the counselor's home, and campers arrive as guests. That sounds like language borrowed from hotels and resorts. However, for the Christian hospitality is so much more than good service. It is the creation of a unique spiritual space in which the usual stresses, expectations and frustrations of the world are held at bay. Call it a "bubble-world" if you like, but it is an environment conducive to change in people's hearts and lives, and God is at work there.

If your parents are active in a church, you are occasionally forced to confine yourself to the family room while the adults of your fellowship converge on the coffee, brownies and weird cracker dip in the living room. Your parents are offering "hospitality." Maybe to you it is just an inconvenience for the benefit of your parents' limited social life, but hopefully to them it is much more than socializing. Hospitality is the creation of an atmosphere of warmth, acceptance, identity and spiritual union.

"No way!" you might protest! "All they ever talked about was politics, people in the church, and us kids!" First, how do *you* know what they were talking about? Eavesdropping, eh? Second, though the more obviously spiritual topics of Christian living and the word of God may not have been their sole topic of conversation, all of life for the Christian is spiritual. Hospitality in the Christian home creates a uniquely spiritual environment, no matter what topics are raised. This is true of the camp context as well.

You might be surprised to note how often hospitality is encouraged in the Bible:

- *Old Testament culture.* In ancient times, hospitality was a way of life and a thing of family honor, as it still is in many eastern cultures today.[53]

- *The Gospels.* Jesus and his disciples depended on the hospitality of his followers.[54] Failure to offer hospitality was a sign of a community's rejection of Christ's message.[55]

- *The early church.* Early local churches had no buildings of their own to meet in, so they usually met in small groups in the homes of believers.[56]

- *The Letters of the Apostles.* The Apostle Paul's command to "practice hospitality"[57] is often listed with other spiritual activities such as patience, faithfulness in prayer, and kindness to those in need. One of the qualifications of church leaders is that they be "hospitable."[58] The writer of Hebrews spoke of some people who had shown hospitality to angels without realizing it! [59]

So, the primary role of the counselor is to help create this zone of hospitality. It is not an easy job. "It is like the task of a patrolman trying to create space in the middle of a mob of panic-stricken people for an ambulance to reach the center of an accident."[60] Hospitality is a spiritual activity in which the Christian's home becomes a place of ministry. The atmosphere created in the home we call "camp" is a safe haven, an open zone in a stressed and oppressive world, a place of welcome and approval and cooperation. When an unbeliever comes into this context, it is not unusual for him to sense the presence of God and to be drawn to him. It is a counter-culture, in sharp contrast to the dog-eat-dog world with which he is familiar.

A SENSE OF TEAM

Imagine a car-load or bus-load or boat-load of campers arriving on the first day of camp. It won't take them long to discover the necessary details such as the location of their cabin and the craft area, the name of their counselor and what happens right after dinner. The other thing they will pick up—almost immediately—is the atmosphere that welcomes them. Is this place warm and friendly, or cold and professional? Are these smiles real, or put on? Are the staff positive and enthusiastic, or is there an undertone of discontent? Are they genuinely glad I am here, or am I in the way?

This "atmosphere" of hospitality is created by the relationships among members of the camp staff, including everyone from cook to counselor. If there is peace among the staff and a commitment to love and support one another and work toward common goals, the campers will quickly sense it. For many, a warm and welcoming atmosphere will be one of their biggest attractions to camp, because the atmosphere at home is so very different from this one. On the other hand, tension among staff may affect campers, causing them to feel hurt, confused and insecure. Good relationships between staff are critical to the emotional health of the camp.

WHAT POSITION DO YOU PLAY?

To become a good member of any team you need to know yourself, your gifts and limitations, and accept your role on the team. Addressing a contentious church situation, Paul scolded, "Now the body is not made up of one part but of many. If the foot should say, 'Because I am not a hand, I do not belong to the body,' it would not for that reason cease to be part of the body... If the whole body were an ear, where would the sense of smell be? But in fact God has arranged the parts in the body, every one of them, just as he wanted them to be. If they were all one part, where would the body be?"[61]

You may be tempted to envy the guy at camp whose position includes driving the ski boat and playing in the worship band, but it doesn't make your role of washing dishes and taking out the garbage inferior to his role. See how he would react if you stopped washing his dishes and emptied the garbage into his room! How would you feel if he refused to drive the boat for a staff ski session? If you think the work at camp is divided unfairly, observe your hands next time you brush your teeth. All that one of your hands ever does is squeeze toothpaste out of the tube and turn on the water! Does the hand with all the up-and-down motion complain about that? No, they work together toward a common goal, each doing their part.

The other side of this body thing is to avoid thinking that some members of the team are unnecessary or that we don't need them. Paul goes on to say, "The eye cannot say to the hand, 'I don't need you!' And the head cannot say to the feet, 'I don't need you!'" On the contrary, those parts of the body that seem weaker are indispensable, and the parts we think are less honorable we treat with special honor." One of the most responsible positions at camp is that of counselor, and counselors are sometimes tempted to look down on those who help in the kitchen or mop the floor. Resist that temptation. The support staff at camp are indispensable, and they may need special encouragement because they see less of the spiritual results of their ministry than you do.

Another important part of being a good team player is knowing to whom you are accountable. Arriving at a camp that was new to me, I had a natural attachment to the first person who took the time to talk with me and show me around. When I ran into problems or had questions, I tended to go to him for solutions. I was puzzled by his response. He seemed to always evade my questions or refer me to someone else. Then I realized that I was going to the wrong guy. I wasn't accountable to him, and he wisely did not want to take responsibility for me.

The person to whom you are directly accountable may be the camp director if yours is a smaller camp. When a ministry increases in size, various levels of accountability begin to develop. As soon as possible, locate the leader to whom you are responsible at your camp. You may need to answer to a program director or a head counselor or a dean. Get to know the person to whom you will go for direction, support and counsel.

HOW TO GET ALONG AS A TEAM

Do you realize what you will *gain* by joining the staff team of a Christian camp? There are not many Christians who have a support base like the one you can have during your ministry at camp. People at home and staff at camp will be praying for you and your campers. You have opportunity daily to encourage one another at staff meetings, or with a few words in passing, or with notes and maybe an anonymous can of Pepsi. Without this support, I don't think many camp staff would still be standing at the end of the summer. Two warnings are in order, however:

- *Keep this benefit in perspective.* Do not allow time with staff to take priority over the opportunity to spend time with campers. Contact with other staff during the day doesn't need to be *long* to be encouraging, and should be kept to appropriate times when crowd control or significant opportunities with campers are not an issue. If there is a break or time off between camps, consider spending that time with staff rather than going away, for their benefit as well as yours.

- *Relationships developed solely at camp may be beautiful, but not deep.* Particularly in the case of friendships with the opposite sex, take the time to build your relationship *outside* the camp context before making commitments or close attachments to one another. The special person whom you think you know so well at camp has another side to his or her life back at home, of which you know very little. Would you have thought to go out with this person if you had met him or her in the larger setting back home? Speaking from the experience of watching many camp relationships over the years, I suggest that you be just good friends at camp and see where the relationship takes you *after* the summer. Otherwise, chances are high that one or both of you will be hurt.

In the book of Galatians, Paul pictures the Christian life as an expedition: "Carry each other's burdens, and in this way you will fulfill the law of Christ... Each one should test his own actions. Then he can take pride in himself, without comparing himself to somebody else, for each one should carry his own load." We are on a journey and we are all responsible to carry our own backpack. The hike is sometimes high risk, and always a challenge and adventure. We need one another. If there was a sign at the head of this trail, it would read: "Danger—do not travel this route alone. Take someone with you." That's the wonderful thing about camp: hiking this road together. It's not only more fun that way, but the risks are substantially reduced when we travel in convoy. Solo expeditions are not recommended at all. Think about what this will mean this summer:

1. We have our own load to carry.

A young guy on a backpacking trip complained to me every step of the way that his pack was too heavy. I finally felt sorry for him and took part of his load. However, I later had occasion to pick up his pack and discovered it weighed almost nothing—he had played the same trick with all of us. We have a personal responsibility before God to carry our own load. We should not be dependent on other people to carry what is our own responsibility. Nobody enjoys a freeloader at camp, one who *takes* more than he gives.

2. We have one another's burden to carry.

At the same time we need to admit that we are not always capable of the load we have to carry and we need to accept the help of one another. How can you tell when the guy or girl in front of you is struggling with the load he or she is carrying and needs help? In my several years guiding backpacking and canoe trips with youth, I got pretty good at differentiating between whiners and people who were genuinely exhausting themselves. The people who needed the most help were usually those in the group who became increasingly quiet, the ones who hardly said boo all through a lunch break. They are the people whose load I would quietly redistribute or take myself. The whiners would get an extra rock or two slipped into their packs instead.

Watch out for the staff at camp who are inexplicably quiet. Sure, some people who need help with their loads will let you know, loud and clear. But the needy ones who are afraid of being a burden to anyone and just keep dragging themselves along are the ones we especially need to notice. In another place Paul put it this way: "Do nothing out of selfish ambition or vain conceit, but in humility consider others better than yourselves. Each of you should look not only to his own interests, but also to the interests of others." The best way for a staff team to **PHILIPPIANS 2:3-4** get along well is to keep an eye on the needs and best interests of each other. It is when we have our eyes only on our own needs and interests that we come into conflict with one another.

3. Be prepared to resolve conflict quickly.

Sometimes individuals staff members stumble, mess up, or get caught up in sin. Paul says in this same passage that it is the job of the "spiritual" (not the "holier-than-thou," but those whose walk with God is firm) to *gently* restore those who are trapped by sin. When you notice someone who seems caught in some device of the enemy, don't look the other way and pass by. At the same time, make sure you are not trying to remove a speck from your brother's eye when you have a plank in your own![62] If you don't feel spiritually competent enough, get help. We do need one another on this journey. Who knows? It might be you in the ditch next time. To carry one another's burdens is to fulfill Jesus' new command to love one another as he loved us.

If someone has hurt you, or if you are the one at fault, don't put off resolving the problem. Camp is too short and too critical a time to afford unresolved feelings and issues. Be quick to forgive, remembering that you will never be asked to forgive more than you have been forgiven by God.[63] If you need to ask forgiveness, don't procrastinate or hope the problem will simply be forgotten. Take the initiative to seek forgiveness, first from the Lord and then from anyone affected by your wrong-doing. Unresolved and unforgiven sin can easily become a root of bitterness that cuts deeply into the ministry of a camp.[64]

What if you have a problem with the way the camp leadership does things? Probably one of the most damaging things you could do would be to go to your friends and start talking about individuals and your concerns about them. There is a term for that. God's word says that *slander* is a form of judgment and condemnation, and a very serious matter. Rumors and gossip are quick and deadly in the camp situation. The trouble with gossip is that we seldom know the whole story and so we are very prone to creating misunderstandings.

When you have a problem with someone above you in authority, go to that person yourself first, not accusing him, but seeking understanding and resolution. If nothing is resolved take it to the people to whom you are directly responsible and leave it with them. Don't make it your secret mission to go talk about it with every camp leader who will listen. This would only create more damage. When someone in leadership makes a mistake that effects you, you still need to support that person, pray for him and seek resolution of the problem in the wisest and kindest way possible. That kind of loyalty is essential to being a good team member.

WHAT IS EXPECTED OF YOU?

Your camp will likely provide materials and training that outline what they want you to do. If you are a little anxious about "knowing what to do," think about this: How much detailed instruction are you expecting? Will you feel secure enough about leading cabin Bible discussions if you are given no material to prepare and use? Do you expect to be told exactly how to set up an activity, or are you ready to apply your own initiative and creativity? Most camps expect counselors to have the maturity and confidence to balance the general expectations of the camp leadership with the counselor's own common sense and initiative.

How *willing* are you to meet the expectations of your camp? Right now it may be easy to say, "Hey, whatever you want me to do, I can handle it." What about in the middle of the summer when you are tired and a little overwhelmed and you start feeling that the expectations are too unreasonable? What are you going to do when you are asked to enforce a rule you think is unnecessary? What will happen if you begin to feel that your personal needs are not being met, and that your personal rights are being violated? What will you do when communications get crossed and one person tells you to do one thing and another tells you something else?

Keep things in perspective. *God's* expectations of you are reasonable,[65] and one of them is to obey those in authority, if it is at all possible.

Camp staff are not slaves, but learn something from what Paul said to the slaves who made up a good portion of the early church: "Slaves, obey your earthly masters in everything; and do it, not only when their eye is on you to win their favor, but with sincerity of heart and reverence for the Lord. Whatever you do, work at it with all your COLOSSIANS 3:22-2 heart, as working for the Lord, not for men... It is the Lord Christ you are serving." Pull your own weight, and do more than what is expected of you, remembering that you are also responsible to God. He is watching even when no one else is.

WHAT IS EXPECTED OF A COUNSELOR

Okay, let's get specific. When you become a camp counselor, what will they want you to do? Some of the following things have been said before in a general way, and will be said again, in great detail! One of my professors in college said that the first law of learning is *repetition*. He said that the second law of law of learning is *repetition*. And the third law? You guessed it—*repetition*!

1. Relationship.

Your primary responsibility as a camp counselor, of greater priority than many other things that may first come to mind (such as supervision or discipline) is to build relationships with your campers. This includes the relationships you have with the individual campers in your cabin and your relationship with the group as a whole, which has a dynamic all of its own. Everything else you do will be based on and CHAPTER 11 will come out of these relationships, from disciplining their behavior to leading them to Christ.

2. Direction.

Even if your camp is primarily a schedule-run camp, your campers will look to you for leadership. Depending on their age and maturity, you will need to find a balance between being *directive* and *non-directive* with them. Being directive means giving them detailed instructions, as you would when teaching a beginner to load and shoot an arrow. Being non-directive means giving instructions that are more general in nature, and leaving the details to the campers' initiative and creativity, such as when you are explaining to them about cabin clean-up. The younger the camper, the more details they will need to feel secure; the older the camper the more they will resent any over-direction.

It cannot be stated enough that you need to know *where* your campers are, at all times, regardless of their age. This does not mean you need to be with them all the time, but you should be with them any time you are not required to be somewhere else. Even when you are not with them, you do need to know where they are supposed to be, and have some way of making sure that is where they are.

Make it an automatic thing to do head counts at meals, group meetings and other occasions where it is possible. If one of your sheep is missing, you must be among the first to notice it and the first to go look for them. They are *your* responsibility.

3. Physical care and hygiene.

Counselors are responsible to make sure their campers follow usual habits of cleanliness, even if these habits are not very usual to them. Younger campers are still used to being told to brush their teeth, comb their hair and use the washroom before going to bed. For junior high and senior high campers, your example and your tactful suggestions will be better accepted than potentially embarrassing instructions.

- *Staying clean.* A swim is not a bath, especially in some of our lakes and oceans! Make sure campers take a shower at least every other day. Younger campers will need the most encouragement. Even kids who are usually clean at home will go for the I-never-even-opened-my-suitcase look by the end of the week. Remind pre-twelve's to wash their hands before meals and after using the washroom. Their parents do so.

- *Clothing.* Make sure they are not wearing the same clothes every day. Also make sure they do not wear to bed the same clothes they wear during the day. Wet clothes should be hung on the line, not left in a corner. If it seems a child has come with insufficient clothes, tell the head counselor. Make sure campers are wearing their cleanest clothes on the last day. It will mean "bonus points" on mom and dad's evaluation of you as counselor when they come to pick up their pride and joy.

- *Bed-wetters.* Make discreet inspections of sleeping bags to see if there are any bed-wetters (you will be able to tell with a sniff—you don't need to touch their bags). Put bed-wetters on a lower bunk, and let them know where you keep your flashlight. Tell them they can get you up at night if they need to go and are afraid. Limit drinks at supper and snack. If a camper gets you up because he has wet his bed, help him hang it up outside and get him blankets from the nurse. A wet bag may need washing. If it cannot be washed, hang it (inside out) where no one will see it, or have everyone in the cabin hang out their bags to "air them out." Be sensitive to the camper's embarrassment and don't make a big deal of it.

- *Cabin Clean-up.* Don't allow your cabin to try to get the least points for cabin check-up. Talk with them about general guidelines for cleaning and decorating the cabin, and leave room for their creativity. If they are not doing it on their own, assign duties. If one camper is not pulling his weight, discipline will be necessary.

- *Appearance.* Campers should go back home the way they came in terms of physical appearance. Do not let them pierce their ears, cut or color their hair, or use permanent ink on their arms and legs. Often campers will attempt to do something they have not been permitted to do at home, and then will blame the camp or counselor when their parents scream! If campers have brought inappropriate clothing (e.g., immodest swimwear, or shirts with rude or obscene designs and words), ask them to leave it in their suitcases for the week. Don't let them get away with wearing it. Use the occasion to teach them why the clothing is inappropriate.

- *Health Care.* Use discretion before taking campers to the nurse for treatment of illness or injury. However, if there is any question about the validity of their complaints, *don't hesitate* to take them. It is also better to *take* them rather than send them if possible. The health care giver can then make the connection that these campers belongs to you, and inform you of any special treatment or instruction.

4. Discipline.

As guests in our home, campers are expected to uphold the house rules. Discipline is not simply administering punishment; it is *training* someone to behave in an acceptable manner. Because discipline is easily misunderstood in our day of abuse-awareness and litigation, counselors need to be very informed and careful in this area.

CHAPTER 13

5. Management.

Control and management of campers—balanced with love and care—are a big part of a counselor's day. You are manager of each individual camper's questions and problems, the steward of his stuff and the organizer of his schedule. How do moms do it? Much of this responsibility involves moment-to-moment common sense and experience. Plus there will be more on this in the next chapter. But here are a few things to remember:

- *Cabin conferences.* You need to have times during the day when all your campers are together in one place to go over things like the day's schedule, what activities each person signed up for, and planning for special events like a sleep-out or skit. Meal times might be appropriate for this, or bedtime or just before breakfast. Conferences are also necessary to work out cabin problems.

- *Camper property.* Be careful about agreeing to hold any valuable items for the campers, even for a few minutes. Just suggesting that they leave a watch or oral retainer in a certain spot may make you personally liable (yes, that means you will have to pay) if it is lost. If possible have campers turn in any valuables, with their names on them, to the camp office for safekeeping. If valuables go missing from the cabin (which shouldn't happen, right?), don't let accusations fly. Get everyone to check their stuff; this may give an actual thief opportunity to return the property without embarrassment. If the item does not turn up, talk with the Head Counselor.

- *Runaway, lost or missing persons.* Contact the camp leadership as soon as you know that campers are unaccounted for, and assist according to camp emergency procedures (make sure you know them). Think through details like their last location, emotional state, who they were with and what they were wearing. The camp leaders may ask you to assist with a search of the grounds and surrounding countryside. This kind of thing can get the adrenaline going, but make sure you don't endanger yourself or get lost! We want no heroes, just a camper returned safe and sound. It is also important to help maintain calm among the campers.

6. Teaching.

There will be times in the day when you will be responsible to lead a Bible discussion, give instruction for a recreational activity or explain how a game works. You will also have many other God-given opportunities to teach campers by your example, by casual observations and by informal discussions.

Simply being attentive to these opportunities demands energy you may not possess at times, so be in prayer each day that God would orchestrate these "teachable moments" and alert you in time to not miss them. Notice in the Gospels how often Jesus used his surroundings to trigger teachings about God's loving care and the nature of his kingdom.[66] Camps generally abound with ready-made object-lessons, images for reflection and metaphors. Make good use of them.

Often the camp program is so intense you may need to provide special space for this kind of reflection and discussion. Cabin time-outs, sleep-outs and other carefully planned cabin events can be significant opportunities. More will be discussed in the next chapters about creating this type of special space for your campers.

7. Training.

The most valuable counselor training a person can get is the opportunity to counsel alongside someone who has experience. Junior counselors should approach their first week of counseling with an open heart and teachable attitude, paying close attention to how the senior counselors handle the campers, how they lead devotionals and how they handle problems. Because of this, senior counselors should do their best to be available, visible and approachable, and to be willing to share the responsibilities and the benefits of counseling with their students.

8. A listening ear.

We live in a hostile world. It is all the more hostile for children and youth because it is primarily an adult world without much room or time for the young. Because camp offers refuge, acceptance and attention, it is likely that a camper who is hurting will want to use this opportunity to talk about it. As you build a relationship with the camper, her primary concern may be to find out if you are a safe audience for some personal issue that makes her feel vulnerable. By the time she gets up the nerve to talk, you have been well-tested and proven! You don't want to miss these opportunities, or too quickly shut off the flow that will come out of her heart. Your principal role is not to give advice, but to attentively listen and to genuinely care.

CHAPTER 12

9. Extended care.

Jesus' famous parable of the "Good Samaritan" is a model of committed love over the long term. He gave immediate care, left the man in the protection of a care-giver, and promised to check up on him again. I suggest that a camp counselor consider a one year follow-up commitment. The counselor gives immediate care at camp, leaves the camper in the care and nurture of a local church, and faithfully checks up on him by means of letters and other contact.

CHAPTER 16

PACING YOURSELF

Maybe it was a crazy thing to do at my age, but one summer recently I counseled at a senior high camp for the first time in many years. One thing that I discovered is that knowing everything a person needs to know about camp counseling (as I assumed I did) is no substitute for continuing experience. Even though I have been training counselors for years, I found my own counseling skills to be as rusty as those of a retired waterskier who hasn't been behind a boat in a long time.

A second thing I discovered was that it takes an incredible amount of energy to keep up with the daily camp schedule. One night early in the week, I had the idea of booking the hot tub for my campers *after* lights out. I invited the camp speaker to join us, and we had a great time discussing deep questions about the things of God until about one in the morning. We had just returned to our cabin and gone to bed when sirens started up and some crazy program director got on the megaphone announcing that "Late Night Madness" was about to commence. The next morning I could hardly drag myself out of bed—after only a few hours sleep—and unlike my campers I never regained that lost energy for the rest of the week!

I say this not to scare you, but to introduce some principles about managing the camp schedule in such a way that you will still have something left to give to your campers by the end of the week. You are no hero if you return home absolutely exhausted. It simply means you have been less effective as a counselor for the last critical days of camp. The effects of exhaustion on a camp counselor are numerous, and all negative:

1. Exhaustion will distance you from your campers.

There is not a thing you can do about it. The more tired you get, the more you will go into "survival mode," looking after your own need for rest, friendship with people your age, space and quiet and even food, at your campers' expense. You will become more concerned with your rights than your responsibilities. I have seen it happen often enough among counselors I love and admire to know that it is an inevitable thing. The only choice you have in the matter is to not let yourself get exhausted in the first place.

2. Exhaustion will rob you of creativity and thoughtfulness.

In this chapter I will offer many ideas for making the basic camp schedule work better by means of your own creativity and thoughtfulness. In other words, this chapter will be a waste of time if you allow yourself to become exhausted. The more tired you get, the more you will just go with the flow of things, riding on the momentum of the program. You will miss so many opportunities to make the camp experience wonderful and to express enthusiasm and the love of Christ to your campers.

3. Exhaustion will make you susceptible to illness and injury.

Coffee and adrenaline will carry you a long way at camp, but in the end you will crash. If you do so mid-week, you have not done a favor to your campers nor to the camp leaders, who will have to scramble to replace you while you recover in the nurse's station or hospital. An exhausted counselor is a hazard, to health and limb. There are too many possibilities for accidents at camp for you to be half-alert or feeling sick due to exhaustion. No one expects you to wear yourself out, and it can be prevented.

4. Exhaustion will lower your spiritual defenses.

Being at a Christian camp is like being on the front line of a spiritual battle. This battle is "not against flesh and blood"[67] (that is, people) but against spiritual forces of evil. Like a stalking lion, Satan is always on the lookout for easy prey, and that is what you will be if you allow yourself to become exhausted. Things that usually don't bother you about fellow staff can cause you to erupt, and temptations that hardly nudged you before can bowl you over.

The secret to running a marathon race is to *pace yourself*. If you attempt to run the full 40 kilometers like a sprinter doing the 100 meter dash, you won't make it. Through experience an athlete learns the level at which he can push himself and still have enough energy to cross the finish line at the end. This is the discipline camp counselors need to develop: the ability to know their own energy level and to hold the maximum pace that will get them capably through the week or the summer. Like marathon runners who have taken into account harsh conditions like rain or cold, counselors need to be ready for the unexpected: an extra late night; a camper who tries their patience; or crows that are worse than roosters outside their window early in the morning.

Pacing yourself is also an attitude that says that I will not allow what is *urgent* to pilfer from what is *important*, or what is *exciting* to burglarize what is *essential*. Camp is fun. We don't want to miss out on a thing, and it seems like the right and godly thing to do to give it everything we've got all the time. The younger and healthier you are, the longer you can keep up that pace, but at some point in the summer you *will* reach a point of exhaustion. Perhaps a day off between camps can be a great time to party with your new camp friends, but you will find that every hour you stay up late robs more of your care and attention from next week's campers.

Part of keeping the pace is taking the *necessary* time to address your own needs, just as a marathon runner will slow down enough to grab that bottle of water or energy bar from the support crew. You need to finish your meals, get as much sleep as you can afford, and enjoy the fellowship of staff your own age. Note: the runner does not stop and *chat* with the support crew for fifteen minutes. As a counselor, you will rarely be able to afford the luxury of long conversations with other staff. But I hope you will offer to one another the thirty seconds it takes to ask how things are going, to tell the latest joke, or to pray right there as you are standing on the path together.

Use your time off wisely. You may be tempted to use free time only to sleep, or only to socialize. It is better to use time off to catch up on whatever you have *neglected*. You may decide to use the time to sleep, or fellowship with other staff. However, maybe you should get some exercise, communicate with people back home, express yourself artistically, have some fun or catch up on your time with God. You are constantly "making space" for campers so that God can work in their hearts; during your time off make space for yourself, and don't feel guilty about doing it.

MANAGING THE SCHEDULE

To help staff and campers pace themselves over the week, most resident camps follow a weekly schedule of events. This schedule is not the *program* of the camp; it is more like a weather forecast predicting what is supposed to happen in the next twenty-four hours or seven days. Sometimes it's about as accurate as a weather forecast too, and camp staff need to be flexible to occasional program changes. However, a schedule is useful to give us direction and allow us to plan and prepare.

Some camps tend to be *schedule*-run camps. In other words, a schedule is posted and campers and staff are expected to follow it without much instruction from the program director. Other camps are more *people*-run. It is up to you as a counselor to make sure your campers know what to do next and where they are supposed to go. Since this method is more common among Christian camps today, I will assume it is your responsibility to transfer the information from the daily camp schedule to your campers.

Here are some practical suggestions to add creativity to the various elements of a typical camp schedule and make the experience more significant for your campers. Not all of these will be applicable to your situation at your particular camp. Nor am I suggesting that your camp program is less than exciting already, nor that you should strike out on your own rather than "go with the program." These are some of the "tricks of the trade" used by experienced counselors to make the camp experience of optimum benefit to the camper, and to you as well.

1. First day of camp.

Try to get yourself behind the eyes of that nine year old camper arriving at camp for the first time. You may have just started thinking about camp a few days before. All the way there you were recalling what you know or imagined or dreamed about this place. Everything you observe in those first few hours at camp is seen through glasses tinted the color of the thoughts and emotions and presuppositions with which you arrived. Whatever happens in that time quickly shapes your initial impression of this place and the people who are in leadership. Misinterpretation is probable. That is why the first day at camp is so important, and why it is so critical that a counselor do everything possible to create a good first impression.

• *Memorize their names.* Names have a mysterious and important quality to people because they represent the whole person. People are surprisingly gratified when we remember their names and use them. Do you find it difficult to keep track of names and faces? This is a discipline you need to learn, in whatever ministry you do. Make it your goal to have all your campers' names and faces memorized and connected by the time you sit down together for the first meal at camp. On that first rowdy night, while they are settling down to bed, rehearse their names and bunk positions in your mind over and over. It is the camp counselor's version of counting sheep!

- *Help them get established and oriented.* Until you discover otherwise, assume that campers don't know their way around. Instead of pointing down the path, *take* them to your cabin and help them get settled in. If they need to do a swim test (and if it is okay with the waterfront staff) get in the water with them. If they are new to the camp take them on a tour. It is not just a matter of being helpful, but these are your first opportunities to build a relationship with your campers. Make the most of them.

- *Focus attention.* The first day of camp tends to be hectic, and people may be after your attention for all kinds of reasons. Some adults complain that when I am listening to a child or youth, no one else can get my attention. I take that as a compliment of the highest order, and wish it were always true. Make time, in the chaos of the first day of camp, to focus your full attention on each one of your campers for at least a few minutes if possible. Younger campers will soak up your attention like a sponge; older campers need time just hanging out with you in a non-threatening way so they can begin to trust you. Make time stand still for them, if even for a few moments, on that first day.

- *Build group identity and dynamic.* Some of your campers probably came to camp with friends or siblings. You need to help the established friendship groups and singles in your cabin connect with one another, especially in those first few hours. The best way is to develop an identity that will make them feel like a cohesive group, rather than small groups or individuals who happen to live in the same room. Examples include everything from painting your noses blue with zinc sunscreen, to making a decision to win the cabin clean-up competition, to coming to dinner wearing boxer shorts on your heads. Your creativity, combined with sensitivity, will make it work.

- *Get them involved in the program.* For various reasons, some children and youth will not readily get involved in what is happening during the first few days. You don't know all the reasons (yet), but you do need to respect their reasons as valid. If you show understanding you will get a lot further than if you make demands. It is more effective to help a non-cooperative camper find his place in your group, or to develop a friendship with another camper who is more involved, than to force him into compliance.

If there are not many activities programmed for the first afternoon of camp (which is often the case as campers arrive and register), try to make something happen with your campers, even if it is just finding some cool place to hang out together. Older campers may not seem to want you around. Respect that, and don't be constantly in their face, but be ever available to them and ready to take whatever opportunity they offer to do things with them.

2. Wake-up.

How do *you* like to have someone wake you up? For some kids, a bad start to the day just means a bad day. Be sensitive to campers who aren't "morning people," and be gentle. Younger campers are likely to get up very early on the first morning of camp. Be prepared, and plan something you can do with them (besides growl) in the hours before breakfast: a short hike, a cabin game, morning exercises or a challenge. Try breakfast in bed one morning (make sure you make arrangements with the head counselor and cook the day before).

3. Mealtimes.

Meals at camp need to be a good balance of fun and control. Try to be the *initiator* of fun ideas at mealtimes, rather than always squelching the campers' ideas of fun. Your camp might have "theme" meals, during which you may have to eat blindfolded or without utensils. Camps also tend to have some spontaneous traditions at meals, like singling out someone for an impromptu song. If your camp doesn't do this sort of thing, some fun activity involving just your table can add to group dynamics, such as talking opera style throughout the meal, or wearing towels on your heads and pretending to be Bedouins. Avoid wasting food or doing activities that will take away their appetites. Starting something messy with food is like taking a megaphone and announcing, "This is okay to do!"[68] Eating is still the main purpose of most meals! Maintain a reasonable standard of table manners, not far distant from what their parents would expect at home. Always keep your campers at the table until they are dismissed.

You are the only one making sure your campers are maintaining a healthy diet. Take note, and if necessary take action, if a camper is seriously overeating or not eating enough. Among teenage girls, watch for indications of eating disorders, which may become more pronounced now that they are not under the supervision of their parents. If you notice eating problems, talk with the camper in private, and if necessary arrange for help and counsel.

4. Cabin clean-up.

It is wise for a camp to provide such incentives as a contest for keeping the cabin clean. Make it a project to keep the cabin not only orderly, but a pleasant, hospitable place to live. Give campers the opportunity to generate any ideas for decorating a cabin, and encourage creativity. Make sure they don't do anything permanent, or use camp supplies without permission.

Unless your cabin group is very motivated, you may need to assign clean-up jobs to individual campers. Make sure they are all doing their share, and don't allow a camper to simply opt out of keeping his stuff in order. Also, it is best not to agree with a plan to go for the non-existent "messiest cabin" award. Be a good model of orderliness for your campers, and never be the *cause* of losing clean-up points for your cabin!

5. Chapels / Firesides / Bible Discussions.

Camps vary greatly in their methods of spiritual instruction. Whether it is you and your cabin having a Bible discussion, or a large program with a worship band and speaker, it is the counselor who makes the program, not the interesting discussion material or the high-tech video equipment. Be enthusiastic! Be less inhibited than you would be in church! This is a special occasion for some unique purposes of God, and it is time to pull out the stops.

CHAPTER 14

For many kids at camp, Bible discussions and worship are entirely foreign and will produce a response that might range from excitement to hostility. Other campers who have grown up with spiritual instruction may assume they have heard it all before and not pay attention. The best way to interest both kinds of campers in spiritual instruction is to carry them along with your own interest, involvement and enthusiasm. For example, getting some ten year old boys to sing is like persuading a cat to take a bath. What will you accomplish by forcing them to stand up and do the actions and mouth the words? It is far better to get into the celebration of God yourself in such a way that they will soon want to imitate you.

Be sensitive to campers whose hearts God is reaching. You can help campers focus on what is being taught by staying focused yourself. At the same time, discreetly observe how the campers around you are responding. Crossed arms and eyes glued to the ground may indicate animosity toward the things of God. Focused attention, nervousness and tears are often an indication that God is at work in a camper's heart, convicting him of sin, or challenging him to obedience. Store up these observations for the sake of future discussions and individual conversations with campers.

6. In-between times.

The camp schedule can be full, but there is always some breathing space between activities. A wise camp leader builds these spaces into the program and plans for them. Some camps increase these created spaces as the week progresses to allow campers to reflect on their experiences, interact with staff, and respond in some meaningful way. Even if these "in-between times" just happen at your camp, be alert to them and be ready to use them strategically.

In-between times are also potential opportunities for trouble. Partly this is because campers are in transition, are harder to supervise and are creating their own entertainment. Also, staff tend to use in-between times as open space for themselves, perhaps to talk together, use the washroom, see the nurse or whatever. This seems only reasonable, but the potential for problems is obvious. These are the times that fights break out, homesickness erupts, vandalism occurs and accidents happen. As much as reasonably possible, be among campers during the times before and after meals, while everyone is waking up or going to bed, when the camp store is open, and between programmed activities. Be alert to problems, and don't hesitate to step in.

Use in-between times as a great opportunity for social interaction. Is there a long line-up for the camp store? Spend time moving up and down the line-up talking with campers. They are a captive audience, and usually like the attention. Before and after meals, be where the campers are if possible, rather than taking advantage of possible special staff privileges. Make "appointments" to spend individual or small group time with your campers between activities. Be sure not to leave anyone out. Watch for the good example of the counselor who is sitting on the grass surrounded by campers! The more tired you get, the more you will naturally tend to distance yourself from campers. Use these times to relax and hang out with them.

7. Recreational activities.

At many camps, counselors form a large part of the activity instruction staff for the recreational part of the program. According to the skills and experience you bring to camp (or gain at camp), you may be assigned to instruct and lead campers in one or several activity sessions per day. Hopefully, you will also have opportunity to simply be with some or all of your campers for one or more activity sessions, allowing you to build relationships with them through your common experiences.

Activities are not an end in themselves. At a Christian camp, the ultimate purpose of the activities is to provide opportunity for building relationships through which God can work in campers' lives. Your camp may also place a strong emphasis on having campers gain certification in outdoor skills and develop character and confidence through adventure activities. At other camps, fun and social interaction are placed higher on the list of goals than education. Find out your camp's philosophy of recreation. Your camp will probably provide some specific training, but here are a few suggestions on leading activities, from archery to bungy jumping:

- *Safety is your first concern.* Go over safety rules in your first session with each group, stressing the reasons for them and the consequences of not following them. Be alert at all times to potentially dangerous situations, and don't hesitate to step in and correct campers who are ignoring safety rules. Take initiative and personal responsibility.

- *Be progressive.* If your activity allows, introduce new skills and challenges each day. Campers will be anticipating new stuff instead of getting bored with the same old thing. Also, adjust your method of teaching to suit the various age levels. Don't expect younger campers to catch on like older campers. Think about what it is like to be their age, and teach your activity as you would want to be taught.

- *Early success.* Try to make it possible for your campers to succeed as early as possible in your activity, without taking away the challenge. For example, if the campers' arrows usually fall short of the target, move the whole group up closer so they can hit it.

- *Think through your method of teaching your activity.* Use your imagination! Create fun! Make it your goal to teach your activity in such a way that campers beg to do it again. Check to see if there are any reasonable innovations you can add, such as offering face-painting in the line-up for the climbing wall, but make sure your innovation doesn't detract from the activity.

- *High expectations.* Your camp's brochure and reputation may create high expectations for the activities in the minds of campers. Make it your goal to run your activity as a quality experience that exceeds their expectations. It should create a good memory that they will talk about for a long time.

8. Games.

Games, wide games and team competition form a large part of many camp programs. As a counselor you may be expected to lead, assist or simply play these games with the campers. It is sometimes difficult for staff to remember that the game is for the fun and benefit of the camper! A counselor who has too much adrenaline pumping while playing a game can be hazardous to the emotional and physical health of campers, and himself. Your purpose while playing camp games is not to win or become the hero, but to make the game the best experience possible for the campers.

Often there will be a meeting for counselors before a "wide game" (a game that ranges over a wide area and takes an hour or more to play) to explain the rules and hand out special assignments. I know from experience that it is most frustrating to have five minutes before the game, ten minutes of instructions to go through, and a room full of counselors who are so noisy and excited you have to yell to be heard. Listen carefully to all the instructions, and save your chatter and questions to the end. You, the counselor, will make or break this game, so it is critical that you and your fellow counselors understand it thoroughly.

If a game begins to slow down, or never really gets going, do something different to spark things again. Gather a few campers together and make a sacrificial, major assault. Watch for kids who are too shy or "too cool" to get involved and take them with you. Even if it means losing, encourage the *campers* to be creative and to do the important stuff in the game rather than you doing it for them.

Above all, don't cheat. It may be fun to stretch the rules, but you will likely hurt someone's feelings (especially among younger campers) and provide a bad example. Go with the program. This is a good opportunity to model the difference that Christ makes in your life. If the game is simply not a great one, your enthusiasm is the key. Try to pump up your team and make it fun. It is the *noisiest* team that usually wins!

9. Special events.

Camps generally have one or several events that require cabin groups to prepare and participate in some up-front production. These include skit nights, cabin "dates," contests, dramatic productions, dress-up-the-counselor events and the like. Often your cabin group will need to come up with an idea to use for such an event. Though you will usually have to be the catalyst for such ideas and get them started, try to promote your campers' creativity as much as possible. If it is feasible, use their ideas. You may want to decide beforehand about your standards of what is acceptable and what is not. Avoid compromise when your campers beg to do something that you (and the camp leadership) would consider rude, violent or offensive, and decide beforehand whether or not you will allow them to shave your head! These events can easily get out of hand, so be prepared to stand your ground and set a firm example of good taste, while making it as crazy and fun as possible.

10. Firesides.

I am not sure what there is about a campfire that focuses people's attention and creates an atmosphere of acceptance and openness. Firesides at camp are a God-given, emotionally charged opportunity for fun, worship and significant sharing of the work of Christ by campers and staff. Staff should arrive early enough that they can spread out among campers. Plan where and with whom you will sit. As always, know where the kids of your cabin are, and sit with them if possible.

Be careful as a counselor not to monopolize fireside sharing times. The purpose of testimony times is to give campers the opportunity to talk about what God is doing or what they are thankful for in their lives. So if you have the chance to speak, use it to provide the campers with an example of a short, simple, to-the-point and from-the-heart account, such as they would be able to offer as well. A three-point homiletic sermon will just discourage them. Be careful not to share negative things such as, "Camp is such a high for me and every time I go home it's such a low, but hopefully this time will be different." That kind of testimony is not encouraging, and may set up campers to expect the same for themselves. Help the sharing time stay on topic; younger campers can pretty quickly turn it into "show and tell."

11. Cabin Devotions.

Cabin devotions are often a traditional way of ending the day. Usually the counselor is responsible to lead these, and may or may not be given material to do so. Make sure campers are ready for bed before you start! Do your own daily routine of brushing teeth and so on *with* them in the washrooms they use, rather than making a detour through the staff quarters. Younger campers are accustomed to being asked by their parents if they have brushed their teeth and have gone to the bathroom. Make sure all your campers have returned to the cabin before you begin evening devotions.

CHAPTER 14

The day's events greatly affect your campers' readiness to discuss God's word in the evening. "Everything you do as a counselor in God's day will feed into the time when you actually open the scripture with the campers. If you wolf down more than your share of the hotcakes at breakfast, make jokes about questionable things or play someone else's position on the volleyball court, you have set up some negatives that will block out your more pious words...["69] The more you work toward peace and reconciliation in your cabin group *before* they arrive for devotions in the evening, the better.

Explain to your campers what this time is about and why it is important, especially for the sake of new campers and those from non-church homes. Explain why you are bringing out this book called the Bible as an authority in life and why it will be the basis of your discussion. Make sure cabin devotions are *their* time, not your time to practice preaching. Cabin devotions should be cabin *discussions*, with everyone talking in turn and everyone involved. Be flexible to the questions, the doubts and the anxieties that your campers express.

Cabin devotions can also be a great time to get to know your campers and build good cabin dynamics. Many counselors do a survey with their campers on the first night, asking questions to find out fun and serious stuff about them, like, "What is something you can do that no one else can?" and "Who lives at your house?" (a safer question to ask than, "Who is in your family?"). Keep discreet (and readable) notes on what you discover about your campers during the week. These notes will give you a better understanding of your campers and their needs. They will also help you fill out camper reports at the end of the week and do follow-up with your campers later.

CHAPTER 16

12. Lights Out.

I have been there. One in the morning. Every camper is still awake. Some are out of their bunks. The director has been by three times to tell you to keep down the noise. You have constantly put out "fires" like rude jokes, pillow fights, flying projectiles and body noises. You wonder why counselors are not issued ear plugs, and you wish you were anywhere but here. Kids who have been active all day, who are outside their comfort zone, and who have just had hot chocolate and cookies (most camp cooks have never been counselors!) do not go to sleep well. How are those other counselors doing it? Here are a few more "tricks of the trade":

- *Help your campers wind down before you expect them to go to sleep.* Camp is exciting! Your campers have been pumped up all day, and cannot just flip a switch and shut down. Help them make the transition from moving to talking, from talking to listening and from listening to sleeping. You can design your cabin devotions toward this goal. *Discussion* will get them talking, and keep them from moving too soon to sleeping!

- *Have a big repertoire of long stories and riddles.* My favorites are "shaggy dog" stories (which begin repeating themselves), long jokes with groaners for punch lines (if anyone is awake by the time I reach the punch line!), spruced-up parables, and two-part stories that keep them in suspense. A good story is worth the time it takes, and will often cause campers go to sleep sooner than repeated threats. Bring a book to read out loud to your campers. I have often used books like C.S. Lewis' *Chronicles of Narnia*, even with junior high campers. The only problem is that they never want me to stop reading!

  Avoid telling (or allowing campers to tell) any stories that involve horror, obscenity, guts and gore, ghosts and the occult, or real-life tragedy.[70] These things have become all too real and close to home in our world. You have no idea of the backgrounds of your campers, nor what stories might trigger terror, shame or grief on their part. There are so many fun and positive stories to tell that there is no need to bother with anything less.

- *Go on a secret mission.* Is your cabin up late every night? Shorten one of those nights by using it to plan a "mission impossible," like a raid of the camp store, a conspiracy to send the director's boxers up the flagpole, a "snipe hunt," or a night out in the forbidden staff lounge. Of course, you pre-arrange everything with your supervisor the day before you carry out your plans, but your campers don't need to know that. You would be amazed how quiet—and how freaked out—they can become trying to pull it off, and how quickly they go to sleep afterward.

- *Sometimes you should stay up late.* When significant discussion is taking place, or an individual camper has chosen this time to open up his heart to you about some issue, most camp directors would only ask that you not disturb others and that you keep the time to a reasonable length. Who knows if the opportunity will ever come again? Be very careful, though, as you do not want to be open to an accusation of manipulating a child through sleep deprivation! Be sensitive to God's leading, and trust him for rest and strength.

13. Overnights / Sleepouts

Campers are often given the opportunity to spend one or two nights of the week away from the cabin in another setting: out on an island in the lake, up in a treehouse, on a boat or simply under the stars in a field. You may get less sleep than you would like on a night like this, but the memories and common ground created by this experience can be well worth the discomfort.

Make it fun! Probably you will be in a place where noise doesn't matter much and the campers have a bit of room to move around. Let them, within safe and reasonable bounds! As suggested above, help them wind down from the excitement of being out of the cabin before expecting them to notice the beauty of the stars or to listen to the special story you saved for this night.

Safety and security are your first concerns, just as if the overnight were a recreational activity on the waterfront or challenge course. If you are staying a distance from the camp, be sure you have first aid supplies and know the emergency procedures and policies of your camp for this particular outing.

14. Last day of camp.

The last day of camp is almost as crucial as the first day. It is amazing how close campers and counselor can become in just a week or two of camp. Those tears on the last day are real tears, and I have seen them on the faces of boys as well as girls. The most important thing you can do on that final day of camp is to remain available to your campers until the last one leaves.

This is difficult, because you have some important responsibilities on the last day. You may be packing up your own things, checking washrooms and clotheslines and looking under the beds to make sure your campers have all of their stuff (the lost and found rooms of most camps are overflowing). The cabin needs a final cleaning, addresses are exchanged, and you want to say good-bye to that staff member you befriended. However, above all, be available to your campers. Be where they are. Here's why.

When I was a youth pastor, I often ended up driving youth home from an event. I always found it interesting how they jockeyed for the position of being the last to be dropped off. Most of the way home we would talk about nothing of any great consequence. But often as we were within a block or two of that last house, the fortunate last-one-to-be-dropped-off would come up with the most important questions about things very close to his heart. Why did he wait until the last few minutes before he reached home? Partly because it took that long for him to read me and see how I would respond to him, but also because he knew that in a few minutes he would have a way of escape if the conversation became too awkward and uncomfortable.

This also happens at camp, only in this case children and youth often wait until that last morning before they are ready to open up about things that are important to them. So you need to be there for them that hectic last day more than any other. Be on the lookout for campers who seem to be seeking your attention. Try to spend at least a few moments of focused attention with each one of your campers. Pray and ask God to make you especially sensitive and approachable, and to arrange significant conversations according to his purposes for their lives.

CREATING SPACE IN THE SCHEDULE

Camp is a space created in the loud and hostile world of the camper, a place where God can reach his heart. However, sometimes the schedule of the camp can become so busy and noisy that people can't hear the "still, small voice" of God even there. The camp program can give opportunity for campers to stop and listen; some camps purposely relax their busy schedules toward the end of the week for this purpose. But it may be left for you as a counselor to create space in the camp schedule so that your campers can listen to God and respond.

This space does not need to be big. It could be a few moments with a camper after everyone else has rushed out of the dining hall, when you were alert enough to notice that this camper was not in a rush. It might be a decision to sleep out in the field one night, rather than in a relatively more comfortable bed, so that you can stare together at the stars until you drop off to sleep. Or it could be a bag of chips shared with a few campers on the merry-go-round in the otherwise empty playground. Fun and wild excitement and making noise are good and essential parts of camp, but they need to be punctuated by a little hush once in a while, so we can pause to understand what it is all about. So that when God whispers, we will still hear him.

---

[53]E.g., Genesis 18:1-8

[54]E.g., Luke 11:37-38

[55]Luke 9:51-56

[56]See Acts 2:42-47 and Philemon 2

[57]See Romans 12:9-13 and I Peter 4:7-10

[58] I Timothy 3:2 and Titus1:8

[59] Perhaps thinking of Abraham and Sarah in Genesis 18

[60] Henri Nouwen, *Reaching Out*, as quoted by Les Comee, "A Philosophy and Theology of Camp Counseling Today," *Training For Camp Counselors*, ©1990 Young Life

[61] I Corinthians 12:14-19

[62] Matthew 7:3-5

[63] See Matthew 18:21-35

[64] Hebrews 12:15

[65] Matthew 11:28-30

[66] E.g., Matthew 6:25-34 and all of chapter 13

[67] Ephesians 6:12

[68] A famous quote from my respected boss, Scott Bayley

[69] Gladys Hunt, "How To Lead Small Group Bible Studies With Campers", *CCI Focus Series #9*, ©1983 Christian Camping International

[70] See Ephesians 5:3-4 for God's standard of story-telling

CAMP PREP #6:
KNOW YOUR JOB DESCRIPTION

Suggestions on how to prepare for your counseling experience.

The "job description" of a camp counselor as outlined above may seem overwhelming! You will be amazed at the grace of God which he will give you as you need it day by day. However, you also need to actively prepare to fill the big shoes of a summer camp counselor!

• Find out if the camp at which you will serve has a written job description for counselors. This may be included in the camp's Staff Manual, or you may need to request a copy.

• If no written job description is available, ask the camp office or former summer staff to outline for you a typical day and week at their camp. Take the opportunity to clarify what will be expected of you during the different activities of the day. Keep in mind that the camper leadership is hoping for a good level of resourcefulness in you, so don't demand too many details at this point.

• As you get a better idea of the camp's expectations through these discussions and the reading of this chapter, take note of areas that will require special preparation or further resources on your part. Make up a "to-do" list that will help you get ready for a summer of camp counseling.

• Check out the ideas and resources listed in the "Resource Section" at the back of this book.

10. The Camper: Understanding Age Patterns

WHEN I WAS YOUR AGE...

Don't you hate that? Think for a moment about why you don't appreciate it when older people try to compare your experience to theirs when they were "your age." First, you are an individual, uniquely crafted by God in his image, but with your very own personality, character, likes and dislikes. If someone were to have exactly the same experiences in life that you do, he would respond differently because he is a different person. Second, times have changed. No other person's experience is your experience, just as you cannot eat the same piece of cake twice. Being 16 years old today is nothing like being 16 years old twenty years ago. No one but God can fully understand your situation as you do.

Believe it or not, things have changed so much since you were 12 that you also have no right to say to campers, "When I was your age..." They will resent it just as you do, because they know that your twelfth year of life does not qualify you to give advice about their twelfth year of life. The older the campers, the less they will accept anything from you but individual recognition.

PEOPLE HAVEN'T CHANGED...

Have you noticed, though, that when you read the Bible you can relate so well to people like David and his psalms, Peter and his struggle to believe, or Solomon and his love life (well, maybe not!)? People are people, and down deep inside we haven't changed since the days of Adam and Eve. We are diverse and distinct from one another, and we need to respect human diversity. However, when you put us all together some patterns emerge, just as the individual lines and dots and doodles on the hearth rug form a pattern if you stand back and look at them from a distance.

If you can learn to understand the patterns, while respecting the diversity, you will gain a good understanding of the campers who are coming to your camp this summer. When they respond a certain way to particular circumstances, you will smile and know why—or at least have an educated guess. You will have gained some wisdom that will help you with the hundreds of daily decisions, big and small, that you must make as a camp counselor. You can become better prepared to deal with each of your campers as individuals, while helping them become a team.

The patterns produced by the individual lives of campers have been interpreted by many experts in many ways. Elsewhere you can find lists of the physical, emotional, social, intellectual and spiritual characteristics of the various age groups. The most helpful analysis I have found is this simple diagram:[71]

Age 0-4	**DISCOVERING**	*(responding to the world)*
Age 4-8	**TESTING**	*(checking out the limits)*
Age 8-11	**CONCLUDING**	*(they are the smartest ever)*

!!! PUBERTY CRASH !!!

Age 11-13	**DISCOVERING**	*(a whole new world)*
Age 13-16	**TESTING**	*(pushing the limits)*
Age 16 +	**CONCLUDING**	*(deciding what is important)*

Two things to note about this wonderfully regular pattern:

- *The ages attached to these stages of life are quite fluid.* The age of puberty itself has dropped by four to five years in the last two centuries, probably due to our raised standard of living (or as some believe, due to the hormones used in food production). In all areas of life, children and youth seem to be reaching these stages of life at an earlier age. It would not surprise me if this trend continues. Children as young as 7 can be quite rebellious and already strongly influenced by their peers. Some teens begin making "conclusions" at age 15, and some reach retirement and still don't have a clue.

- *The stages themselves seem to be quite constant.* That is, children and youth seem to all move from one stage to the other in the same order, though (as you will note in the chart) some overlap is always there and regression is possible.

Let's look at this pattern more closely, and later we will discuss the implications it has for each age group that will arrive at the average camp:

1. Discovery (age 0-4).

Someone has said that in his first year of life a child processes the equivalent amount of information needed to earn a Ph.D. What a wonderful (and for the young parent, terrifying) time of life! Everything from big toe to grandpa's false teeth in a cup is a new discovery, seen, touched and tasted for the first time. Why do babies put everything in their mouths? For the same reason dogs sniff everything: some senses are more to be trusted than others. This is an age of extraordinary sensory perception and response.

Okay, for a young parent this age is not always terrifying. It is also very fun. I will not forget the expression on my son's baby face when he tried puréed blueberries for the first time. Or the way his eyes lit up when he realized the tricycle was for him. Notice that it is the more experienced parents who don't react when their toddler is waddling toward your priceless vase. They know that discovery is worth everything at this age; and besides, it's not their vase.

2. Testing (age 5-8).

Once you discover the world, it is time to see just what it will do. Bedtime is a good example. Kids of this age know exactly how many things they can contrive to do after the first time mom or dad says, "Go to bed!", and they are pushing for a new record every night. They don't easily give up gained territory either. Once I had established the evening "sock war" with my youngest son, there was no avoiding it until the last sock bounced into the hamper.

Much of a child's morality is established at this age, and this too is conquered ground not easily surrendered. If you serve at a camp that has weeks or weekends for this age group, you may be surprised at what some of the kids talk about. When a young child pushes the barriers and finds they move, he cannot be expected to have the maturity to stop pushing. It is not his responsibility.

At the same time, this too is a fun age. "What happens if..." is fun at any age, and counselors for this age group have opportunity to make the "experiment" both safe and an adventure at camp. The greatest challenge will be holding the boundaries for a half dozen kids who are used to the boundaries being set in different locations than you have placed them.

3. Concluding (age 9-11).

It makes sense that after eight years of exploration, analysis and investigation anyone would begin to come to some conclusions (except perhaps a federal committee). By the time a child reaches this age he has come to know practically everything, in his opinion. How can you tell a ten year old? Sorry, you can't tell him anything. However, there is a strong likelihood that he will adore the ground you walk on and that your influence will carry much weight.

One of the "concluding" aspects of this age group is that their bodies still work like they came from the factory, and after years of practice and training, junior campers know just what they can expect from them. They never seem to stop moving until they drop from exhaustion, and before you know it they are back up and going again and leaving you behind. When I give in and play road hockey with the pack of eight to eleven year old boys on my street, I have to play hard (and avoid knocking them over—they get very upset). In a couple of years when their bodies start changing I know I will be able to score with one hand. Can't wait.

4. Puberty and Discovery, Part Two (age 12-13).

There was a time when no one knew what a teenager was, but "coming of age" was a big deal. Our culture has identified and classified a group of people with the syllable "teen" in their age, and labeled it as a difficult period of life. At the same time we have largely swept under the rug the event that marks the beginning of this age category: the milestone of puberty.

Nobody threw a party when I hit my "change of life." Instead I was thrown a book and told to read it. Because my parents seemed embarrassed about it, I never did read that book (it's okay—I know now what it was about). So the thing that was happening to my body and emotions and social structure was mostly a mystery to me and a little frightening. No one told me—though I soon found out—that life would never be the same again. My experience was a far cry from the days of "Bar Mitzvah's" and other rites of passage that celebrated a child's journey to manhood or womanhood.

Puberty is hard because suddenly the world is not what you thought it was, back when you were ten years old and knew all. Everything has fallen to pieces, and anything is up for grabs—even your faith in Christ. It must all be re-explored and rediscovered, which is why many parents panic, just as they did back when they came upon their toddler exploring the medicine cabinet. Yet this process of rediscovery can also be an opportunity for God to reach young and sensitive hearts. Junior high camps can be simply amazing that way.

5. Testing, Part Two (age 14-16).

It was hard enough when they were five to eight years old, trying out and pushing the boundaries. Now they are old enough and big enough to do some real damage to others and themselves if they step too far over the line. This is a difficult age, but if you think it is difficult for you to handle as a counselor, try being a teen. I personally have no desire to re-live this period of life. You would think that if anyone had the ultimate method of dealing with this age it would be a guy like Dr. James Dobson, but even he is often quoted as saying, "Just get them through it."

Of course, our culture intensifies the problem by making the boundaries so vague or by refusing to set them at all. Dr. Dobson invites us to imagine walking down a long dark corridor with many doors on either side, doors labeled with every harmful and addictive behavior you can imagine: drinking, pre-marital sex, drugs, pornography, the occult, gambling, homosexual experimentation. Behind those doors you can hear your friends (or people you want as friends) partying it up and having a good time. All you have to do is turn the handle and open the door. No one can stop you, and few people are giving you any reasons not to, at least reasons you take seriously.[72]

That is the world in which junior high youth live. Thankfully, many of them have had enough childhood direction, personal integrity and pure grace from God to not push the boundaries too far even though they know they could. Many adults are appalled at the immorality of youth; I am amazed at how moral they are considering the opportunity they have to be immoral, and I wonder how well most adults would do in their shoes. Still, this is a fragile age, and I have seen simple hurt feelings turn into disappointment, rebellion and disaster. The camp counselor of this age group needs to be much in prayer for wisdom, compassion and patience.

6. Concluding, Part Two (age 17+).

The significant thing that happens as youth get older is that they begin to make decisions about what is *true* and what is *important* to them. That is, they begin to determine their own set of principles and values. That sounds good—and it can be—but not necessarily. Senior high youth often choose beliefs and practices different from or even contrary to those of their parents, and they don't easily change them again.

Senior high campers tend to choose friends who have views similar to their own. Therefore, the emerging values and principles of the older youth are reinforced daily, while the parent's influence becomes less and less. This is hard for parents to experience, especially when they are not especially happy about the direction their teens have chosen. That is the point: they have chosen, and that is as it should be. More and more, senior high youth are coming out from under the parent's responsibility and must be left in God's hands.

Another factor in this process is that as they determine what matters to them in life, they begin planning and working seriously toward significant achievements. There was a time when they were bored if the right people weren't there. At this age they are bored when they sense that what they are doing has no significance and achieves nothing that matters to them. Senior high camp better be a significant experience, worth taking a week off the summer job.

A CLOSER LOOK

Perhaps my description of these age patterns fails to include all the details about physical abilities and intellectual capacities at the various age levels, but I have never met anyone who can remember all those facts and figures anyway. I personally find a description of the big picture more helpful, but if you want the facts and figures, they are available in most psychology textbooks and camp staff manuals. From here, let's take a look at the implications of these patterns to you, the counselor of real kids at camp.

THE PRIMARY CAMPER—AGE 6 TO 8

A growing number of camps are welcoming younger children for day camp programs and even longer overnight sessions. Primary campers are not difficult to please, and the camp program is generally more relaxed than it is for older children. However, supervision is almost constant and will demand the counselor's full attention and boundless energy.

Children of this age are exploring the perimeters of what is acceptable behavior, and they need the security of definite rules and limited space. If these are not provided, many children will quickly step over the line to see how far they can go before they are stopped. Younger children have a limited sense of responsibility, particularly when stimulated by other children. A small group of young children can get into much more trouble—or have much more fun—than they would ever dream of attempting on their own.

Here are some of the needs of primary children and how to provide for them as their counselor:[73]

1. They need basic care.

All the care a parent would usually provide for this age group will be required of the counselor. Staff who are used to campers caring for their own basic needs may be surprised the first time a six year old camper asks for help washing the shampoo out of her hair. Going to the bathroom, washing up before meals and getting ready for bed become small group events, done together. It is not likely that a younger camper will be willing to make the trip from the cabin to the washroom in the dark by himself. You as a counselor will be with your campers all the time, which is why many camps provide two counselors per cabin for this age group.

One of the basic needs of younger children is rest. They seem to have all the energy in the world, but they tire more quickly than older children and need regular breaks. You will be amazed at how quickly they bounce back, however, and are ready to go again long before you! An after-lunch "down time" as a cabin group is a wise plan for this age. Make sure you have with you a good variety of resources—things to make, paper to draw on, quiet games to play, a story to tell or read—to keep the children quiet and resting , and to make it fun.

Bedtime is generally not as much of an issue with younger as with older campers. Campers are exhausted at the end of a long day, and only a limited number of them will test the boundaries when it is time to sleep. Again, bedtime needs to be a group event at this age. Take them through all the steps of washing up, brushing teeth, using the toilet and every other routine they are familiar with. Finish off the day with prayer and a bedtime story that will calm them and ready them for sleep. Kids of this age are used to some form of affection such as bedtime hugs, which will give them a sense of being cared for and secure.

2. They need warmth and affection.

Maybe the reason God made little boys and girls so cute is that they have an inherent need for lots of affection. Both the girls *and* the boys need hugs at this age, and will want to crawl on your lap, hold your hand and sit close to you. Some will squirm and wriggle, but need and appreciate physical affection just the same.

Of course, in our day of alarm about sexual abuse, caution is needed and some children may be resistant because of the anti-abuse training they have received, or their home situations. Physical affection should never be forced on a child and should not be prolonged. Consider the amount and style of affection a parent would offer, and do not step beyond that standard or give in to a child's demands for more.

For the most part, children will naturally initiate the hug or other sign of affection they need, and you simply need to respond. With children who are too shy or too busy to initiate affection, it is appropriate to offer it yourself. But be mindful of how the child and those around may read your actions, and be careful that your own motives are always pure.

3. They require short-term and simple expectations.

Primary children do not have high programming needs. Simple is better, and young children will be happier and feel more secure when the program or activity is relatively easy. They love to be made the "experts" at something they can do well, and can be easily overwhelmed if the activity is too challenging or complicated. They like repetition and routine, and will not mind playing the same game or singing the same song again and again.

Set out your expectations early, and break them down into small enough pieces that they can digest and understand what you want them to do. For example, saying, "Let's clean up the table" may be rewarded by blank stares or a rush to the playground. Instead say, "Jackie, could you stack the plates; Mary, you gather the cups; and Sue, please put all the cutlery in a pile."

Like all children, primary campers require discipline to maintain order and teach them appropriate behavior. But they are very concerned about fairness. Many of the discipline issues and conflicts you will encounter have to do with whose turn it was, who it belongs to, and whether everyone got their fair share. They will look to you for judgment on these "major issues," and may be upset at the outcome even when you have been as fair as possible. Part of your discipline will include encouraging them to share and to consider the feelings of the other children. Don't wait for campers to step over the line, but offer them warnings (not threats) when they are nearing a behavioral boundary.

When discipline is needed, be very specific and concrete about the issue you are addressing. Children in the new context of camp may not know or remember your expectations, and will need to have the situation explained very simply and plainly. When there is more than one child involved, it is usually better to talk with them separately, and deal only with their own part of the problem. Ask for their suggestions as to the outcome of what they have done. When deciding on consequences for their behavior, be sure not to embarrass children or single one out for punishment. See the seriousness of every issue from their young eyes, and trust God for wisdom in making decisions.

4. They want to please you.

Not only will young children easily trust you, but they will also quickly seek to please you and win your approval. There will be much competition for your words of praise and your attention. Children of this age are very perceptive of when your attention is divided, and will not be satisfied when they have you in body but not in mind. Be very careful not to show favoritism—at any age, but particularly with this one. Primary children read your actions and attitudes more than they give credit to your words.

One of the best ways to express love for these campers is by your enthusiasm. Get excited about the rock they found, laugh with them when they tell jokes and silly stories, and motivate them with your excitement about the next activity. Rather than hound campers to get them moving, make it a game and they will want to move with you.

Realize the opportunity you have to help these children formulate their young concepts about what is right and wrong, true and false, good and bad. When you show pleasure about their good attitude and behavior, and disapproval of what doesn't meet your expectations, it carries a good deal of weight with young children. Use your influence with care, avoid manipulation, and keep in mind Jesus' warning about millstones.[74] But use the opportunity to be an example that they may retain long after they forget your name and face.

5. They have varying degrees of skills.

If you have young cousins or nieces and nephews whom you see only occasionally, you know that children of this age grow and develop a great deal over a short period of time, both physically and intellectually. Because of this, your cabin of primary campers will vary greatly in terms of their physical and intellectual skills. It is not unusual for one five year old to be reading fluently, and another eight year old to be hardly reading at all. In choosing activities, don't assume that the children can read the words to the song or understand the meaning of your object lesson. Games should be designed so that special skills with equipment or with balance and timing are not required.

As stated before, with this age simple is better, and easy is fun. Children will be better stimulated by your enthusiasm than by the challenge of the activity. Young children are happy doing things at which they excel, so try to find activities for each camper in which he or she can succeed. Be reasonable in your expectations. A large part of the enjoyment primary campers will carry away with them is the feeling that they have done well.

6. They are at different levels of spiritual perception.

To the chagrin of his disciples, their esteemed rabbi Jesus didn't mind when people brought their children to be blessed by him. You can imagine Jesus with a lap full of children, telling them stories and easily winning the trust of these perceptive little creatures. He warned his disciples not to hinder even little children coming to him, for the kingdom of heaven belongs to those who become like children.[75]

We also should not under-estimate a primary child's ability to have true spiritual awareness. It is important to realize that children of this age are able to differentiate their beliefs from those of their parents: I have known children who demonstrated more genuine and personal faith than their parents! It is true that some primary children are not yet able to grasp the seriousness of sin and their need for faith in Christ—but some children are ready, and we should not forbid them. The glory of the gospel is summed up in Jesus' prayer: "I praise you, Father, Lord of heaven and earth, because you have hidden these things from the wise and learned, and revealed them to little children. Yes, Father, for this was your good pleasure."

MATTHEW 11:25-26

As you share the gospel simply and clearly with young children, ask God to enable you to discern whether they are responding to the work of the Holy Spirit in their young hearts, or to the simple desire to please you. Be supportive of new believers at this age, but don't offer them so much special attention that you suddenly have the whole cabin wanting to get in on this, for the wrong reasons. Be as accepting of the child who is not ready to respond as you are of the one who does.

THE JUNIOR CAMPER—AGE 9 TO 11

I shouldn't play favorites, but this has always been one of my favorite age groups to work with because they are so incredibly responsive. If you do even a reasonable job as a counselor they will love everything you do for them and give glowing reports to mom or dad at home that would make you blush. Imagine what will happen when you do a *great* job. Here are some things to watch for, based on the patterns discussed above, and some suggestions on how to respond as a camp counselor:

1. Junior campers are at the center of their own world.

Junior campers tend to see life from a subjective point of view. How many junior campers does it take to change a light bulb? Just one—he holds the light bulb and the whole world revolves around him. What are the implications of this kind of perspective at camp?

* *They talk all the time.* There is nothing on earth smarter than junior campers, as they will soon let you know. It is because after nine or ten years of sifting the evidence, they are finally ready to give their verdict on practically every area of life. They pre-judge everything; that is, they "know" first and experience second. Sometimes it appears they are lying when they are simply assuming something to be true of which they have little or no knowledge. If they are proved wrong about what they thought they knew, they will likely have an immediate excuse to bring forward. They have good ideas, even good intentions, but often fail to follow through on projects.

    Why do junior campers find it necessary to fill up every silence with anything that comes to mind? It is their way of keeping an adult's attention, like the annoying sales clerk who puts you on hold so you have to listen to his company's ads while you wait. When a camper knows he has had you heart and soul for a period of time, it has been a significant experience for him, and probably an uncommon one.

    Junior campers often engage their mouths before putting their minds in gear, and leave their mouths running long after they have nothing left to say. Does anything they constantly talk about matter to you or anyone you know? Probably not, but your *campers* matter to you. When you listen attentively to their chatter and humbly let yourself be instructed, you communicate that you care about them, and they will love you for it in return.

* *Junior campers can be very critical.* Remember, junior campers are at an age of making conclusions on everything; therefore, they tend to be idealists with often unreasonable expectations. They have especially high standards for anyone they look up to, which of course includes you. Your junior campers will probably respect you as a counselor, but don't be surprised if they frequently challenge or correct what you say—if you can get a word in edgewise. They can also be very critical of themselves, not

meeting even their own expectations. They have very little patience with failure and may not be quick to forgive and forget. They can make life miserable for a fellow camper who doesn't measure up.

This can help explain situations you might face in the cabin group. Why do they all pick on that little guy in the cabin whom you really like? Perhaps he failed to make a good first impression on them and they are unwilling to give him a second chance. In the meantime he is slowly shriveling up inside and becoming an easier target. Because you are defending him, the other campers feel slighted, and so they take it out on the little guy whenever you are not around. Somehow you will need to elevate this camper in their eyes, or at least disperse some of the criticism against him. It may be time to find some way he can make an important contribution to the group, like help the cabin win a contest, or perhaps you need to increase your cabin's sense of identity by writing up together a pact of cabin loyalty.

- *They have a heightened sense of fairness.* It is extremely important to junior campers that people treat them fairly, or even a little better than fairly. For example, I was once playing roller-hockey in the rain with a group of kids ten years old. Every time anyone took a slapshot he would hit a puddle and soak everybody. It was great fun, except for one fellow who got mad and had the nerve to complain to me (while I'm wringing out my shirt), "Everybody keeps getting me wet!" He didn't think getting wet was fair to him, but didn't even consider that we were all in the same condition.

  Anticipating this attitude, follow the Apostle Paul's advice: "If it is possible, as far as it depends on you, live at peace with everyone."[76] Not that you should compromise yourself in order to please every camper, but make every effort to be fair and equitable with junior campers. As fun as it may be, don't cheat at games. Watch that you don't play favorites in the cabin; give your campers equal time and attention. You should anyway, but since fairness is an inherent value at this age, make it your goal to be as fair as fair can be in their eyes.

- *They have great capacity for learning and memorization.* After your eleventh year, you will never again have such a great ability to retain and recall information. Most kids this age still enjoy learning; only a handful are "too cool" to engage their brains. Put much effort into making cabin discussions, devotions and events into learning experiences, but also challenge them to live out what they claim to know. Challenge them to memorize Bible verses; if this is not part of your camp's program, make it a contest for your cabin with an appropriate reward at the end. They will retain those words longer than you, and God knows how much they will need them in the years to come.

- *They are likely to reach some wrong conclusions.* Junior campers have been collecting information over the years from people such as parents, siblings and school teachers, and also from non-personal sources such as television, magazines, movies, music, video games and the world wide web. It is from this info that they are making their first conclusions about life. Much of the information they have accumulated is simply not true, or based on wrong assumptions and principles. TV morality is generally several degrees worse than morality in the real world. World views such as evolutionary theory and new age beliefs permeate everything. As a Christian camp counselor you have the opportunity to offer them absolute truth and the example of your own integrity and moral values. However, do not be surprised if a junior camper challenges things you assumed everyone thought were true or good.

2. Junior campers' most significant relationships are with adults more than with kids their own age.

Junior campers have friends and would say their friends are important to them. However, their primary relationships—the ones that most influence them—are usually still with their parents, teachers and other adults.[77] When these adults have neglected them, some kids turn to their friends for identity and self worth at an early age. But at camp, the primary relationship of most junior campers will be with *you.* This is what it will mean at camp:

- *A junior camper's week at camp often revolves around their counselor.* Have you ever seen pictures of a momma lion being pulled, climbed on and chewed on by her cubs? Younger and less mature campers can also be very clingy. They will do anything to get your attention, including jumping on your poor back and constantly getting in your face. They will look to you for direction on what to do next, come to you with every scratched knee and make you the mediator of every dispute. You are their substitute mom or dad, as if their parents were gone for the day. You are their older brother or sister who has been given the job of looking after them.

- *They will want to hold your attention.* The world is increasingly becoming an adult place where there is little room and time for kids. People used to work so they could raise and support their family; today many people work to give *themselves* comfort, satisfaction and status. Kids don't fit that plan very well. So in more and more families, children get farmed out to daycare, plunked in front of the TV set or computer monitor, put on sports teams, and sent to camp as a substitute for time with parents. In the end, the kids have had lots of thrills, lots of opportunities and lots of fun—but it is meaningless to them and makes them feel insignificant. Their experiences are lacking *relationship* with the people who matter to them.

  Many kids this age are easily bored, even at camp. You can do some very exciting game and you ask a camper how he liked it, and he will say, "Okay, I guess. Kinda boring." Probably the game was exciting enough, but it made him feel alone and now he is hungry for conversation and relationship. The word "bored" is usually a clear signal that a child desires some attention from you, not that he needs more thrills. Time with you, doing just about anything that will hold your attention, will satisfy him.

- *Some junior campers are starving for a sense of self-worth.* For some kids, summer camp is like a refugee camp. The camp counselor is often called on to be a refugee worker among kids who have just come out of horrible conditions and are starving for attention, some care and understanding, a bit of tenderness and compassion. It is not always comfortable to work among these campers. However, just as some well-off people opt to work at refugee camps rather than play at a resort, we go to camp to serve—not to be served—because Jesus has ransomed these kids for himself.

Think of the incredible opportunity this presents! There are kids out there who want to spend time with you, who desire your attention, and who are ready and willing to learn from you. In a few years, none of that may be true of them. I guess that is why I find it so upsetting when I run across the occasional counselor who seems to have time for everything except simply being with his campers. The opportunity lost in these years will never be seen again. Use it wisely.

3. Junior campers know their rights, but not necessarily their responsibilities.

Junior campers have been taught ever since Sesame Street to be "empowered," and to take charge of their own lives. At school they are encouraged to think for themselves, make their own decisions, and work at their own pace. Many kids today are enjoying the absolute height of material prosperity and opportunity. Many of their parents own their own homes, and even the relatively "poor" kids seem to have all the toys: rollerblades, Nintendo, big screen TV's. To the average North American junior camper, having stuff and being comfortable is a "right."

• *They may not respect you as an adult.* Kids this age may not expect to have to do what they are told by adults. The point of practically every kid's TV show and movie is that adults don't have a clue and need not be respected. Our nation's emphasis on human rights, combined with an erosion of moral boundaries, has encouraged kids to think very little (and care very little) about the consequences of their actions. There has seldom been a generation of kids so aware of their human rights, and so ignorant of their human responsibilities.

• *Kids are capable of hurting kids.* Examples abound in the news every day: kids beating up kids and damaging property and stealing cars at incredibly young ages. Many elementary school teachers spend more time trying to maintain control than teaching their classes. The privilege of freedom has become more important than duties like kindness and honesty. Their world is sometimes violent and insecure, and it will take firmness and compassion on the part of the counselor to ensure that camp is a place of refuge and safety for the camper.

4. Junior campers are facing stresses they are not ready for.

Young campers sometimes face decisions they are too young to handle, such as which parent to spend Christmas with, or whether to start smoking or not. Their schedules are packed with school and sports teams and dancing and swimming and staying out of the way of mom and dad's schedule. They know too much about issues like global warming and drugs and sexual orientation. TV commercials and movies pressure them to dress and act like compact adults. They are forced to contain adult-size stuff in junior-size packages. For example:

- *Opposite sex relationships.* Sure, when I was in grade three I did have a crush on a girl, but nobody would have expected me to ask her to go out with me and be my "girlfriend." Increasingly juniors are pressured to be like junior highs, and to value their peers—including the opposite sex—as the most important people in their lives rather than their parents. We need to encourage junior campers to have junior relationships. It may be cute to watch them write love notes and hold hands at age 10, but it is inappropriate to support this behavior. Encourage junior campers to focus on their relationship with you and your cabin group, because these are the natural primary relationships for this age group.

- *Pressure to succeed.* Who are the parents of junior campers? They are "baby-boomers" or "echo-boomers", who for the most part are just big junior campers. Like their kids, these parents think the world revolves around them. They talk positively about things like being success-oriented and profit-driven. As the saying goes, they tend to "worship their work, work at their play, and play at their worship." Put these people in charge of 9 to 11 year olds, and what do you have? Kids who already put pressure on themselves to know everything and do everything flawlessly, and parents who exert more of the same pressure on them. You can see it at a kids' soccer game where parents scream at their children from the sidelines, or in the sign-up for junior dance lessons where parents fight over their place in line.

Camp should be a place where kids have some space, where they aren't pushed to perform, and where it is okay to be late for class. It should be a time to be quiet, go nuts, be alone, stay up with their friends, be mellow, be wild, let go. Camp should be a place where they can just play and nobody thinks it's a waste of precious time. Where kids can be kids.

Junior campers have a deepening need to be loved and accepted for who they are. They don't need more pressure to succeed from their summer camp counselor. Personally, I think camp should promote fun and relationships over achievement and competition. Where I'm from, it tends to be the loudest team that wins, not necessarily the most talented one.

5. Junior campers are at an age of spiritual commitment.

The highest percentage of campers coming to know Christ at camp is in this age group. Almost all junior campers are old enough to understand the gospel and to know what they are doing when they sign their lives away to Jesus Christ. They have the ability to be sure of their decision, and the capacity to be very dedicated to living the Christian life.

- *They want reality in their faith.* Church kids at this age will be bored with the same old stories and pat "Sunday school" answers that many of them have heard all their lives. Challenge them with the deeper truths of God's word; show them that what you believe really does affect the way you live. Campers with little or no church background will be hungry for some spiritual meaning in their lives. Don't act bored when you are talking with them about the things of God, or they will look for spiritual food elsewhere.

  The best way of convincing this age group of the truth of the gospel is by the faith displayed in the lives of adults. At camp that "adult" is primarily you, but the more good relationships they have with other staff, who show their faith by what they do, the better. Whether you are counseling or teaching archery or washing dishes, your influence will be what gives them a firm place to land when the world crumbles beneath their feet, which it is about to do.

- *They need to hear the gospel clearly.* We will discuss this more thoroughly later, but it is so important that you as a Christian counselor know how to share the gospel in a clear and simple way. It is especially important that you avoid phrases that will give the wrong impression to junior campers, who do not grasp symbolism well.   **CHAPTER 15** What does it mean to "ask Jesus into your heart"? You may understand that this involves a realization of your sin and your need for a Savior; they may see it as the equivalent to inviting a friend for a sleepover. These are concepts they have the capacity to understand, but our Christian lingo can confuse and mislead them very easily.

  John 3:16 is a wonderfully simple explanation of the gospel, but do your junior campers understand what it means to believe in God's Son? They will not find it hard to accept that a man named Jesus died on a cross to take away our sin, but do they realize that putting their faith in Christ is a lifetime decision to live for him? Perhaps we assume that these doctrines are too weighty for young minds. Not only can junior campers understand these ideas, but they can receive God's grace by faith as well as any adult—no, probably more readily than any adult. We must let them come to Jesus and not forbid them by being less than clear and up-front about the gospel.[78]

- *They may need to regain assurance of their faith.* Though junior campers are at an age of making conclusions, they also tend to be self-critical. It will not be unusual to find campers who are not sure if they are Christians, or who have serious doubts about their faith. Usually these will not be rebellious doubts, but searching ones: Can God really love me? How can I know for sure that I am a Christian? Am I going to go to heaven someday? Why does God let bad things happen? Is God listening when I pray?

Your growing influence will give you an audience when it comes time to answer questions like these. Be careful to admit the limits of your own knowledge. If you don't have an adequate answer to one of their questions, tell them you will ask someone else—and be sure you do. Also be ready to admit some of your own times of doubt, and how you have dealt with them. Junior campers will not be satisfied with pat answers. They want to *know*.

THE JUNIOR HIGH CAMPER—AGE 12 TO 14

How can we describe the transition from junior age to junior high? A junior camper is like someone who spends a long time preparing a cake, shaping it, icing it, decorating it just as he wants it to be. It is a perfect masterpiece, and no one can tell him otherwise. A junior high camper is like one who is carrying the cake out to the living room—and drops it on the floor. It splats hard, icing flies, decorations go rolling down the hall, and he spends the next several years desperately trying to gather all the pieces together again and remember where and if they belong.

For a society so pre-occupied with sex, we sure don't talk much about this transition, known as puberty. Except for a few cultural exceptions, we have no ceremonies or traditions to mark this rite of passage and make it a matter of family pride. Puberty is the subject of crude jokes and insensitive remarks about cracking voices, racing hormones and emerging body hair. Sex education for the adolescent is a sensitive issue for parents and teachers; most schools would rather not get involved. Except in the case of a few conscientious parents, my experience is that most of them do not provide much if any instruction and counsel for their emerging adolescents, leaving it for who-knows-who to take care of this responsibility. It is like neglecting to tell someone with a big load in his arms that he is approaching the curb on the sidewalk.

So this cute, happy and bubbly little kid you remember from last summer returns to camp three inches taller, wearing weird clothes, and she has forgotten how to speak more than a few basic words. What's up? Over the winter, puberty struck. It is important to realize that the changes connected with the start of adolescence are not just physical. Rapid development is taking place on the emotional and social level too. It can be very upsetting and scary for these new teens, especially if they think that they are the only ones experiencing these changes.

It is also important to realize (and it is sometimes very obvious) that not all kids change at the same rate. Girls go through puberty much earlier than boys—as early as 9 or 10—and tend to develop more rapidly. So in a group of 11 to 14 year olds you can have little boys who like to burp and make other rude noises, in with young guys who are ready to shave and sing bass. With them are small giggly girls that stink after the third day of camp, alongside girls with model figures who are ready to break hearts.

Is it any wonder, then, that we have so many difficulties with this age group? Tell someone that you plan to spend the weekend in a secluded place with 200 junior high campers and they may try to admit you to the psych ward. What they don't know is that along with the difficulties of this age are opportunities to see miracles happen and lives transformed. To sit in a front row seat and watch God perform his wonders with junior high campers is a privilege you will not forget. Here are some things to observe about this age group, and some appropriate ways to respond:

1. The priority of friendship.

It is at this age that friendship becomes the first competitor to the camper's relationship with his own parents. Is it a bad thing to place so much value on friendship? It can be very bad, or it can be very good. Friendship at this age is an all-powerful force. For example, I have noticed as I plan events for junior high youth that it doesn't matter what they are doing; what counts is who is there. They could have a great time playing tiddly-winks in the corner of a basement, or a bad time on the rides at an amusement park. It all depends on the combination and dynamic of the people who are there.

Because friendship is so powerful at this age, junior high youth tend to become like their friends. The influence of the parents, though still strong, is waning. If it came to a choice between the opinion of their parents and that of their friends, there is no guarantee that the parents' opinion would prevail. The warning, "Do not be yoked together with unbelievers" shows that the Apostle Paul knew the power of friendship. He is not saying that we should have no unbelieving friends, but he knew that *committing* yourself to your friends—being "yoked" with

II CORINTHIANS 6:14

them—means committing yourself to their values and lifestyle. It is very difficult for a junior high youth to avoid that kind of commitment.

As much as youth of this age are influenced by their specific peer group, the group itself is in a constant state of change. The forces that draw a group of junior high campers together are a mystery. How can they all love each other one minute and be fighting the next? Their commitment to one another can cause them to do things they would never dare on their own, and yet they dump one another over the smallest issue. The group dynamic of junior high campers is a challenge for their counselor. Perhaps they asked to be in the same cabin when they registered for camp, but by the time they arrive they may be entirely indifferent to one another, or perhaps even mortal enemies.

What can you do about these hyper-group-dynamics? Nothing, and so you are better off working *with* friendship groups rather than working *against* them. For example, some of your campers might develop a bond with others in the cabin next to you. Are you going to spend the entire week trying to keep them apart, or will you work with their counselor to accomplish something together? Are you going to insist on trying to talk about spiritual matters individually with each of your campers—as they claw the walls in desperation to get away—or will you sit with them as an identifiable group of friends and challenge them together? Here are some suggestions for making friendship groups work for you at junior high camp:

- *Find out who in your cabin came with whom.* As I said, there is no guarantee that campers who asked to be together will arrive at camp as friends or stay friends during the week of camp. However, knowing who came together will help you to understand the dynamics at work in your cabin. Watch the friendship groups form and change all week, whether within your cabin group or with those in other cabins. Take note especially who among the opposite sex is included in the group.

- *Jesus worked through friendship groups; why shouldn't you?* Next time you are frustrated with the junior high politics taking place in your cabin, think of what Jesus would do. Can't you imagine him—a complete stranger—sitting down among a group of fishermen, or "tax collectors and sinners" or children? He listens, he observes, he waits as they become comfortable with his presence. He throws in a comment, asks a question, and listens and observes some more. Soon they are asking him questions and offering him food, and before you know it he is being condemned by the Pharisees for letting himself become one of the crowd, a "glutton and wine-drinker" like the rest.[79] The crowd itself knew better. Jesus was their friend, and so they claimed him as their king.

The best counselors I have known have been like Jesus the Counselor, the "one who comes alongside."[80] He related to some people as individuals, such as the woman at the well, or Nicodemus in the middle of the night. However, he identified with others in their peer group: the tax collector Matthew and his friends; a swarm of children on his lap; the fishermen among their nets. It works so well with junior high campers. Sometimes you will have opportunity to talk with them alone, but expect most often to relate to junior high campers as groups of friends.

- *Don't censure friendship when you discipline.* That is, remember how much they value their friendships when it comes time to correct their behavior. Unless it is a serious matter, don't separate a friendship group as a form of discipline. Be careful to avoid the appearance of favoritism, such as when two friendship groups co-exist in your cabin and one is easier to handle than the other. Sometimes it is better to discipline a group rather than single out their apparent "ring-leader." Treat their friendships with respect.

- *Take your time.* It's the first day of camp, and you know exactly what to do: greet your campers; make them feel at home; get them involved. Trouble is, this is junior high camp. You introduce yourself and they don't even offer their names in return. In fact they seem a little embarrassed about being seen with you, and quickly go off in several little groups. Juniors camp this is not.

By the time most kids reach this age they have been hurt by adults they once trusted. They have not yet realized that pain is part of any relationship, and so they may be reluctant to get close to their counselor. They might seem unfriendly; it may be that they are afraid. They are entering—if they haven't already entered—the school of hard knocks. People let you down. They don't do what they promise. It can be painful to get too close to someone. Part of that sensitivity comes from their rapid development. They can be touchy when attention is drawn to their fickle emotions and new body.

Be patient and sensitive. Give them some time and space so they don't feel as if you are policing them. Be ever available. In those times that they want to spend time with you, put everything else aside—especially other staff who want to socialize—and listen and observe attentively. Don't push yourself on junior high campers but be there as a guide, a brother or sister, a boundary-setter, a teacher. Make sure it is respect, not just their approval, that you are earning.

2. Submission to conformity.

It makes sense that if acceptance in a group of friends is important to you, it may cost you something. The cost to a junior high camper might be anything from a type of behavior to a style of clothing or standard of achievement. For example, one group of junior high youth might all wear clothes made for someone twice their size, carry skateboards where there is no pavement, and never do homework. Another group could practically live at church, excel in academics and music, and wrap people's houses in toilet paper at night. I knew one group that listened to classical music, kept their hair long and amused themselves by asking each other trivia questions.

These types of conformity are not too serious; others are. Many schools have a "Dungeons and Dragons" gathering; some have gangs; and you can be pretty sure that a youth who starts smoking is in with a crowd that is morally as well as physically unhealthy. There are friendship groups that spend all week deciding which parties to crash and spend the weekend in oblivion. Athletes are a world to themselves. Style of music is a strong factor binding some friendship groups, which of course could be a positive or negative thing, but can also be a clear expression of the mood, attitude and priorities of a particular group.

As a counselor it is not necessary to take on the "baggage" of a particular friendship group. Unless you are close to their age you will probably not carry it well and it may take away from their respect for you. Junior high campers retain their ability to be critical, and they will read you like a book. Disguising yourself as one of them may raise their suspicions of your intentions. At the same time, it is good to be observant of the trends in a group. Watching your campers may even help you with ideas for their activities or cabin devotions. Sometimes your own enthusiasm will carry an activity they consider stupid, but often it is better to find out from *them* what is the cool thing to do, and adapt it to what you want to accomplish.

There is usually another group at camp: those who don't fit in anywhere. They are not hard to spot, but they may be very hard to motivate. Some of these kids will be familiar with being left out of things; for others it is a new experience caused by some unfortunate circumstance, a sheltered home life or some key person who has decided not to like them. They have all had the wind knocked out of them by general rejection, and would probably rather go home. These kids will need extra attention from staff to get them involved and help them feel accepted. This can be so time-consuming that some camps assign special workers to spend time with campers on the sidelines. Be prepared to give these kids some extra encouragement.

3. Confusion about morality.

Sin has become so much a part of our culture that many youth no longer know what it is. It's like trying to see a black object on a black background—it blends in with daily life and hardly even tickles their conscience. Even those who were raised within the church context are very fuzzy on where the boundaries lie. They can step over them with little awareness of what they are doing to themselves, to their friends and family, or to their relationship with God.

Junior high campers sometimes don't make the connection between their faith and their actions, especially when they have grown up in Christian homes. They might party it up Friday night and help in children's church Sunday morning, and not notice that the two don't correlate. Right and wrong are a non-issue to many youth, like the girl who answered in a survey, "The things I enjoy the most are skiing and sex."

What *reasons* will you give them to live moral lives? They have heard about the dangers of sexually transmitted disease, the effects of drugs, the consequences of dishonest behavior. They can always find arguments to satisfy these kinds of reasons. Sometimes the reason they get involved in immoral behavior is that we give them reasons not to, and rebellion is fun.[81] Perhaps we can't expect morality from youth who have no place for God in their lives, though as guests in the house we call "camp" they must live by the house rules. But what does a counselor say to the Christian kids who want to maintain the same lifestyle as those without faith?

Josh McDowell in his book *Right From Wrong*[82] offers reasons no believer can argue against: Christians need to be holy because God is Holy. We need to be kind and thoughtful because God is Love. We need to avoid sexual immorality because our bodies are indwelt by a pure Holy Spirit. We need to be honest because God is Truth. We need to respect life because Life is from God. For junior high youth, as much as for you and me, "The fear of the Lord is the beginning of wisdom."

Josh also points out the *evidence* that God's morality is the right choice: that God protects those who choose to obey him from the consequences of sin (such as guilt and low self-esteem); and that he provides them with benefits they would not otherwise have (such as the feeling of having done the right thing, or being noted as a person of integrity). This is a good approach to discussing morality with Christian youth who are searching for reasonable boundaries in a world that says there are none.

4. Re-evaluating their faith.

Are you afraid that your junior camper who returns the next summer as a junior high has lost her faith because she is suddenly doubting or challenging the Bible, or flirting with the world? She may not have exactly "lost" her faith; it just crashed down around her ears along with everything else. She is picking up the pieces, examining each one and wondering if it is a piece that fits or one that just happened to be on the floor. On the outside, her faith looks as if it may be on the brink of disaster; in reality, this is a world of discovery.

This age group has some things in common with toddlers and pre-schoolers: both are in the process of discovering and testing their new world. Parents of young children like to give them room to explore. They set firm boundaries but allow much freedom within those boundaries. Junior high campers need the same encouragement to explore, though within larger limits, of course. Be willing to give them room to find reasons for their faith, to question some things, to have differences of opinion from you and to challenge your beliefs and lifestyle. In return, don't be afraid to ask the hard questions about what they say they believe compared to the way they live.

And pray hard. This part of a youth's life is very precarious, and what he does now will have implications for years to come. You will sometimes feel as if you are over your head trying to rescue him from drowning in his adolescent sorrows, and he will occasionally need more help than what you can offer on your own. You will, of course, pray for all your campers, but I hope that your work with junior high campers will drive you to your knees in prayer like never before. Ask support staff at the camp to pray with you, call home to the prayer warriors there, and meet with another counselor to daily pray together for your campers.

The wonderful thing is that as we pray and make ourselves available to God, he works through us in incredible ways at junior high camp. I have known over one half of a camp of junior high youth make a commitment to Christ during the week, and I have heard many testimonies of others whose faith became real and personal to them through some event (often camp) at this age. Wherever spiritual battles wage the worst, the greatest victories are won, for the battle is the Lord's.

THE SENIOR HIGH CAMPER—AGE 15 TO 18

If the junior high camper can be described as a person who has dropped the cake, you might think of the Senior High camper as one who has picked up most of the pieces again, arranged them according to his own tastes, and is now having the cake bronzed as some people do with their baby's shoes. That is, not only is the senior high youth's life coming back together again in a different form than it was before puberty (and different from what mom and dad would have made it), but the choices he or she is making are much more permanent than ever before.

Not that a person at age 18 is what she will be for the rest of her life (heaven forbid!), but from this point on any changes in character will be slower, more costly and more painful, as the bronze coating begins to set. By the time she reaches her twenties, she has already mostly become the person she will be in terms of personality, lifestyle and spirituality. All that is left is to mature.

This age group can become very annoyed about being "labeled" by adults. When you have been painted with the same brush as street gangs and party animals, it doesn't help you establish your own identity as an emerging adult. I am very aware that many who are reading this chapter are part of the senior high age group, and may feel I am just another adult labeling them. I invite those who feel that way to take a look at their lives and see if I am in any way close to the mark in my observations, and to let me know if I am not. I respect your individuality and your opinion.

This is an age group that is capable of great things, and knows it. They *want* to do great things, and find it frustrating to be held back or not allowed, or not given the credit they deserve. Probably what attracts so many of these young emerging adults to camp ministry is that they are allowed greater responsibility as camp staff than they would ever be offered in their church or at their job back home. Camp is a closed system, like a rock climber attached to a belay rope, enabling the participant to do more daring things than would be sensible if they were "off belay." The thrill of climbing is still there, but in relative safety.

As a counselor to this age group at camp, here are some things to watch for:

1. Priority of choice.

This is an age of forming personal values, and there is nothing on which senior high youth place greater value than freedom of personal choice. This is a definite change from the junior high years, when their interests and priorities were governed largely by their group of friends. In direct contrast, the senior high camper's group of friends is largely determined by his or her personal interests and priorities. The result is that they tend to have fewer but closer friends.

It is almost a given these days that someone who is 15 to 18 will have a part-time job. I personally think that is not a good assumption, and that there are better things to do with young time and energy than expand the number of years they have to work. It does mean, however, that senior high campers have money, mobility, and options that they didn't have in junior high. And they like it.

The number of options available to them is increasing on every level. Just try and call a large corporation or government agency, and by the time you "press one" for every option offered, you can't remember why you called. Senior high campers are reaching this age in a flood of options, and they know how to access their options and process them better than any generation before them. The opportunities available to the average senior high youth are utterly amazing and enviable. As a result, however, they tend to be extremely busy people, especially since their time-management skills are still maturing.

Senior high campers are dealing with many decisions. Some of these are the usual ones, like which of several hundred classes to take in grade 12, or whether to buy the Ferrari or the VW bug. Senior high campers are also making life-long decisions about what they believe in and what they are going to *do* about what they believe in. They are making these decisions in what amounts to a moral vacuum, and often will not seek advice from people with experience.

What kind of help do senior high campers want from a counselor with these decisions? The last thing they want is people telling them what to do, what to believe, and how to think. Every attempt on the part of another person to force a decision on a senior high youth will be met with resistance, even if they agree with the decision. They want people to listen first, listen with understanding, give advice if and when asked, and let them make some mistakes of their own. They are ready to discuss and defend their views on things. Lecture is not a good method of doing cabin devotions at this age (nor any age). Senior high campers can get pretty heated about things like racism and women's rights and sexual orientation, but will appreciate the opportunity to be heard.

A counselor of senior high campers should be kind of like a bungy jump cable—he should let the camper fall a long way, but not hit bottom. They want freedom, but they are not ready to be without boundaries. As a counselor, set the guidelines wide at first, and narrow them only if the campers' behavior warrants it. Give them lots of room to run, but have lines that must not be crossed, and consequences if they are.

At the same time, the camp counselor needs to be careful not to belittle senior high campers, treat them as children or put them in situations where they will feel lowered before people. Remember when mom brought your forgotten lunch right to your home room at high school? Or when your little brother brought out your baby-in-the-bathtub pictures to show your girlfriend? Be very alert to the sensibilities and perceptiveness of this age group, and preserve their dignity even when you are out having fun.

2. Chosen friends.

I have asked many youth about this and have discovered that sometime around grade ten or eleven, the nature of their friendships begins to change. Instead of becoming like their friends, they increasingly begin to choose friends according to their personal values and principles. Do you want to know what is going on in the heart of a grade twelve youth? Check out the friends he chooses to be with, and that is who he is—for better or for worse. It is no longer so much a matter of being influenced by friends, but making a conscious decision to think and act a certain way and to do it with like-minded people.

Friendship is valued just as much as it was in the junior high years, if not more. Relationships are capable of becoming deeper and more intimate and long-term. Of course, this is the age that guy / girl relationships usually become more serious and long-term, and less dependent on a larger circle of friends. As a counselor at senior high camp, you can expect some of your campers to have a boyfriend or girlfriend who will draw their attention away from you and the cabin group. You will also need to be aware of couples with a tendency to wander off together. Make sure they are at every event, and don't be afraid to confront them if necessary. Your camp will have its own policies on physical intimacy among campers, and will expect you to step in and enforce them.

What kind of relationship does a camper want with his counselor at senior high camp? They may not accept you on the same basis as they would a friend their age, but more like a big brother or sister. Be the kind of person they will want to be someday, but also someone who loves and accepts them as they are. Let your authority come out of the respect they develop for you, the respect which you have earned.

3. Concern for significance.

Senior high campers have made some conclusions about the things that are important to them—a career, an issue, a car, a sport, a hobby, a guy or girl—and they are investing time and resources into those interests at the sacrifice of others. They are in pursuit of things that *matter* to them.

Because of this, senior high campers tend to be fairly serious about life. Many of them feel that the generations before them have handed them a mess, and that if it is to be fixed they will have to take up the responsibility themselves. As in the case of their junior counterparts, they may not always follow through with their idealism and good intentions, but if given the opportunity their accomplishments will often amaze you. Many youth are very good self-starters, not only because it is the character of their age, but because the lifestyle of their parents has forced them to be independent and self-reliant.

Senior high campers are still young, and as much as they demand independence, they also want guidance and structure in their lives. For example, encourage senior high campers to explore options that you know will give them a sense of real significance. They could earn money at a fast-food joint and meet the expensive expectations of their peers, but they will gain greater satisfaction working as a volunteer in a career area in which they are interested. Challenge them to consider what they can do to serve other people and achieve a sense of accomplishment. There is no better time for them to get involved in Christian ministry than this age. They are people with time, and it would be a shame for them to waste it simply earning cold cash at a job that means nothing.

4. Incredible optimism.

In his 1995 study,[83] researcher George Barna discovered that youth are incredibly optimistic about their future. Four out of five describe themselves as "excited about life"; three out of four claim to be "optimistic about the future"; two out of three see themselves as "a leader" and the same ratio believe they are "physically attractive." However, this rosy self-portrait is far from realistic. Barna claims that youth paint this picture of themselves not so much to mislead others as to "anesthetize" themselves against the harshness of life in this world.

However, there is no denying that this generation of youth does not share the despair and "I just don't care anymore" attitude of their immediate elders, or at least not yet. They enjoy a standard of living that is higher than any North American generation before them, with options and opportunities to do almost anything they can imagine. Reality is, they will probably not enjoy as high a standard of living when they are adults as they did while growing up. When it comes time to apply for the job for which they have been preparing, chances are it will not be there and they will have to find something else. They know that, but tend to respond by deciding to worry about it when (and if) it happens, and to focus on life in the here and now.

5. Disappointment on hold.

Beneath the busy-ness and enthusiasm of many youth is an underlying sadness and disappointment. It has a remarkably small affect on their daily lives, but it shows itself on special occasions. I see it more in letters and e-mail than in conversations, but I can imagine that on late nights when the party is over, disappointment is the topic of choice in many teen circles.

They have this huge natural urge to get out there and do something significant, and pressure from parents and teachers and peers to do the same, but the opportunities are limited. Even some of the high achievers are quite cynical about life, wondering if it will be worth the effort. They work hard at school, but are told that no matter how hard they work there will be no jobs for them on the other side. Career-type jobs are becoming scarce, being replaced with work-by-contract, which demands mobility and special marketable skills. They have always wanted freedom, but as they try it out their anticipation is not satisfied and their idealism falters. This is a generation very much in need of hope and faith.

Pray that they will be willing to talk with you about their disappointments in life, and when they do, try to listen, offering faith and hope rather than advice. What they really want from you is to know you are there, and that you understand and care. They feel safer at the wheel of their own car, and will not want you grabbing it from them and trying to steer like so many adults do.

6. Highly spiritual, but not necessarily Christian.

Youth do not lack spirituality. The majority of youth have a deep interest in spiritual things, and nearly all believe in God. They often simply have their own views of who God is—which range from orthodox Christianity to eastern mysticism—or they are in the process of deciding for themselves who he is. The notion that there is one true God, who has told us conclusively who he is and what he is like, is offensive to many youth and rejected along with organized religion and churches. The majority believe that when people of various faiths pray, they all pray to the same comprehensive God. About 80% agree that the Bible is a clear and accurate description of truth, but many of these would say the same thing about the Koran.

As a result, I am discovering that many older youth are seriously disappointed with God. If asked why, they will point to unanswered prayers or a discouraging circumstance, but the impression I get is that their real beef is with God himself. As they make conclusions from the world around them and their experiences of life, many youth develop a picture of God that is not what they had expected and hoped for. They feel he has let them down, that he pulled away when they needed him most, or simply remained silent. The answers they learned to parrot in church do not satisfy them, but neither does the "God" they have made in their own imagination. Their deepest spiritual longings go unfulfilled.

At a Christian camp, it is necessary to take spiritual discussions beyond the topic of "God"—which can mean anything to anyone—and focus on God's special revelation of himself, which is his Son, the Lord Jesus Christ. Who is Jesus? That discussion takes spirituality out of the realm of the nebulous. If God really did send his Son to be the "exact representation of his being,"[84] then he can be understood and believed in and loved. Even the demons believe in God, but at least their view of him makes them shudder.[85] The average youth's view of God apart from the truth revealed in Jesus Christ will lead only to disillusionment. Tell him about his Savior.

FAMILY CAMPERS

Not all camps offer programs for families, but enough camps do that it is essential to discuss the nature of families today, and how we can best serve them at family camp. Those ministries that can afford (in terms of time in the summer schedule and economics) to offer the camp experience to families are doing them a great service and should think twice before retiring such a program. However, camps also need to be careful not to become just another family resort. The *spiritual* opportunity is just as great for family camp as it is for any children or youth camps.

We are told that the definition of "the family" is changing, and certainly the families that come to camp are a mixed bag, including single parent, widowed parent, divorced and remarried parents, mom-and-her-boyfriend, grandparent families, foster families and every other combination you can imagine.

Therefore, camps have to be very careful not to design their family program around the idea of "couples," or to assume that each dad will be there to take his son fishing, making the single-mom family feel like the odd one out. At the same time, the program should support the dynamic of the nuclear families made up of mom, dad and two-and-a-half kids. It is difficult to do both. Here are some things to consider about families, and how to make their week at camp wonderful:

1. Stresses and pressures of family life.
It is getting tougher all the time for families to balance work, household duties, hobbies, recreation and family time together. Many parents are exhausted by the time their kids go to bed, and have very little time or energy for one another. Guilt is the usual feeling experienced by the busy parent, because they know they are neglecting the important things—such as time with their children—for the sake of the urgent things, such as getting their tax returns done on time. The pressure is very tough when spouse, children, work and church are all demanding the same narrow block of a parent's time.

More and more single parents are coming to family camp these days, especially as there is much less stigma today about being a single parent. Other families come to camp as a last-ditch effort to keep from splitting up, which is occasionally successful. It is not unusual for a family to arrive totally unprepared for the relaxed atmosphere of camp. At eleven o'clock in the evening of the first day they are still at "warp speed five" and hardly able to sit still. It may take several days before they stop jumping at the sound of a phone, and begin spending time in meaningful conversation and pure fun together. Families need camp.

2. Why families come to camp.
What are family campers looking for?

• *Time and space.* Family campers come to find space and relief from the pressure they experience at home. The schedule should be relaxed, with lots of free time. It should allow many options, including the option to opt out. Family campers shouldn't be made to go to events—even spiritual ones—if they would rather do something else. Camp staff need to be aware of this change in policy from kids' camps, or they will begin putting the same pressures on family campers that they came here to escape.

• *Fellowship with Christian adults (including each other).* Why do the adults stay in the dining hall until midnight, talking and laughing and making more noise than junior campers? Because they are starving for adult Christian friendship. A young family has very limited opportunity for this back home, because it usually means having to get a baby-sitter whom they can't afford. If you serve as a "baby-sitter" at family camp you are performing a very important ministry to the parents as well as their kids. Don't grumble when they come in late, well-fed with the encouragement they need to face the next year.

- *Time for their kids.* Many parents cringe whenever they hear the musical introduction to the "Focus On The Family" broadcast, because they know they never spend enough time with their kids. Many hardly see their kids during the week, except in the rear-view mirror of the car as they drive them from daycare to swimming lessons to kids club. Make it your goal as a staff member to give them great times and great memories together. They will have extra-high expectations of the events and activities offered by the camp because they are trying to make every precious minute count with their families. Be on time if you are in charge of an activity, and go the extra mile to ensure that it is the highest quality experience. Enable them to focus their attention on one another, without the distractions of shoddy service or poorly run activities.

3. Family ministry at camp.

The spiritual opportunities at family camp are numerous. However, because it is usually a more relaxed atmosphere than children or youth camps, many camp staff are tempted to sit back and miss these opportunities, and even slip into spiritual lethargy themselves. Here are some ministry opportunities to watch for at family camp:

- *Put your heart into the children and youth's teaching ministry at family camp.* The family camp program usually offers some kind of Bible teaching for the children and youth, either as a separate program while the parents listen to a speaker, or as a program for the whole family. In my experience, staff have a tendency to put less effort into these programs than they would at a children or youth camp. Partly this is because of the relaxed pace of family camp, but also because it may be a different program than what they have used all summer and so it demands preparation and work at a time when staff were expecting a break.

What a wasted opportunity if staff do less than a quality job of presenting God's word to these children and youth! Don't assume that these are Christian families who have heard it all before. Many families with no church background choose camp as an inexpensive "resort" holiday. For the sake of the kids who do seem to know it all, make the program challenging and fun, and much more than just another long lesson. Employ all the resources you are learning to use at camp, such as skits, object lessons, crazy games and challenges, music, dress-up and drama. Spend time with the kids you teach during other parts of the day, so that the message you communicate will be driven home by your life and relationship with them.

- *People come to faith in Christ at family camp.* It is not just at youth camps that you will have opportunity to lead kids to faith in Christ. A majority of children who grow up in Christian homes and put their faith in Christ make this commitment at camp. Be sensitive, though, to parents who are not believers and who may be suspicious of your attempts to "indoctrinate" their kids. Do your sharing openly, not excluding the parents, and if there is any resistance then back off. You do not want to push a family further away from faith because of the pressure tactics of a Christian camp.

- *The male staff can build relationships with the kids of single moms.* A couple of years ago, my family and I sat at the lunch table with a single mom and her only son. I chatted with the son practically the whole meal, along with my own two sons. Later she came to me in tears to tell me that I was the first man to whom her son had opened up since the family break-up. Single moms are often concerned that their kids do not have enough male adult influence and role-models. Male counselors should try to spend extra time with the kids of single moms, especially individual time. Ask for addresses so you can write to their children—and make sure you do! Your special attention will mean the world to these moms.

- *Watch for families or family members who seem alienated.* True, some families choose not to participate in some activities at family camp because they have their own ways of spending time together. But because most families tend to be focused inward at camp, it is very possible that other more dependent families may feel left out. A family may be for some reason not especially attractive, due to undisciplined or hyper kids, or family habits that are unusual. Jesus said it was the sick who need a doctor, and these families need you as staff to come alongside them. Your love and care may be just what they need to draw them to a lifestyle set in order by the Lord Jesus.

- *Be available to listen with care and understanding to the children of hurting families.* Children are often the most damaged victims of family break-up. In the "safe" setting of camp, they may want to talk with you about their hurts, so be ready to spend time just sitting and listening. Especially because the parent(s) are right there at camp, be careful not to take sides on any issue, and be slow to offer advice. Just listen and care, because that is what they need most. You may also sense a need to let the parents know that their child has been talking with you, but use wisdom and tact in this, and get advice from a camp leader if needed.

- *Be aware of families under tension.* Do what you can to not add to the tension. This takes sensitivity and wisdom. Pray for these families regularly, that their camp experience would draw them closer to one another and to the Lord. Offer to look after their kids for an afternoon if you can, and be careful not to pressure them to participate in activities. If you are aware of tensions and feel that they might be open to counseling, talk with the camp pastor or speaker or the appropriate administrator.

4. I Timothy 4:12.

"Don't let anyone look down on you because you are young, but set an example for the believers in speech, in life, in love, in faith and in purity." This was Paul's advice to a young "counselor" named Timothy serving a church of families. Your very presence at camp is of incredible encouragement to the adults there, as they watch your dedication and faith and your ministry to their kids and themselves.

So be very careful not to take away from that example. You are staying on the same camp grounds as they are, and they will not be so encouraged if you keep them and their kids awake at night while you take advantage of having no campers of your own to look after. Be gracious and warm and friendly as you serve them. Be thoughtful towards them, creatively satisfying their needs. Be absolutely pure in your relationships with other staff—above all *reasonable* suspicion (family campers are not always reasonable). Take time to share with them how your summer is going and the incredible things God is teaching you. Your testimony and example may be what they remember most about their week at camp.

---

[71]Sorry, I don't know who owns this little chart. The best I can offer is that it came from the *Youth Specialties National Resource Seminar* notebook by Youth Specialties, Inc., who also don't remember where it is from

[72]James Dobson and Gary Bauer, *Children at Risk*, ©1994 Word Publishing, p. 7-8

[73]My thanks to Juli-Ann Oldham and Jen Witbeck for their first-hand insight into working with this age group

[74] Matthew 18:6

[75] Mark 10:13-16

[76]Romans 12:18

[77]Helen Bee, *The Developing Child*, 7th edition, ©1995 HarperCollins, p. 324-325

[78]To see how strongly Jesus felt about this, check out Matthew 18:1-6 and 19:13-15

[79]See Luke 7:34-35

[80]Remember? That is the meaning of the word "counselor" in John 14:16, as discussed in Chapter 1

[81]An example would be the increase in the percentage of smokers among teens and young adults, despite all the campaigns against smoking

[82]Josh McDowell and Bob Hostetler, *Right From Wrong*, ©1994 Word Books

[83]George Barna, *Generation Next*, ©1995 Regal Books, Ventura, CA 93003. Used with permission

[84]Hebrews 1:1-3

[85]James 2:19

CAMP PREP #7:
DEVELOP YOUR AGE AWARENESS

Suggestions on how to prepare for your counseling experience.

What you have just read in these last two chapters is a ton of information that will quickly slip out of your grasp again unless you do something with it. Here are two suggestions:

- *Memorize the chart at the beginning of the chapter.* It's simple, but get it in your mind so you can refer to it.

- *Do some people-watching.* Next time you are in a public place, such as your church or the mall, take time to observe the children and youth around you. Can you identify these characteristics in the various age groups we have discussed?

PART THREE:
COUNSELING SKILLS

"Relationships are the building material of God's work here on earth."

11. Building Relationships: Individual & Group Dynamics

Relationships are the building material of God's work here on earth. Jesus said that the two most important things in life are a loving relationship with God and a loving relationship with our neighbor.[86] Through relationships, God peopled the world, described himself to us, communicated his will, defeated sin and death, and established his kingdom. God himself is a relationship, a unique and mysterious unity of three Persons in one Being: the Triune God.

Relationships matter to people too. When the house is burning, most people ignore every material thing they own, grab their children and spouse and get out, and leave everything else to burn. If there was any material possession they would miss, it would be the picture album—the memento of their relationships.

When you have served at the same camp for years and years, you get to watch certain campers grow up and mature as they come each summer. Some of them eventually take a counselor-in-training course and become staff members. It is possible that some of you who are reading this book are campers whom I have known for years. Good to see you again!

What amazes me is that, though I am with these campers for only a week or two each year, we develop a close relationship. Campers and staff often call me up to talk about a problem or to ask me to write a letter of reference for them (of which I do dozens every year). We have developed a trust relationship in a very short time. There is something unique and powerful about the relationships created at camp. The most significant thing you can do for your campers in one week is to get to know them.

WHAT IS UNIQUE ABOUT CAMP RELATIONSHIPS?

1. Compression.

At camp you tend to get to know one another very well very fast. The tears on the last day are real tears. But it is more like seeing the movie than reading the book. There are so many details about your campers' lives you will not get to know in a week, and the memories don't last. Still, at the end of the week it will *feel* as if you have known them a long time, and they will feel the same about you.

2. An agenda.

You have some goals for this relationship, and so you can create an agenda for it. For example, you want the relationship to help the campers understand who Jesus is, so you decide to treat them as Jesus would in everything you do. You want to develop trust and respect between you and your camper, so you offer him your own trust and respect. You want to avoid having too many distracting discipline issues; therefore, you aim for a balance between love and control so your campers will like you but not walk all over you.

3. Trust, mixed with suspicion.

You are an adult who wants to spend time with kids. That is unusual, and though the campers will likely be glad about your offer of friendship, they may also be a bit suspicious. Things like this may not have always gone well for them in the past. It might take time before they trust you, but you will be amazed how quickly most of them do. They will trust you initially because they trust the camp, so be sure to deserve their trust and not damage or abuse it. Failed trust is not quickly regained. You have incredible power to make or break a kid's week.

4. A foundation to share Jesus.

The basis of the Apostle Paul's ministry was not just great preaching, but an open heart and life to those who listened. "We loved you so much that we were delighted to share with you not only the gospel of God but our lives as well, because you had become so dear to us." It may seem unlikely that you will feel affectionate about your campers after just one week, but I bet you will. As a result, you will have opportunity to share with them your relationship with Jesus.

I Thessalonians 2:8

SOME TRICKS OF THE TRADE

Here are some tried and proven ways of building relationships with kids, developed over many combined years of ministry by many people. Keep as many of these up your sleeve as you can!

1. Focused attention.

Younger campers will compete for your attention every moment of the day (if not the night)! Even older campers will want more and more of your time as they get to know you better. Particularly at juniors camp, this cry for attention can become unbearable. Here's how to survive: All they want is your undivided attention, so *give* it to them!

Is that crazy? Yes, if you did it all the time you would soon die. So instead of trying to give them *all* of your attention *all* of the time, give them *all* of your attention for *some* of the time.[87] This will be much easier on you and much more satisfying for your campers than giving them only part of your attention all day long, while the rest of it is taken up with various duties, a book you are trying to finish and conversations with staff. Your campers will only be frustrated if they feel they are constantly competing with something else for your attention.

Learn the secret of setting everything else aside on various occasions all through the day to give your campers 100 per cent of your attention for a short time. This could be just a few minutes or as long as a half hour or more. Then excuse yourself and turn your attention elsewhere for a time. The result? Satisfied kids (for a while), and a less-frazzled you.

2. Undistracted attention.

When you are focusing attention on one person or a small group, be "undistractible." Other staff may thoughtlessly interrupt a conversation to bring you a message they consider important, or other campers will try to drag you away. But in my experience, most things can wait (unless the building is burning down!). When I stay focused on the person who is talking to me in spite of the threat of interruptions, it says worlds to that person about how important he is to me.

3. Initiated Attention.

Some campers belong in *Star Trek*. They are "Cling-on's" who will be all over you no matter how much focused and undistracted attention you give them. Beam me up, Scotty! What can you do? To a point, put up with their clamoring out of compassion for their need. But be firm, and be in charge. Try to find times when campers are not being clingy and *initiate* some attention, perhaps by going up to them and giving them a hug for no apparent reason, or turning and asking their opinion on something. Hopefully these campers will soon come to realize that your time and attention are offered freely and generously, and they don't have to beg for them.

4. Threesomes.

There is an awkwardness that occurs when you and another person (who isn't your boyfriend or girlfriend!) are face to face and attempting conversation. This is especially true when one is an adult and the other a camper. Face-to-face conversation makes kids feel uncomfortable; it invades their space. They will avoid eye contact and will start playing with anything in reach.

Try adding a *threesome* to your twosome. The third party in your conversation could be almost anything, such as another person, a can of Coke, a ping pong table, a meal in front of you, a bag of gummy bears to share, or the dark of the cabin as you lie on your bunks. Sometimes just facing the same direction instead of toward one another helps, such as sitting in a canoe, or looking out the windshield of a car, the path you are hiking, the view from the top of a mountain, or sitting around staring into a campfire. When you add the third factor, it removes the awkwardness you both feel and promotes good conversation. Try it!

5. Remember their name.

Names are our spoken identity, and for some reason are very important to us. You know the warm feeling you get when someone you haven't seen for a while remembers your name, and how deflating it is when someone who should know forgets. Bad memory is no excuse. You have only a week, and you better know the names of all your campers in the first hour or so after they arrive! Go from there to remembering other campers' names too, and don't forget the staff! I have found that those who know names tend to also get to know people better on a personal level. There are many ways of remembering names—try some of these:

- *When you meet someone new, make a conscious decision to remember his name.* If you don't, his name will leave your mind five minutes later and you will have to ask again (which is very awkward—if I miss a name I usually ask someone else what it is rather than ask the person again).

- *When you first meet a camper, use his name as many times as you can.* As you talk with him, include his name in the conversation in a natural way (not so often that you feel stupid!), and look into his face every time you say it. Soon your brain will begin to make the association between his face and his name.

- *Try "memory by association."* This is connecting a camper's name with something else about her, like remembering that you met "Sandy" on the beach, or that "Tamara" carries a camera. Names by themselves are hard to picture, so get a picture in your mind that will help you remember the name.

156 PART THREE – COUNSELING SKILLS

- *Do frequent self-tests.* When you are sitting in a group at a meal or meeting, use the time to silently recite all the names of everyone in the room, and take note of those whom you don't know so you can add them to your collection.

- *If you have a list of campers' names, keep it in your pocket.* Occasionally take it out and mentally picture each person on the list. Check off the ones you have memorized until the whole list is done.

6. Transparency.

So that you can be a good example and role model to your campers, they need to be able to see you as you really are, like first thing in the morning when your face looks like a puffy mushroom. Tell them that embarrassing story about the time you lost your shorts in the pool when you were a kid. Being a good example to them does not mean you must put on a show of being perfect. Part of personal maturity is learning to laugh at ourselves and admit our deficiencies. I'm bald, okay? And I can give you ten reasons why being bald is better than having hair any time![88]

Be careful, though, not to hang out your "dirty laundry" before your campers. They don't need to know your deepest darkest secrets, and you don't need to answer all their curious questions. However, what will you say to a camper who asks if you have ever made out with your boyfriend, or if you have ever been abused? If they are clearly not asking out of mere curiosity, but are looking for help, it may be time to swallow hard and answer.

Balance your transparency with a bit of intrigue and mystery (does she or doesn't she?), which usually motivates people to want to get to know you better. Don't be afraid to be goofy, but retain a reasonable dignity at the same time, so your campers will not only enjoy you (at your expense) but will respect you too.

7. Approachability.

To have friends, you must be friendly. Do a bit of self-examination, or even have a close friend evaluate you, because it is hard for us to see ourselves objectively. Are you approachable? Are you usually happy and smiling, or sarcastic and negative, or moody and unpredictable? Do people easily get the impression that you are interested and care about them, or do you tend to distance yourself from people until they have earned your trust? Though some of these traits have to do with your personality, many have to do with attitude, which is something you can change.

8. Interest.

A large part of relationship-building is accomplished through conversation, but dialogue is not enough by itself. We can quickly tell if the person who is asking the questions about us is truly interested or is just being polite or simply performing a duty. Demonstrate *interest* by giving a person your full attention while she is speaking, and by referring to your growing knowledge of her on later occasions. For example, if you learn that a camper is in a swim club at home, on a later occasion challenge her to a race at the waterfront.

People who take a genuine interest in others are rare,[89] but taking an interest is an essential expression of love and it is following the example of Jesus: "Do nothing out of selfish ambition or vain conceit, but in humility consider others better than yourselves. Each of you should look not only to his own interests, but also to the interests of others. Your attitude should be the same as that of Christ Jesus..."[90] There are people just like you all around. Take an interest in them, just as you hope they will with you.

9. Common ground.

You shouldn't try to look or act like a kid or youth, unless you are one. It robs you of your identity and dignity when you try to relate to campers that way, and they usually resent it. Instead, simply seek common ground with them, matching your identity and interests to theirs. Paul, the great relational missionary, claimed this as his method:

> When I am with those who follow the Jewish laws, I do the same, even though I am not subject to the law, so that I can bring them to Christ. When I am with the Gentiles who do not have the Jewish law, I fit in with them as much as I can. In this way I gain their confidence and bring them to Christ. But I do not discard the law of God; I obey the law of Christ. When I am with those who are oppressed, I share their oppression so that I might bring them to Christ. Yes, I try to find common ground with everyone so that I might bring them to Christ."[91]

I COR. 9:20-22

Camp itself is great common ground, because all week you gain experiences that you can share and laugh about together. The whole purpose of the recreational activities at a Christian camp is to create this common ground that draws people into a relationship with one another.

Use your common experiences to build bridges between yourself and your campers as a basis for sharing the love of Christ.

10. Physical altitude.

No typo here. I mean physical *altitude*. When children rushed up to meet Jesus, what do you imagine he did? Did he stand there and pat them on the head, or did he get down to eye level with them and let them crawl on his lap? It is interesting that the Gospels say that (contrary to most movies about him) Jesus *sat down* to teach the people.[92] This was not an uncommon practice among rabbis, but Jesus embraced the idea of getting to or below eye-level with people so that he could relate to them better. It works!

11. Look me in the eye and smile.

A common complaint I hear from youth is that adults who pass them on the street or in a store will not look them in the eye (and if they do they quickly look away) and that they rarely smile at them. I think that many adults are just so pre-occupied with adult stuff that they don't realize their coldness toward younger people. Perhaps some adults fear confrontation, keeping in mind that a person should never look a mean dog in the eye because it might take it as a challenge. It is true that there are a few gang member type youth who are like mean dogs. But most youth are not, and will greatly appreciate a steady and warm glance from you as you pass by, and an appropriate greeting.

12. Consistency.

Treat your campers with respect no matter where you are or who is with you. Your campers believe they are the greatest kids on earth in your sight. Imagine the potential to destroy that relationship if, when you are with other staff (or with your friends in the mall back home), you don't have the time of day for them, or you refer to them as "those rotten little ankle-biters." You work hard at building rapport with your campers and they come to trust and respect you, so be very careful to be consistent in the way you treat them.

13. Avoid favoritism.

Some campers are "cool." Some are cute. Some are plain obnoxious or smell bad. However, it is an extremely serious offense as a counselor to show favoritism, and it can destroy your relationship with all your campers. James explains the seriousness of "pre-judging" (or prejudice) like this:

My brothers, as believers in our glorious Lord Jesus Christ, don't show favoritism. Suppose a man comes into your meeting wearing a gold ring and fine clothes, and a poor man in shabby clothes also comes in. If you show special attention to the man wearing fine clothes and say, "Here's a good seat for you," but say to the poor man, "You stand there" or "Sit on the floor by my feet," have you not discriminated among yourselves and become judges with evil thoughts?

JAMES 2:1-4

Favoritism is contrary to the law of Christ, which is to love one another as he loved us. Jesus loved us no matter how spiritually sick, sinful and repugnant we were. Take the time to get to know *each* of your campers—that is why you were given just a few. Don't let a week of camp go by before you realize that there is a child or youth who has received almost no attention from you, while other campers have been your obvious favorites.

14. Be a playing coach.

Be careful not to expect your campers to do what you are not ready to do yourself. For example, if you are not willing to use the same bathrooms they use but decide to go to the staff bathrooms instead, what does it communicate to your campers? By doing the same things you expect them to do, you get into your campers' world (and maybe you will begin to feel sorry for the guy who cleans their bathroom).

I knew a wilderness guide who would always choose the worst equipment for himself so that he would be experiencing what the least-prepared hiker was experiencing. Do what you can to reduce the distance between you and your campers. Be the one among them who plays the hardest, gets the dirtiest, is served last, and takes the thing no one else wants. They will love you for it, because it shows that you love them.

15. Empathy.

It doesn't take long to get seriously annoyed by a camper. Before you blow up at him and say things you will later regret, take a deep breath and try to get behind his eyes. See past his behavior to why he might be acting that way. Try to get at his real needs, not just the symptoms he is acting out. Bad behavior may be a sign of deep-rooted anger created by his home-life, or a desperate attempt to get the attention he is starving for, or plain ignorance of your expectations. A half hour of listening might change your opinion of that camper forever. Feel his pain!

16. Helpfulness.

Look for every opportunity to do "random acts of kindness" toward your campers. Help with a suitcase, take time to look for a lost item, give your opinion on the T-shirt a camper printed. A moment's interest and kindness speaks volumes to a camper and will be substantially constructive to your relationship with her. Maybe it is because our world is so self-centered much of the time that even small kindnesses don't go unnoticed. Be the servant-leader who is always there for campers.

17. Constructive language.

"Do not let any unwholesome talk come out of your mouths, but only what is helpful for building others up according to their needs, that it might benefit those who listen." Our tongues are powerful instruments, for good or for evil.[93] Watch carefully what comes out in your speech. Some kids can't handle teasing or sarcasm. They get enough criticism about everything at home. It is easy to undo all your relationship-building in one moment of anger. "Be quick to listen, slow to speak, and slow to become angry, for man's anger does not bring about the righteous life that God desires."[94] Make sure that your speech builds up your campers and doesn't destroy them.

EPHESIANS 4:29

18. The teachable moment.

Do you remember those moments in your life that were a turning point, or a time when you suddenly understood something that you had never grasped before? These special occasions can often happen at camp, and we need to be ready for them. "Teachable moments" are most likely to occur when we have spent lots of time with someone. *Quality* time happens where there has been *quantity* time.

For example, you may walk all the way up a mountain and back, and talk the whole time with a camper about skateboarding (heaven forbid). Just as you round the last corner, something comes up in the conversation that has real significance to the camper: a problem at home; a fear he has; maybe his desire to put his faith in Jesus. The time spent hiking has been worthwhile because it has created one of those precious moments of interaction he may always remember.

As previously mentioned, kids often bring up something very important to them at the strangest times: just as everyone is dropping off to sleep; or five minutes before the bus leaves. They do this because they know they will have a way of escape if things are not working out, or if the conversation becomes awkward or uncomfortable.

The trick is to recognize these moments, use them tactfully, even create them if possible. We can recognize them by the hints campers usually throw out, like the question that starts, "I've got this friend who has a problem with stealing, and I was wondering...?" Or the old standby: "By the way...?" If you ignore these "moments," you will kick yourself later. They are your best opportunities to build a relationship, be an influence and create a memory.

19. Giving advice.
Do you like getting advice from adults? To a camper you *are* an adult, and he may not want your advice. Give advice when it is asked for, but even then remind the camper that you are only giving your objective opinion and that you may be off the mark.

There is a way to communicate unasked-for advice without being offensive. For example, if you suggest deodorant to a camper with stinky armpits, you will embarrass him to death. But you could diffuse the offensiveness of your advice by giving it to the whole cabin, and by making it fun.

20. Enthusiasm.
It shouldn't happen, but what if the camp program is boring? What if the activity bombs, in spite of everyone's hard work? What if the game someone brought to camp with him turns out to be hopeless? Or the food at lunch is wretched? Would it be possible for a counselor to make a great week out of what should be a disaster? When all else fails, don't forget the first rule and bottom line of camp work: *enthusiasm.*

Tim Hansel says that though kids need love and attention from the adults in their life, most of all they need enthusiasm from them.[95] Enthusiasm *communicates* love and attention. Kids need someone who is enthusiastic about being with them, who can occasionally let loose with them, and who is excited about what they think is important.

Here are some of the ground rules for enthusiasm:

- *Throw yourself into every activity.* But as a leader stay in control so things don't get out of hand.

- *Be spontaneous.* Not thoughtless, but able to do things at the spur of the moment. This is learned through experience. If you are not usually a spontaneous person, it is time to surprise everyone!

- *Be willing to look foolish for their sake.* For example, when I'm playing with my kids and I'm self-conscious, I both look and feel foolish about it. If I get into it without thinking about who is watching, my goofiness seems natural and right.

- *Even if you don't like the activity, get into it.* Your enthusiasm will be copied by your campers. Even if the activity is really dumb, they will have a good time if you do.

- *Get excited about the ideas your campers offer and implement them if you can.* They will be enthusiastic about doing something that they came up with, even if the idea itself seems less than professional to you. Kids are pretty good at knowing what kids like, and sometimes their ideas are what work best.

21. Perseverance.

Not every camper will respond to your best efforts to befriend him. Some will test you to see if you are genuine, or to check out the boundaries of the camp policies and your patience. Some will not respond readily to the gospel. You may have one or two who seem hopelessly bad or irretrievably lost. Think of how far Jesus went to love the unlovable, heal those whom society had cast out, and forgive those whose sins were many. Don't give up easily on a child, or write him off as an enemy. Ask God for the patience to work slowly and carefully to build a relationship with the resistant camper.

THEIR RELATIONSHIPS WITH ONE ANOTHER

"Group dynamics" is the term used to describe the power of a group to be and accomplish more than they could as individuals. The whole is greater than the sum of its parts. You need to build a group relationship as well as individual relationships with your campers. The dynamic formed by a group is a powerful thing, and it is important to ensure that it is a positive force. Here are some ways to make it work for you:

1. Become part of your own cabin group early.

On the first day, before cabin dynamics start to form without you, spend time earning a place in your cabin group. If you are not available to them that first day as they arrive at camp, you may find it harder to fit in with them later.

2. Develop a sense of belonging.

The old TV show "Cheers" is not the only place "where everyone knows your name." People everywhere have a deep need to belong to one another, and to be recognized as part of a group of others. Make it clear from the start that everyone owns a place in your cabin, that you accept each one, and that you won't put up with anyone being excluded. Coming to camp is an event that has probably upset your campers' sense of security. Many kids will have difficulty if they are thrown into activities that threaten their security even more (like jumping into a cold lake or climbing a rock wall) if they have not established a sense of security in their own cabin group.

3. Create identity.

Do special and creative things together as a cabin that no other cabin does. Dress up in some crazy way, or come up with a cabin song or password. Plan experiences unique to your group, like arranging to meet in some special place for cabin devotions, or standing and singing a loud and silly song in the middle of breakfast. Having a unique and separate identity draws the group together.

4. Create opportunity for each person to have his personal role and make a contribution to the group.

Some campers will need more help establishing their place in the group, and so you might assign them a special responsibility such as getting desserts for everyone, or the opportunity to be the flag-bearer for your team. By the end of the week, the group should be capable of identifying how each person fits the puzzle that forms your cabin group.

5. In every cabin a natural leader will arise.

Most often the leader in the cabin will not be you, and very often it will be a camper whom you would rather not have as the natural leader. For example, I was once involved at a kids club for children in a low-income housing project. Every few weeks the natural leader (usually the toughest guy) would get asked to leave because he had become unmanageable, but someone would always take his place. I soon discovered that if I patiently befriended the natural leader and spent extra time with him outside the club, he would not only stay (or at least stay longer), but the group itself also became more manageable.

Don't let the natural leader in your group become your enemy, or you may find the whole group against you. Exercise firm love to keep the leader from working against you, and to keep him from intimidating and manipulating the rest of the group. Let that person know he has your trust and you are counting on him, and he will often respond by doing things your way.

6. Make the campers in your cabin accountable to one another.

For example, during cabin clean-up, make it a matter of cabin loyalty that each person is expected to do his part. Rather than getting after the camper who isn't doing his share, let the group work it out. Of course, kids can be cruel and you will need to keep the experience from becoming negative. However, you can use group dynamics to maintain control in your cabin group in a very positive way.

7. Unite multiple groups in the same cabin.

More than one group might form in your cabin, especially at junior high camp where friendship groups are a dynamic all of their own. As a whole cabin group, do activities that will help draw them together: a night out on the field or dock; or an "appreciation time" where they encourage one another. When a friendship group spans two cabins, it is sometimes wise to team together as counselors to work with that dynamic. You will often have one or two campers who don't fit into any natural group in your cabin, but if you take the lead, the group(s) will usually include these campers as well.

8. Teach them their responsibility to love one another.

Our world is becoming so inward and self-centered that kids are becoming dangerous in their irresponsibility to one another. We have an opportunity in the small cabin group to turn them outward, and to teach them by word and example to love as Jesus loved. Rather than letting them cling to their personal *rights*—or imagined personal rights—make them aware of their personal *responsibilities* to the people around them.

9. Encourage them when love hurts.

> "To love at all is to be vulnerable. Love anything, and your heart will certainly be wrung and possibly be broken. If you want to be sure of keeping it intact, you must give your heart to no one, not even to an animal. Wrap it carefully around with hobbies and little luxuries; avoid all entanglements; lock it up safe in the casket or coffin of your selfishness. But in that casket—safe, dark, motionless, airless—it will change. It will

not be broken; it will become unbreakable, impenetrable, irredeemable... The only place outside heaven where you can be perfectly safe from all the dangers of love is hell...[96]

Love can be painful. Love cost God his own Son, and yet he considered it worth the price. Kids can seem very resilient, but despite your best efforts they do occasionally get hurt emotionally at camp, and the hurt can last a long time. If they entrust you with even a little hurt they are feeling, count it an honor, give them time to talk about it, and work with them towards a solution. Encourage them to forgive and to restore their relationships with other campers, rather than take the world's usual easy way out, which is to get back at them or walk away. If it is you who have hurt their feelings, be quick to admit you are wrong and make it right with campers. They will trust you more if you ask for forgiveness than if you just let it ride. Even a counselor can learn from his mistakes.

---

[86]Mark 12:28-31

[87]This essential concept was first introduced to me in the classic by Ross Campbell, *How To Really Love Your Child*, ©1977 SP Publications, Inc.

[88]Hah! I made you check the footnote out of curiosity! Here's reason #1 - I am always the first person in a crowd to know that it is starting to rain!

[89]See, for example, Paul's commendation of Timothy in Philippians 2:19-21

[90]Philippians 2:3-5

[91]I Corinthians 9:20-22, *NLT*

[92]See Matthew 5:1; Luke 4:20 and 5:3; John 8:2

[93]James 3:1-12 points out that a person who can train his tongue can train his whole self

[94]James 1:19-20

[95]Tim Hansel, *What Kids Really Need in a Dad*, ©1984 by Tim Hansel, published by Fleming H. Revel Co.

[96]C.S. Lewis, *The Four Loves*, ©1960 Harcourt, Brace, Jovanovich

12. Helping Individuals: Becoming A Caring Listener

Camp is a safe place away from home where an adult (yourself) is giving campers more concentrated attention than they may have had all year, and they may never see you again. Because of this, it is likely that some of your campers will confide in you concerning their personal and family problems. They may have questions that have gone unanswered for years. When children or youth show this kind of trust and confidence in you, it is a compliment, but it was probably not easy for them to do. The camp counselor must be ready to take up the role of "people-helper" when individual campers come to talk.

HOW QUALIFIED ARE YOU TO OFFER "COUNSELING"?

You are probably not a psychologist; or not even a trained "counselor" in the therapeutic sense. How should you respond to the child or youth who comes to you with a problem? You may feel less than qualified to deal with many of the issues campers bring up, which may be entirely out of your realm of experience. But because it is no small thing for a camper to get up this kind of courage, never put off a camper who comes to talk with you about a problem. If you feel it is too big for you to handle, you should at least help him find the counsel he needs, and check on him later.

However, you are probably more qualified than you think, because the help you can provide to the individual camper is mostly a matter of *listening with care and understanding*. As a Christian, you have experienced solutions and a changed life through faith in Christ. It is not so much that you have answers and advice to offer the camper, but rather compassion for his situation and hope for his future. You also have the word of God and can ask for wisdom from the Holy Spirit to help campers discover solutions. God will do his work of encouraging, convicting and comforting the camper as you make your time and your attention available to him. This type of "counseling" or "people-helping" will come out of your relationship with the camper. He is not going to a trained psychiatrist but to you as his friend and example, as he might go to a big brother or sister.

The problems that some campers bring to you may be too difficult to deal with yourself. You should be able to recognize problems that need referral or even immediate protective measures,

RESOURCE C

and know where to find help for them. There are also problems you might come across that will demand further action or long-term help and care. Even if you give a camper's problems into more competent hands, you as his camp counselor will still have a responsibility to pray for him, deal with the questions and emotions of the rest of your cabin, and be involved in the follow-up process.

A MODEL OF PEOPLE-HELPING

Jesus told a story that is a great description of what to do for a person who is in need or facing a crisis. A man was walking the dangerous desert road from Jerusalem to Jericho and he fell into the hands of robbers, who left him half dead. Most people who passed by avoided him, but one—whom we have named "The Good Samaritan"—stopped to help. He offered the injured man three things:

LUKE 10:25-37

1. Immediate care and attention.

Just stopping to help was a risk that several others in the story had thought too great a risk. The Samaritan not only inconvenienced himself, but ran the risk that the robbers might still be near by, or that this might be a trap. Nevertheless, he pulled out his first aid kit—perhaps a strip of cloth from his own garment, a bit of oil for softening and wine for washing and disinfecting—and bandaged the man's wounds. He was no doctor, but he offered what he could, which was mostly just care and attention. Then he took him to a place of refuge and continued to care for him all night and as long as he was able.

2. A long-term care-giver.

Realizing the man would need more care than he could give him at the time, he left him with someone who could provide that attention. It was not unusual for a keeper of an inn to be recognized as a "horse doctor" of sorts, and this inn-keeper was left with the instruction, "Look after him." The Good Samaritan did this at his own expense—two silver coins.

3. A promise to check up.

Having done all that, the Samaritan did not wash his hands of the invalid and forget about him; he promised to return. In Jesus' story, the Samaritan promised to repay what he might owe the inn-keeper in addition to the two silver coins. It is notable that he intended to come back and check on this man and offer further help if needed. Jesus told this story as a description of what he meant by his command to "love your neighbor as yourself," the greatest duty of mankind toward one another.

Keep the story of the Good Samaritan in mind to help you remember the process involved in offering care and help to a camper who comes to you with a question or problem. What follows is a description of this process, and a story to serve as a running example of a counseling situation.[97]

TAKE ON THE BURDEN

When a camper comes to you for help, take seriously the responsibility you are accepting. You may need to give this person a chunk of your already busy day; there may be unforeseen risks in helping her. You may need to make difficult decisions and do follow-up in the future. Make the conscious decision to take up this camper's burden and help carry it for a while.

In most cases, there will be no need for you to tell anyone else what the camper will tell you, and she needs to know that she can trust you to keep confidential what she shares. Be careful not to give details to other staff, for example, in a staff meeting. Simply ask prayer for that camper without going into specifics.

You will often be the only one who needs to offer help to a camper, but you may need to involve others if the matter is more serious. Because of this, *offer conditional confidentiality*. Stop a camper who says to you, "Don't tell this to anyone, but..." because you don't know if you will need help or not. Let the camper know she can trust you to stick with her and tell only the people who need to know, and only out of her best interest.

Usually it will be your own campers who will come to talk with you as their camp counselor. Occasionally you (or one of your campers) will develop enough of a relationship with someone from another cabin that she too might come to you. That is fine, but be sure you let the other counselor know enough of the situation that she can provide additional support. *Under no circumstances* should you provide counsel to campers of the opposite sex, beyond answering a casual question. There is simply too much potential for problems such as emotional attachment and dependency. Refer them to their own counselor, and later check to see if they have confided in their counselor.

Be careful of the location you choose to offer help. You need to be separate from other people so that the camper will feel free to talk, but you should avoid a location that could leave you open to any suspicion. Sit out in the open away from others, or in a place where people know you are there and could walk in if they wanted to. If a camper insists on talking behind closed doors, there may be more to the situation than meets the eye, and you should either refuse or ask to bring in another counselor or the head counselor right from the beginning. Occasionally (especially in the case of teens), a camper may want to bring along a friend for extra security; usually you should agree to that.

> *Sue was ecstatic about her new cabin of senior high campers. They were a cabin made in heaven, and it seemed that this week at least would be smooth sailing. Every camper was enthusiastically involved in the activities, and participated in Sue's discussion of the word of God with interest. So she was taken off guard when she found under her pillow a note from Erin, a confident and beautiful camper from a strong Christian family, whom all the other girls looked up to. She wanted to talk with Sue in private, and in her note begged for complete confidentiality. Sue placed a note of her own under Erin's pillow, suggesting that they meet in the middle of the main field during the open activity time tomorrow. In her note she promised confidentiality, but reserved the right to find extra help for Erin if it became necessary. At supper that night, Erin was nervous and did not want to make eye contact with Sue.*

OFFER IMMEDIATE CARE

What kind of care can you offer someone who is hurting emotionally, socially or spiritually? Mostly he needs your attention and understanding, in the form of listening and help in exploring solutions. What do you imagine were the first questions the Good Samaritan asked as he reached the man in the ditch? You can bet he asked, "Are you okay?" and "What happened?", and listened intently to the man's mumbled reply as he began cleaning and comforting his wounds. That is a good start for you as a camp counselor. It will demand skills that you probably already have, such as these:

1. Show that you are available.

Often it will be with great reservation that a camper will come to you for help. He may drop the most discreet hints that he has something to talk about. Be alert for these indicators, especially in those "in-between times" we have already discussed (e.g., before or after a meal, between activities) or towards the end of a week (even the last hour before he leaves). He may hang around you rather awkwardly, or try to pull you away from the crowd, or start out with, "By the way, I was wondering..."

If possible, drop what you are doing immediately and show him that you have the time and opportunity to talk right then. If that is not possible, set a definite time and place to meet and talk. Make it your goal to communicate to the camper that he will have your full and undivided attention for the time you will be listening to him. Don't refer to a deadline or someone you have to go and see. The best way to show you have time is to sit down with him. Avoid looking at your watch or at people who are passing by, and avoid silences or motions (such as standing up) that indicate you are eager to leave. If it does become necessary for you to leave, make a definite appointment to meet later.

Just showing that you are willing to give your time and attention is a huge encouragement to a hurting or confused camper. Often children or youth will clutch onto a problem for a long time simply because no one has shown that he has the time to listen. As one child wrote in an essay, "Everyone should have a grandparent, because they are the only grown ups who have time."[98] Be one of those unusual adults in their lives, and give them your unlimited time and undivided attention.

Remember that you can reduce awkwardness in a conversation by making it a "threesome"; that is, by adding the view of the ocean or a bag of candy or the focus point of a campfire while you talk together. Focusing on something other than the person we are talking to is our usual way of making ourselves comfortable with him. Also, use his name occasionally as you converse together to express your care for him and his importance to you. Your warmth and acceptance toward a camper are the keys to helping him relax and begin talking.

Sue wasn't sure if Erin would show up after her reaction to Sue's note the day before, but she did. People were in the vicinity, but involved in their own activities, and so Erin seemed to relax. Sue told her that she was all hers for the next hour and a half, and offered Erin a Coke and a bag of chips to share. At first, Erin only gave answers to Sue's direct questions and seemed preoccupied, playing with the tab on the Coke can and offering no eye contact. Then she looked up and blurted out, "I think I'm pregnant!", burst into tears, and got up and ran in the direction of the cabins.

2. Show that you are paying attention.

How can you show someone that you are paying attention as she speaks? We do it through eye contact and our physical and verbal responses to what she says. Eye contact is looking without staring. There is a mysterious and powerful connection made as we catch someone's eye. If there is no eye contact, we assume the person is not listening to us, because we know that our eyes wander as our minds wander. If there is too much eye contact, we feel uncomfortable and over-exposed by the implied intimacy, as if someone was looking into our very soul. Learning the right balance of eye contact is simply a matter of practice, but it is essential in a counseling situation.

Physical and verbal responses are also a matter of practice. Physical responses include a nod of the head, facial expressions such as a genuine smile or look of concern, and posture that shows you are intent on what she is saying (for example, lying stretched out with your hands behind your head and your eyes closed won't do). These responses need to be natural and not put on, of course, but they can still be deliberate and intentional. Avoid expressions and gestures that show disapproval or disbelief. You want her to know by your "body language" that you are paying attention and you are accepting (even if not agreeing with) what she is saying, so that she will keep talking.

Some verbal responses are a matter of habit to us: whether you say, "Uh huh" or "Hmmm" or "Eh?" you are telling the person you are with her and that you follow what she is saying. Add to these responses some questions and statements of clarification: "So are you saying that...?" or "I think I get what you mean..." Other responses reveal your empathy for the person and show you care: "Wow, that must have been very difficult for you..." All of these will encourage her to talk more, which is the whole point. You want her to talk about her situation and feelings as much as she can, while you listen.

There are other verbal responses that will make a camper feel that you are paying less attention to her than you are to yourself. Isn't it annoying when someone interrupts you, assuming he knows what you are talking about, when it is obvious he hasn't been listening at all? Or when he brings up his experience as if it is the answer to your own situation? Doing this to a camper will damage her trust in you, and perhaps end the conversation. It will show that you are not willing to take the time to listen before you jump to conclusions about what she is telling you and what she should do about it. When someone is speaking to you, it is natural that what she says will bring to your mind similar experiences and feelings. Resist the urge to mention them; instead, use those mental images to add to your understanding and empathy. Be slow to speak, quick to listen.[99]

When Sue entered the cabin, Erin was on her bunk sobbing. Sue just held her for a long time until Erin was able to talk. Another camper came in at one point and Sue asked her to let the head counselor know that she would be occupied for the afternoon and to make arrangements for her. As Erin began to talk, Sue found that many things came to mind that she could say, but she wasn't sure if they were the right things, so she simply kept asking questions and responding to Erin.

3. Show that you care and are trying to understand.

Sometimes a camper will indicate that she wants to talk, but she can't get started. Ask questions to get her going, starting with questions on a casual level (e.g., "What's the most fun thing you have done all week?"), and moving to deeper questions about her needs and feelings (e.g., "Would you like to tell me about what was bothering you this morning?" or "What was it like when you heard that your family would be moving?"). Sometimes a camper needs to think a moment or two before answering; give her time without letting the silence become so long as to become awkward. If you sense you have tried to go too deep too fast, move back to a more casual level, perhaps by joking about something or by referring to a topic on safer territory.

Listen to body talk and emotions too. Communication is much more than words. Do the camper's words misrepresent her apparent feelings or the way she is acting? Is the camper hard and defensive, or soft and dependent? Sometimes it is good to tell her what you observe, not in a judgmental way, but to show that you want her to feel free to say what is really on her heart. Be careful of trying to read between the lines too much, or pretending you are a psychoanalyst. You are not, and she didn't come to you to be diagnosed. But do try to understand what she is communicating, and attempt to identify with her feelings.

Show your desire to understand by saying back to her in your own words what she has said, and asking if you have it right. Ask questions that will get to the *meaning* behind what she is saying, not only so you will understand her, but so she can better understand herself and see things more objectively. For example ask, "Do the things that have happened to your family ever make you feel guilty, as if it was your fault?" This is a question that may help her identify her feelings as *guilt*, enabling the camper to deal with it. She might respond, "No, I guess it is more that I'm just angry all the time that my parents are doing this to me," and then you can explore her feelings of anger. Don't give up easily when you are confused. Stay with her until you understand what she is trying to communicate or describe.

At one point, Erin asked Sue if she thought that what she had done was wrong. Sue opened her Bible and showed Erin from I Corinthians 6 that sex outside of marriage was not what God intended for his people. This put Erin on the defensive: Why would God give someone these feelings and desires if they were not to be used? Sue wasn't sure how to answer at first, then asked how Erin had felt since the incident. Erin talked about feeling guilt and dirty and a number of other negative emotions, and Sue asked if her emotions indicated that God was right or wrong about sex outside of marriage. As they talked, Erin came to see her need to confess her sin to God and regain her purity. But as they prayed together, Erin suddenly stopped and said, "But what if I'm pregnant?", and seemed ready to burst into tears again.

4. Offer to work with the camper toward a solution.

Be sensitive, not critical. You are not there to pass judgment on the camper for what he has told you, but to help resolve the guilt or pain. Also, be slow to give advice. Instead, work with the camper to find a solution. You could offer good advice, but he may not see it as good advice or may not want to follow it. The solution he "discovers" together with you is the one he will try, not your pat answers. If you can come together to an understanding of the problem and issues involved in his situation, this may be all the solution he needs. If not, start discussing together possible ways of resolving the problem. Set some definite goals, if possible. Avoid making up his mind for him by your suggestions.

Somewhere in most problems there is sin involved: either that of the person you are helping or someone else, or both. All problems are partly spiritual, because we are spiritual beings. So things like forgiveness and repentance, taking a stand against the enemy and submitting to God, are probably at least part of the solution in every issue.

At some point during almost every counseling session, I bring out the word of God so it can shed light on the problem. Use your Bible not as a weapon, but as a scalpel to perform needed surgery,[100] or as a lotion to bring comfort and healing.[101] Show him that God offers love and *forgiveness* in Jesus Christ, if we will confess and turn away from our sin. He can forgive those who have hurt him for the same reason he has been forgiven: a decision to love those who don't deserve it.

Comfort campers with the comfort God has given you.[102] Though it is not right to assume that your experiences and solutions in life match the camper's problems, you do probably have more life experience than he does. Draw from the assurance and grace that God has given you in hard times and use it to bring hope and comfort to your camper. For example, you may not have been disappointed in the same way he was, but you know the feeling of disappointment. Try to remember what it feels like, and think about ways that God and people brought you hope and strength. This will give you wisdom for bringing comfort to your camper.

Exercise firm love. Sometimes you will need to be frank with a camper and help him see things about himself that he will not want to see. If it is done tactfully, thoughtfully and out of love, it will help and not destroy your relationship in the long run. Watch that you are not being manipulated by a camper who has learned to control people who offer him help. If you need to be critical, be careful not to be judgmental. Even God places his heavy hand on us not to condemn, but to discipline us. Be sensitive, but be realistic about what you see in the camper's life and don't whitewash sin or sinful attitudes. You have no right to try to pluck a speck from his eye when you have a log in your own eye.[103] If you want him to be transparent with you, be willing to show him an appropriately honest picture of yourself.

Where did we get the idea that saying, "Let's pray about it" is a cop-out? The Bible clearly teaches that going to God with our crises is the first thing we should do, not the last resort. Teach the camper to go to God with his problems. Never end a counseling session without having taken him to God's word and having prayed together about it. You don't want the camper becoming dependent on you for the resolution of his problem, but on God.

Erin was terrified at the thought of her parents knowing what she had done. As they talked, Sue realized that Erin could not be pregnant, but many questions still remained: Would Erin continue this relationship? Should she be tested for sexually transmitted diseases? Should her parents know? Sue had to bite her tongue when Erin said she wished she hadn't said anything and begged her not to tell her parents. Regaining her composure, Sue began discussing the pros and cons of telling her parents, and slowly Erin began to see that she could not confess this to God and yet keep it from her parents. She would need their support for some time to come, and this secret was affecting her relationship with them.

LEAVE THEM WITH A CARE-GIVER AND CHECK BACK

In some cases, the problem will be more serious or long-term and more help will be needed than you can offer in one week at camp. There will be times you will wish the camper could just stay with you forever, especially when you know that the tears on the last day are not only because she is saying good-bye to you, but because of what is waiting for her at home. Be assured that God is watching her—he sees the sparrow when it falls—and his angels seem to keep a special eye out for children.[104] He loves them more than any counselor is capable.

However, when you have counseled a camper who will need more help, you do have a responsibility to see that she will get the help she needs. How this is done depends on the policies of your camp; if you are unsure about the process check your camp's staff manual or talk with your head counselor or administrator. In the case of some camper problems, the camp's follow-up process will be enough to ensure the camper will get adequate support at home; in more serious matters the parents, authorities or government services may be contacted.

Unless instructed otherwise by your camp, do follow-up with campers who have brought their problems to you in the same way you would if they made a decision to accept Christ. If the home situation is part of the problem, be aware that the letters you write or calls you make might be monitored by suspicious parents, so be careful to provide encouragement without siding against a parent or giving advice that might be misconstrued. The main thing is to let campers know that you are still thinking about and praying for them, and that you invite them to write back and let you know how things are progressing. Just the knowledge that you are still there will be of great encouragement.

By Sue's suggestion, Erin called her parents and asked them to pick her up in person at the end of camp, so that Sue could be with her when she told her parents. It was a very emotional meeting. Sue was relieved that Erin's mother was compassionate and understanding of Erin's repentant spirit; however, she was a little concerned about her father's angry expression. Both parents thanked Sue for her involvement, and were grateful when Sue asked if she could keep in touch with their daughter over the winter. Erin wept on her shoulder for a long time when it was time for her to go, and Sue felt that Erin was really coming to terms with her situation. She and Erin wrote each other regularly all winter.

TYPES OF ISSUES YOU MAY ENCOUNTER

In Resource Section "B" is a list of several camper issues and problems you may encounter as a camp counselor. This is, by necessity, a limited description of problems and solutions. For more resources on dealing with these and other issues, I would recommend:

- Josh McDowell and Bob Hostetler, *Handbook on Counseling Youth*, ©1996 Word Publishing

- Joan Sturkie and Siang-Yang Tan, *Advanced Peer Counseling*, ©1993 Youth Specialties

- Gary R. Colins, *Christian Counseling: A Comprehensive Guide*, ©1980 Word Books

- Dr. G. Keith Olson, *Counseling Teenagers*, ©1984 Group Books.

COUNSEL FOR THE COUNSELOR

Sometimes during the summer you may wonder if it is *you* who needs counseling! Camp counseling can be stressful and constantly demanding. Counselors sometimes say to me that they never have opportunity to deal personally with crises as they happen, because they are the ones who always need to restore things to normal for the campers as quickly as possible. Most camps have a head counselor or camp pastor who have as part of their responsibility the emotional and spiritual health of the staff. What are the signs that it is time to pay them a visit?

1. When you are exhausted.

Your camp appreciates your dedication, but it isn't looking for heroes, especially exhausted ones. If you are becoming over-tired (for example, you can't get up in the morning, you are getting sick, you are snapping at your campers, or you find yourself blanking out) go talk with your head counselor. They can offer you support, perhaps adjust your schedule, and discuss with you how you can better pace yourself.

2. When you are facing strong temptations.

The devil loves to get his foot in the door of a camp, especially among tired counselors. If temptations such as lust or dishonesty or substance abuse are at your door constantly, don't wait until you give in the first time before you go talk with someone. Better the small "embarrassment" of going to someone for help than embarrassing your whole camp and destroying its testimony. Swallow your pride, and find someone to whom you can confess your problem, and to whom you can become accountable in overcoming it.

3. When there are anxieties that are infringing on your daily routine.

Maybe you are under pressure to make career or education choices for the fall. Perhaps events back home are occupying your mind all day long. Other staff and campers will watch you pull away from them and not know why. It is far better to go *early* rather than later to talk about these issues with someone and get them praying with you, so you can regain the peace that is greater than your limited understanding.[105]

4. When you are having spiritual doubts or questions.

Another strategy of our enemy is to assail us with doubts about what we believe in, or about our self-worth. He may work on our minds about a question a camper asked, or about some disappointment we experienced. If your own time with God is not addressing these doubts, and especially if your doubts are taking away your motivation to share Christ in the cabin, go talk with someone. Be honest with him, so he can help provide the assurance you need in order to serve Christ effectively.

5. When you are experiencing trauma from a crisis.

One of the signs of a great counselor is an ability to empathize, bearing the griefs and joys of her campers along with them. This can be emotionally draining and even traumatizing. It is not "being spiritual" to give everyone the impression that you are okay and handling your emotions well if you are not. It is no sign of weakness but only wisdom to go and talk about your emotions with someone.

6. When you are having trouble getting along with other staff.

People are people, and even the best of them will occasionally let you down. The Bible warns us not to let any "root of bitterness" gradually grow and cause trouble in a Christian fellowship, making the ministry ineffective.[106] Start by going to the person yourself; if there is no response, talk with your supervisor about the situation. A camp cannot afford resentful feelings to continue among staff. There is too much at stake. Be an example of what it means to forgive as Christ has forgiven you.[107]

---

[97]You will find the story throughout this chapter, in italics. This story is fictional, based on a composite of real counseling situations, so that any similarity it bears to any real persons or situations is entirely coincidental

[98]James Dobson, *What Wives Wish Their Husbands Knew About Women*, ©1975 Tyndale House Publishers, Inc.

[99]James 1:19

[100]Hebrews 4:12-13 rather than Ephesians 6:17

---

[101]Exodus 15:26

[102]See II Corinthians 1:3-4

[103]See Matthew 7:1-5

[104]See Matthew 10:29-31 and 18:10-14

[105]Philippians 4:6-7

[106]Hebrews 12:15

[107]Ephesians 4:31-32

CAMP PREP #8:
BECOME QUICK TO LISTEN

Suggestions on how to prepare for your counseling experience.

"My dear brothers, take note of this: Everyone should be quick to listen, slow to speak and slow to become angry..." (James 1:19). This takes practice! It is more natural for us to be quick to draw attention to ourselves, and slow to pay attention to others.

• In your conversations in the next while, practice good listening skills, as discussed above. Bite your tongue when you want to jump in with comments about yourself before adequately listening to the other person. Work on suitable eye contact and response; try out the idea of adding a "third something" to your conversation to reduce awkwardness. Become a good listener.

• If you feel inadequately informed about some of the issues discussed in this chapter, see Resource Section "B" for more information, or do some extra reading on the various issues campers might bring up with you. Your pastor or the local library may be able to point you to further resources.

13. Discipline: Principles Of Correcting Behavior

Perhaps the part of camp counseling you are not looking forward to this summer is camper discipline. Camp is supposed to be fun, and the thought of enforcing rules, breaking up disputes and deciding on suitable consequences for bad behavior seems contrary to the idea of fun. However, if discipline does not happen at your camp this summer, I guarantee that very few of your campers will have any fun (and for those that do, you will not share their idea of fun). We live in a fallen world. The sobering book, *The Lord of the Flies*, demonstrates that people who live without boundaries and authority structures quickly begin to dominate and use and hurt one another.

What is the purpose of disciplining campers? The word "discipline" is related to the word "disciple" or student. It has more to do with instruction than simply maintaining control, and is more concerned with future development than dealing with a past event. Discipline is teaching better behavior, not simply administering justice or handing out punishment.

Even God "does not treat us as our sins deserve,"[108] but "disciplines those he loves, as a father the son he delights in."[109] "Our fathers disciplined us for a little while as they thought best, but God disciples us for our good, that we may share in his holiness."[110] God is holy, and so he is concerned with justice; but he is love, and so he is also concerned with mercy. Out of mercy for his people, he disciplines them, so they will not be condemned with the world.[111]

Punishment without discipline is child abuse. A counselor has no right to apply disagreeable consequences for a camper's behavior apart from the loving purpose of teaching him correct behavior and improving his relationships with people. By disciplining the camper, he should have a better week at camp than if you had failed to discipline him, and a better relationship with you than before you disciplined him.

STYLES OF DISCIPLINE

Discipline of your campers takes a careful balance of two things: *support* as an expression of love for the camper, and *control* in the form of definite boundaries and consequences for crossing them.

This balance of support and control can be ordered into four distinct styles of discipline:[112]

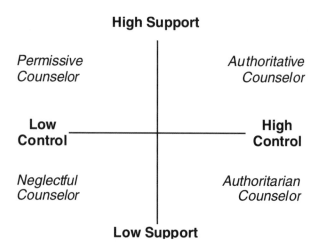

1. The permissive counselor.

This counselor offers high support but low control. Campers tend to walk all over the permissive counselor, but at least they know he loves them.

2. The neglectful counselor.

This one provides very little of anything: low support and low control. He is probably at camp for all the wrong reasons, or is simply not suitable for the task. There is minimal time and attention given to campers, and they suffer for it.

3. The authoritarian counselor.

The counselor demands high control but offers low support. Campers usually respond to this counselor one of two ways: they either fear or rebel against him. The counselor is demonstrating immaturity and misusing his or her authority.

4. The authoritative counselor.

The ideal discipline method offers high control while also offering high support and love. Campers feel secure in firm boundaries, but also know that their counselor loves and cares about them. Obviously, this is the best of these four styles, but it is not always the style that comes to mind when campers begin to get out of hand.

In a study of parents and children,[113] it was found that the *authoritative* parent ranked first in establishing their children's sense of self-worth. Children who experience high support and high control in the home are the most likely to conform to their parents' authority and accept their parents' faith, and they are the least likely to rebel.

So which is the *second* most effective of these counseling styles? Surprisingly, it is the *permissive* style, which means that it is more effective to let kids walk all over you but love them than to try any other method but not show them love. The *authoritarian* parent, who exercises high control but offers low support and love, comes dead last in every category of child development.

Of these four styles of discipline, or discipleship if you like, Jesus consistently used only one in his ministry. Like his Father, Jesus was the Authoritative Counselor, firm in his stand against sin, but displaying incredible love for sinners. As in other areas of camp ministry, Jesus is the prime example of the kind of counselor we should be.

PROBLEM PREVENTION AS DISCIPLINE

The best form of discipline takes place *before*—not after—a problem occurs with your campers. There are several things you can do to teach better behavior before bad behavior happens, and to correct wrong attitudes before they get a camper in trouble. I have known counselors who are just waiting for their campers to make a wrong move so they can pounce on them. Don't stalk your campers. Instead, do whatever you can to keep your campers happily involved in the program within the boundaries that have been set for them.

1. Get to know your campers.

The more observant and communicative you are with your campers, especially in the first part of the week, the better you will be able to catch problems before they start. Take note that little Ryan is very sensitive to teasing and tends to lash out at campers who bug him, and then set the standard that negative teasing is outside the boundaries for your cabin group. Observe that Jenny and Crystal chose to sit among a group of disruptive boys during fireside the first night, and make it a point to talk about the "guys" topic in your cabin devotions. The more they know you understand them, the better they will respond to your authority.

2. Let them know your expectations, and the consequences of falling short.

In a culture that avoids the topic of morality, you should not be surprised that some kids have no idea of the kind of behavior you expect of them. A boy I brought to camp from a housing project was sent home after punching the lights out of another boy. In the world he came from, fighting was the "right" thing to do when someone started pushing you around, and he was very surprised that *he* was the one to be punished.

Early in the week, sit down with your group and establish some guidelines together. Involve your campers in setting the rules. Ask them, "How do you want to be treated by everyone in our cabin group?" which leads to the biblical standard, "Do to others what you would have them do to you."[114] Decide together the consequences of stepping outside these boundaries, and come to an agreement about what is right and fair. Make sure that the boundaries you set provide enough room for your cabin's age group to feel free but safe. The more mature your group, the broader the boundaries should be.

Offer reasonable explanations for your guidelines. Don't give in to the temptation to say, "Because I said so!" which is not satisfying to anyone. Of course, there will also be rules set by your camp, which may be posted or announced on the first day. Campers do not often pay much attention to announcements and signs, so be sure to bring these up with your cabin personally. Make this a brief and fun discussion time, not "laying the heavy" on them. Let them know that the purpose of the guidelines is to ensure maximum fun for everyone.

3. Give those with a bad start or bad reputation a fresh chance.

On their first night of camp, one of my groups of CIT's (Counselors in Training) sneaked out of their rooms and joined some other staff for a late-night party. Though I felt like writing them off then and there, I re-affirmed the rules with them and they humbly continued the program—to become some of the best counselors I have known. Sometimes well-meaning people will tell you all the horror stories about a kid who is going to be your camper. Here's a good response: "So you are Kevin. I've heard all kinds of things about you, and you know what? I don't believe a word of it."[115]

It may be that your first impressions or the things you have heard about a camper prove to be justified. But give him a chance, and resolve your own opinion of him. Sometimes people behave badly simply because it is what their leaders have come to expect of them. Believe in your campers and expect the best of them, and they will more likely respond positively to you.

4. Be with your campers, especially during in-between times.
This is worth repeating. In my experience, most problems occur while campers are waiting for something to happen. You will be able to prevent many problems if you are with your campers during those "in-between times," before and after meals and activities, and as campers are getting up or going to bed. Don't be afraid to step in and use your authority when necessary. At the same time—especially among older campers—avoid policing them or bossing them around. Spend the time building on your relationship with them, not just watching for trouble.

5. Praise good behavior.
Positive reinforcement is not limited to dog training; people respond well to it too. When someone notices and draws attention to something you have done well, you want to do it even better next time. If a camper shows kindness or patience or decides to side with forgiveness rather than revenge, draw attention to it and let your campers know you are impressed and happy about it. Show that your expectations are not just negative ones, but also things you hope they *will* do.

6. Avoid allowing your campers to become over-tired.
More problems usually occur toward the end of a week of camp because campers are getting tired. They have less patience, they tend to not think before they act, and they become more selfish (which is what will happen to you too if you let yourself become exhausted). Problem prevention is mostly helping campers pace themselves so they will not end the week snarling at one another. If you see that they are getting over-tired, call for a nap time, or arrange a sleep-in and serve them breakfast in bed. Talk with the head counselor about other alternatives.

7. Teach campers how to have constructive fun.[116]
Some kids have learned only destructive ways of having fun, such as wrecking things, hurting people, and having fun at others' expense. Don't tolerate this behavior, but at the same time teach them new ways of having fun without damaging property and people. Destructive kids need more structure and specific things to do, even when the program is unstructured. This will demand more enthusiasm, spontaneity and flexibility from you,

but you will also spend less time repairing the damage if you can keep them constructively involved.

CONFRONTING A CAMPER

When a camper has stepped over the boundaries, you are the person who will usually need to confront him. This is a difficult task because of the personalities, possible risks and especially the emotions involved—yours as well as those of the camper. You will do well to think and pray beforehand about your approach to this kind of confrontation. It is difficult to decide what to do when you have left all your decisions to the heat of the moment. What should be your first concerns, attitudes and actions when approaching a camper who is out of line?

1. Remove any danger to the camper, others around him and yourself.

For example, if a fight is taking place you will need to stop the fight, but not if doing so would endanger you. Get help, and clear away campers in the area so that they will be safe and the fight won't escalate. Watch also that campers don't immediately seek revenge on one another, which seems to be the way many kids deal with perceived wrong.

2. Stop the camper from doing wrong.

Even if the camper is not endangering anyone physically, it may be up to you to stop him from doing the wrong in which he is involved. Don't hesitate to step in and end verbal abuse or threats, or to make a camper stop destroying property. As a counselor you *have* authority, but it is up to you to be *authoritative*. Raise your voice if needed, but avoid yelling or going on the offense with your language. If what he is doing has made you angry, there is nothing wrong with letting a camper see your anger (it would not be healthy for you to fake calmness), but stay in control of your anger. Make sure your anger is directed at his *behavior*, not at the person himself.

3. Communicate understanding or at least a willingness to understand.

"What's going on here?" is better than quick accusations that you may have to swallow later when you understand the whole story. Do you really know what happened and who is at fault? Let those involved in the problem know that you want to be fair and get all sides of the story. If necessary, separate those affected and talk with them individually, and "reserve judgment" until you have heard them all. Sometimes it is better to let emotions cool before discussing the problem with the campers involved.

4. Be tentative.

Avoid saying things that will be hard to mend later, such as threats of dire consequences, hurtful words, and quick pronouncements of judgment. "The world's future doesn't depend on how powerfully or decisively you react in a problem situation. Stay calm, take a few deep breaths... Realize that your relationship with the problem person after the incident is more important to his future behavior and spiritual growth than the problem itself."[117]

GETTING THE RECORD STRAIGHT

Once the immediate situation has calmed down, it is time to talk about the problem with those involved. If campers have been involved in a problem together, usually you will talk with them together. If there has been a dispute between campers, it will likely be better to talk with them individually first before bringing them together. Do this privately and confidentially, but as we discussed in the previous chapter, do it in a public place away from other people rather than behind closed doors. Here are some things to talk about:

1. Communicate your expectations and how the camper(s) failed to meet them.

What is the rule or expectation they failed to meet? If you have already talked as a cabin about that expectation, you will have a stronger base from which to work. For example, you could say "We decided that we need to be able to trust one another in this cabin." Don't assume that they know what you expected of them, or that they should understand the difference between right and wrong. Be careful to avoid language that is judgmental, sarcastic or that will cause anger. For example, saying that they are "*always*" doing this thing, or asking "how come you *never...*" is not realistic and will only put them on the defensive.

2. Identify the problem.

Describe to the camper(s) the situation as you see it, and then ask them if they think you have it right. This will give you opportunity to discuss and explore the problem together and come to a mutual understanding. In some cases you might ask the campers to summarize the problem instead. When there are two campers involved in a dispute, do this with them separately and then bring them together, so that you can clarify the problem on both sides, and so that they can come to understand the other person's point of view. Stay on top of this discussion; don't permit accusations to fly and emotions to rise again.

Talk about the natural *results* of the problem, such as who was hurt by their actions, the damage that was done and what it will mean from this point on. For example, "Jon, if you have been helping yourself to Joe's clean socks, it makes it hard for the rest of us to trust you." This may seem too obvious to you, but often kids have given no thought to the natural consequences of their actions, and part of the learning process in discipline is to bring this to their attention.

It is not up to you to make them feel guilty about what they have done, but to show them *why* what they did was wrong. Avoid language that tears them to shreds; instead keep your language constructive, encouraging them to do things better than before. Take time to find out *why* the deed was done before you decide what to do about it. There may be reasons that you couldn't imagine, such as deep-seated anger over a situation at home.

DECIDING ON CONSEQUENCES

Is it essential that there always be consequences when disciplining a camper? Sometimes the natural consequences of her behavior will be enough to correct her. Many kids are sensitive enough that your obvious disapproval—perhaps simple eye contact and a frown—is all they need to mend their ways forever. You will use your own judgment, but if it seems that there is true remorse on the part of the camper, she may have suffered consequences enough to have learned her lesson. It may be appropriate to talk about confessing to God what she has done, and about how his forgiveness erases her guilt. She will also need to apologize to anyone who has been hurt by her actions, if she can do it honestly.

Sometimes you will get the sense that the camper is more sorry about getting caught or about having to talk with you than she is about the wrong thing she has done. She might simply remain resistant or rebellious, and ready to do what she did again. In these cases the natural consequences of her behavior are not enough to teach her, and you will need to add consequences that will drive the lesson home a bit better. You want her to learn that bad decisions have uncomfortable consequences, and if she doesn't seem to be getting the idea, you will have to help her. In many cases, you will create a consequence to *end* bad behavior, such as when you separate a pair of trouble-makers. Sometimes you can involve the camper in the decision about the consequences, but usually you will need to choose them yourself.

In some cases, it is better that there be no consequences to a camper's bad behavior at all. For example, if the camper is simply out to get your attention by negative means—such as shining her flashlight in your eyes during devotions—you will reward her if you bring attention to her. It may be better to ignore her, or walk over and take away the flashlight as you speak. At other times, a potentially bad situation can be creatively diffused, such as when two campers are sizing one another up like a pair of fighting hens and you start a rousing water fight. Ask God daily for wisdom and creativity in dealing with camper problems.

1. Disciplinary consequences at camp that are appropriate.

These fall under several categories:

- *Limiting activity.* Probably the most consistently effective means of correcting the behavior of active kids is putting temporary limits on their activity. "Time out" is the punishment of choice in many homes and daycares, so most kids are familiar with having their activity curtailed because of bad behavior. It usually works. For example, if a camper has been cheating or acting violently during a game, it would be appropriate to have him sit out ten minutes of the game while you talk together. A camper who is being disruptive in cabin devotions might have to sit on your bunk with you during the discussion.

  Sometimes all that campers need is some re-direction of their energy. The camper who has been trying to pick a fight can be given the job of cleaning the cabin, or the one who pushed his way into the line-up to the camp store could be told to pick up 25 pieces of garbage before he will be allowed to return to the end of the line or buy anything. Make sure the "punishment fits the crime." It would be a fairly serious thing for a camper to have to miss an entire activity. Be careful to choose consequences that will correct behavior, and not just create resentment.

- *Separation.* It can be effective to simply remove a camper from an environment where he has gotten (or will get) into trouble. For example, if a camper is being disruptive at a fireside, get up and trade places with him. By doing this you separate him from the temptation to fool around, and you become a calming influence in that location. Separation should be temporary, and suitable to the seriousness of the problem. Remember that friendships are so important to junior high campers that any long-term separation would be a serious matter to them. It is not appropriate to *isolate* a camper, which is like sending him to solitary confinement. If a camper must be sent to his cabin, usually someone should go with him.

- *Making restitution.* The camper who has caused a problem can often be disciplined by making him part of the solution. For example, it is not inappropriate for a camper who has spray-painted offensive things on a wall to be responsible for cleaning it up or repainting it, and apologizing to his fellow campers. Insisting that a camper make amends may mean more work for the counselor, but this is part of "coming alongside" your camper for his long-term benefit.

   Make the restitution suitable to the offense, or it will become abuse instead of a teaching opportunity. Parents are sensitive to stories of campers having to dig ditches or polish pots as punishment for some minor problem. The consequence you choose must be reasonable enough to satisfy any parent who might inquire about it. Think about what discipline method the average caring parent would use at home.

- *Withdrawing privileges.* I have seen counselors use the withdrawal of privileges as their primary method of discipline, but I believe this should be reserved for more serious matters. An example would be not allowing a camper to go to the camp store for a day. To a junior camper, whose visit to the store is a big highlight of the day, this is a harsh punishment. Older campers will just get a friend to buy something for them. Another example would be denying access to an activity area. Again, this should be reserved for a serious offense, such as acting dangerously in that area. There should possibly be some way of earning the right to regain the privilege.

- *Talk with the head counselor or director.* This should also be reserved for serious matters, where all other disciplinary methods have failed. Realize that taking a camper to the head counselor or director is the step before a camper is sent home. The possibility of being taken to talk with him (or being sent home) should never be used as a threat. In fact, threats have no place in discipline. If your campers know your expectations, there should never be a time you say to them, "You guys do this one more time, and this is what will happen..." Don't hesitate to go to your head counselor or supervisor for advice concerning a difficult discipline situation, and don't allow a problem to continue unchecked. If the head counselor agrees it is necessary, take the camper to talk with him privately, and without drawing the attention of other campers.

2. Disciplinary consequences at camp that are *not* appropriate.
Watch that you avoid even the appearance of these "methods":

- *Any form of physical punishment.* Handling a camper roughly, shaking him, hitting him, or almost any other physical action is not only inappropriate but also illegal. Be very careful when you are angry with a camper to avoid all physical touch or even threatening actions. Kids are trained from an early age to be alert to any hint of abuse.

   It is also inappropriate to force him to do things that are physically demanding or threatening, such as running up and down stairs, doing push-ups until exhausted, staying out in the rain, "running the gauntlet" or being forced to jump into cold water. These are punishments that may be traditional in some camps, but they involve a high risk of physical and emotional injury to the camper, and will also upset his parents. What do these methods teach campers? Simply that they should not trust their counselors.

- *Verbal or emotional abuse.* This form of abuse includes shouting, name-calling, labeling, taunting, ignoring or embarrassing a camper in front of others. Avoid trying to make a camper feel guilty, which is the job of the Holy Spirit. Be careful not to make a big deal out of nothing. If you find that you have over-reacted, take a step back and apologize, and deal with the real issue. Many kids have to face put-downs and yelling every day at home; don't let that become part of their camp experience too.

- *Retaliation.* Occasionally a camper may do something that will injure you, your property or your pride. Be very careful not to discipline a camper more strongly than you normally would simply because you were the one hurt. Never use discipline as a means of getting back at a camper; this would be a very wrong use of your authority and a breech of trust with the camper. Stay as objective as you can.

- *Unfairness or favoritism.* Be as fair and equitable with your campers as possible in matters of discipline. Some counselors impose adult standards on campers' behavior, forgetting that they are children. Avoid disciplining campers for their actions one moment but changing your standards the next. Aim for consistency, and treat your campers equally.

Some kids are more fun or popular and it may be a temptation to let them get away with more than the ones who are hard to control. There is such a thing as campers earning the right to have more space, but be sure it is offered to them for the right reasons, and not just because they are "cool" kids.

- *Bribery.* Bribery is always wrong, but *reward* should not be mistaken for bribery. For example, a desperate counselor might be tempted to offer his campers candy the next day if they will just be quiet and go to sleep. That would be bribery, because it is offering them something to stop their bad behavior. On the other hand, it would be appropriate to offer a reward for exceptional behavior, such as being the best encourager, or memorizing verses to get the most points for your cabin.

- *Disciplining personality.* Some campers do not only make loud noises; they *are* loud. Others are extremely excitable or talkative, or hesitant about getting involved. Discipline kids for what they *do*, not for who they *are*. You want to teach kids better behavior through discipline, but you will not change their personality, and it would be unfair to try.

AFFIRMATION

Most parents understand the concept of affirmation naturally. They have punished a child they love, who is sorry and wants to do better. So they take the child in their arms, reaffirm their love for him and tell him how glad they are that he is their son. After disciplining campers and seeing response, it is essential to let them know that you still love and accept them, that all is forgiven and the slate is clean. Kids will not always respond to discipline. Even then they must know that you love them, though you disapprove of their attitude and behavior. Discipline should always result in a better relationship with your campers.

---

[108]Psalm 103:10

[109]Proverbs 3:12

[110]Hebrews 12:10

[111]I Corinthians 11:32

[112]Taken from: *The Seduction of Our Children* by Neil Anderson and Steve Russo, Copyright ©1991 by Harvest House Publishers, Eugene, Oregon. Used by permission

[113]Taken from: *The Seduction of Our Children* by Neil Anderson and Steve Russo, Copyright ©1991 by Harvest House Publishers, Eugene, Oregon. Used by permission

[114]Matthew 7:12

[115]Based on a story about Howard Hendricks, as quoted by Stan White, "The Counselor's Role in Camper Discipline", *CCI Focus Series #5*, Christian Camping International

[116]Alison Short, "Kids Want Fun, But Need Help To Have Fun", reprinted in *Journal of Christian Camping*, Nov. - Dec. 1988, p. 21

[117]Gary Richardson, "When You Have a Problem With Someone," *The Group Retreat Book*, ©1983 Thom Schultz Publications

CAMP PREP #9:
DO SOME ROLE PLAYING

Suggestions on how to prepare for your counseling experience.

Many camp staff have found it helpful to use role plays or case studies of real-to-life camp situations and problems to help them think through their personal responses ahead of time.

- Several role plays are included in Resource Section "D." In addition, see Resource Section "C" for a description of discipline issues you may face this summer and how to deal with them.

- If you have friends who are also planning to serve at camp this summer, perhaps you could get together and do a few role-plays with them. Okay, it sounds boring and nerdish, but it can be very fun. I dare you to try it!

- At the very least, read some of the potential camp situations in Resource Section "D" and think through your responses. It may be helpful to write down your responses as a continuation of the story.

14. Leading Bible Discussions: Helping Campers Discover Truth

Here I am, Joe Counselor surrounded by a group of campers in a sunny spot on the field, or sitting on bunks just before lights out. The camp wants me to lead these guys in a devotional or Bible discussion. Maybe I was given a lesson sheet to follow; maybe not. It doesn't matter, because two of my campers are still mad at me about the discipline I had to impose this morning, three more couldn't care less about anything I could teach them, and the rest have heard it all before. I am sitting here looking for the fortitude to get started and wondering if it will be worth the hassle. I have my doubts.

However, I have seen a counselor holding her Bible and reading, and all her campers looking on, listening and attentive, asking questions and offering answers. I have seen and experienced small group discussions that made me want to dance for joy when they are done. There is nothing more stimulating than watching young faces in the circle light up with understanding as they grasp some critical principle of the word of God. I wonder why it isn't always like this.

LESSONS FROM THE MASTER TEACHER

There is no doubt that Jesus Christ was the greatest teacher the world has ever known. The truth he communicated on flowery meadows and dusty streets turned lives upside-down, even when it was passed on second-hand years later through his apostles. Many centuries have passed, yet people who hardly know who Jesus was unconsciously use his sayings as part of their daily vocabulary. He was a master of relating the truths of heaven in earthly terms, drawing crowds wherever he went. Jesus was the greatest Communicator who ever walked our planet. As John described him, he was "the Word."

When you read his teaching in the Gospels, do you think of Jesus more as a lecturer or as a discussion leader? How do you carry on a discussion with 5000 men, not counting the women and all those children running around? However, when you take a close look at the Gospels, you will be surprised how seldom Jesus sounds like our idea of a preacher or lecturer. The people didn't call him "The Teacher" for nothing.

Look at the teaching methods Jesus employed:

- *Object lessons.* Whatever was at hand—lilies in the field, an empty picnic basket, the child on his lap—became a means of bringing to light the deep truths of God.

- *Challenging questions.* Jesus often met question with question, motivating the listener to think through the issue for himself.

- *Provocative statements.* What else did Jesus have in mind but to stimulate a response when he promised to rebuild the temple in three days? It worked!

- *Case studies.* Several times Jesus presented a scenario—a man getting mugged on his way from Jerusalem to Jericho, or an accident in which eighteen people were killed by a falling tower—and then asked the people how they read the situation.

- *Paradox.* He caught their attention by pointing out that those who are first will be last, that the poor are rich and that those who claim to be able to see are blind.

- *Metaphor.* Saying that we are *like* little lights in the world would have been boring; Jesus said we *are* the light of the world, and we imagine it better in our minds.

- *Proverbs.* Much of Jesus' teaching was in the form of short, effective and memorable statements like those given by King Solomon in the book of Proverbs.

- *Parables.* Jesus was famous for practical stories with a spiritual point. Think of how many complex truths you understand and remember because of "The Prodigal Son" and "The Sower and The Seed."

- *Demonstrations.* It was not enough to give a lecture against merchandising in the courts of the temple of God, or to simply talk about servanthood. Jesus gave full-out isomorphic demonstrations, and no one missed the point.

All of these are the stuff of discussion, and they are the choice of the world's greatest teacher. Maybe discussion has its place in the camp setting after all.

THE PURPOSE OF SMALL GROUP DISCUSSIONß

What do you want to accomplish by the method of small group discussion? I have witnessed too many discussions that were nothing more than a time-filler, that almost immediately degenerated into lecture by the counselor, or became a question-and-answer period. Ask yourself some tough questions about the purpose of your small group discussion:

- *Will I allow my campers to wrestle with God's word for themselves?* Will I let them discover truth, or just tell them things?

- *Will they only learn facts that they can accept or reject?* Or through my relationship with them will they become convinced of what I am teaching?

- *How can I get everyone participating in the discussion?* Will I allow campers to teach one another? Will it be a guided discussion, or just a wide-ranging sharing of ignorance?

- *Will I expect them to do something with what I teach them?* Do I expect to influence their thinking about God, and change their lives? Or is this just their daily spiritual fix, prescribed by the leaders of the camp? How can I help them put God's word to work?

- *Am I willing to be taught by my campers?* Or do I act as if I have a monopoly on spiritual wisdom?

- *Will they learn to study the Bible for themselves?* Will my example and instruction equip them to continue reading and learning from the Bible when they get home? Will they learn how to pray?

- *Will my campers come to know God better, or just know about him?* Will they understand the gospel and how to make a personal commitment to Christ? Will the Christians be challenged to grow this week and make new commitments to their Lord and Savior?

THE DYNAMICS OF A DISCUSSION

A small group discussion does not simply mean that more than one person is doing the talking. You could say the same of a dialogue or an interview or a brawl. It is also not one person asking questions and each person responding with an answer; that could be called an oral exam. In a true discussion, the leader simply gives direction to a group of people who contribute and develop ideas, ask and answer each other's questions and come to some conclusions. If a discussion was a kind of road, it would look more like a multi-leveled interchange than a straight freeway. Information travels from each participant to every other, not only from teacher to student and back again. In a discussion, the topic is reduced to the language of the campers, as they wrestle with an idea using their own terms.[118]

Discussion may sound complicated and a little risky. Interchanges are like that, but they are an effective way of getting where you need to go in a crowd. The reason many people shudder at the idea of leading group discussions is the same reason some people avoid interchanges on the freeway: they haven't given them a fair try. The more practice you have with discussion, the more comfortable you will become with using this incredibly effective tool.

GETTING TO KNOW THE NEEDS OF YOUR CAMPERS

Because group discussion is an interpersonal activity, the better your group knows one another the more freely discussion will flow. Counselors who at the start of the week despair at getting their kids talking often find in a few days that they simply needed more time to warm up to one another. When you are living with one another 24 hours a day this shouldn't take very long! You can help the process by deliberately getting to know the characteristics and needs of each of your campers.

1. All kinds of backgrounds and personalities.

Where are your campers coming from? Of course, knowing the family background of your campers will help you in many ways. When you know whether they come from a stable home situation or a dysfunctional one you will also be better prepared to lead discussions that are relevant to their home life and sensitive to the hurts or challenges they may be experiencing. Also, get to know each camper's personality through some discreet observation. How do they normally react to other people? Who do they remind you of? This will also give you clues to their style of learning, as follows.

2. Various learning styles and abilities.

Every person, according to his background and personality, has a preferred way of learning. My two sons are near the two ends of the scale in this respect, which makes things interesting for my wife as she teaches them at home. My older son is highly logical and analytical; give him ten steps to follow and he will fly through them in no time. My younger son is very intuitive and hands-on in his learning, and needs to see the whole picture before he can do anything with it.

Your campers will be somewhere along that scale, and it will help if you know where. One way is to talk with them about their interests and hobbies, or their least favorite subjects at school. Kids who know the stats of most hockey stars or who have to get all the creases smoothed out of everyone's sleeping bag each morning may be your analytical ones, and will respond better to underlining key words and doing crossword puzzles. Kids who dislike details and who love play will be on the intuitive end of the scale and will want hands-on experiences.

You will also run across kids with learning disabilities and short attention spans. Watch out for kids who might become embarrassed if asked to read a verse. Be sensitive to campers who don't know what to do with their hands when sitting down; give them a big piece of paper to doodle on or some other object to help them concentrate on the discussion better.

3. Wide range of spiritual knowledge and awareness.

You will have campers who know all the answers but don't seem to care, and other campers who thought "Jesus" was just a swear word. It can be tough to interest the one end of the scale without losing the other and all those in between.

It is a little sad that those who have been taught from the Bible all their lives can sometimes be the larger problem. "It's as if those who have the best diet can afford to make fun of food."[119] Remember that they are still kids, and that they may simply be testing you or questioning the validity of what they have always been taught. Challenge them, don't put up with "Sunday school" answers, and let them be convinced of what they have been taught by the evidence that Jesus is alive and well in your life.[120]

Church kids can also be challenged by interaction with the kids who have never heard of baby Moses or bulrushes before. Good discussion at camp can show church kids that they are less sure of themselves than they thought. This can also be an opportunity for them to share the wealth of their Bible knowledge with the camper who has limited church background. Have them help look up verses in the Bible, or share their testimonies, or talk about what happens in a youth group or church kids club.

4. Individual feelings, concerns and interests.

Spend time listening to your campers. What seems to be on their minds? What do their conversations tell you about their priorities, and how does that compare with what they say in group discussions? When they ask a question on a spiritual matter and you haven't the time to answer right away, write it down, get advice if needed, and bring it up in a cabin discussion.

Of course, it would be very easy to let cabin discussions range over the vast sum of campers' individual interests and concerns. You can start out talking about honesty and wind up with a debate on the meaning of the number of the beast in Revelation. Discussion without direction is fun, but it is often a sharing of ignorance rather than real teaching. Instead, take their interests and emotions and concerns and address them with a directed discussion of a particular topic or Bible passage that relates to those needs. Have a deliberate goal in mind for every Bible discussion to help you stay on track and make your teaching more effective.

At the same time remain sensitive to the leading of the Holy Spirit. Sometimes the best preparation has to be set aside because it simply doesn't address the immediate need. When the discussion takes an unexpected turn and it seems important to let it go that way, don't insist on getting through the other nine questions on your sheet. If the new topic is valid but can wait, decide as a group to talk about the issue at another time.

USING PREPARED CURRICULUM

Sometimes counselors are given materials to use for evening devotions and other small-group discussions, though many camps leave it to the counselor to prepare their own. Don't assume that getting something pre-packaged means that you can wing it. When you take a discussion sheet sight unseen to your cabin group, it means that you are trying to communicate truths that you have not wrestled with yourself. Your campers will sense that you are simply parroting words that mean little to you, and will have every reason to yawn.

You may not have much time to prepare, but there are some things that you should do to make prepared curriculum more effective:

1. Pray about these times all week.

Cabin devotions are much too big a responsibility to take on entirely yourself. You need God working through you. Ask him before you use his stuff.

2. Before reading the study material, read the Bible passage it uses several times.

Do this even if this is all you have time to do. Ask God to speak to your own heart through his word, and be accountable for what he is saying to you through it.

3. Glance through the study material.

What is the central idea the author of this discussion wants to communicate? Are there any materials you need to gather, such as pens, paper or Styrofoam cups? Do additional Bible passages come to mind?

4. Feel free to make reasonable changes to the *method* of communication.

Sometimes you will think, "This just isn't me—I can't do this." You may decide that the way the topic is presented will not reach your campers where they are. Feel free to make changes in the method of presenting and discussing the topic, but *make sure you still communicate the central idea that the writer intended.* You may think this central idea is irrelevant or not important, but remember that the camp speaker or pastor probably plans to follow up that discussion with a related topic, and is assuming that the campers have all discussed certain things together. So don't mess him up by talking about something entirely different. Instead, if you wish, make changes in the *method* by which his ideas are presented.

5. Use the material as a guide, not a script.

Some materials you are given may look like a script, with all the things you are to speak in bold print and "stage" instructions in italics. If you use prepared material in that way your campers will soon have reason to yawn loudly, and to question the reality of what you are communicating. Use the material as a guide, but avoid reading the sheet out loud to your campers. Ask questions in your own words, do activities as if they were your idea, and add and delete as the situation calls for and as the Holy Spirit leads.

PREPARING YOUR OWN BIBLE DISCUSSION

It is not unusual for a camp to leave evening devotions and other Bible discussions entirely up to the counselor. You may need to choose a topic and passage and determine a method of teaching and applying it. This is a large expectation, but not an unreasonable one. A camp counselor should be competent at pulling together a Bible discussion whenever necessary, and often very quickly. This ability will also enable you to use prepared discussions in a more effective way.

Preparation is necessary for a good small group discussion. Deciding what to talk about on your way from the bathroom to the cabin is sheer negligence, no matter how busy your day was. If you start off cabin devotions by saying, "So, what do you all want to talk about tonight?", it is an invitation to swing from the rafters, shoot spitballs, belch and make other rude body noises. And the boys are even worse.

1. Decide what you want to accomplish.

Go to cabin devotions praying and expecting that your campers will be influenced by what will happen there, and that they will do something about it. Cabin devotions must be much more than a duty done or a stamp on the day to make the experience "Christian." What are your goals for your devotional? What do you hope will be different in the lives of your campers as a result of this time with them? In what way are you asking God to move in their hearts and lives?

2. Support the camp speaker.

If your camp features a speaker in the evening, listen carefully to what he is communicating. Take notes if that helps. Try to notice how your campers are responding, or as you are getting to know them try to imagine how they are responding. While you listen, be thinking about questions that you could ask your campers to help them wrestle with these ideas, and jot them down if needed. Try to fix in your mind the one central idea the speaker is communicating.

Also, be careful about voicing any possible disagreement or complaints about the speaker to the campers, and even to other staff. We need to work as a team. If you have problems with the speaker or what he is saying, go to him personally. When you are with campers and staff, express your support and enthusiasm for the topic he is teaching and the way he is handling it.

3. Choose a Bible passage and topic.

No matter what you do in cabin devotions, you should focus on the Bible. It is not enough to give your own answers to campers' questions or to provide them with your opinions on a topic. Your authority on every topic needs to come from the word of God.

Sometimes it is best to begin with a Bible passage (perhaps one from which God has been teaching you personally) and determine your topic by studying it. Other times you will begin with a topic pertinent to your campers and look for a Bible passage that addresses that topic (a Bible concordance is helpful for this). Both methods are valid, as long as you develop the topic from your study of God's word and not just from your own experience or opinions.

You have quite a number of discussions to prepare for in a week of camp! Here are some suggestions to help you think through an entire week of cabin devotions:

- *First Day.* What do you want to accomplish on the first night of camp? This is a great time to get to know your campers and for them to get to know you. It is also important that they get a good first impression about what cabin devotions are all about so they will look forward to this time of day.

  One way to get to know your campers is to do some form of survey, keeping discreet notes as you ask a variety of questions. Maybe you could pose as a reporter on the street, asking things like, "What would you wish for if you had Aladdin's lamp?" and other fun but informative questions. Tactfully seek information on things like their home situation (a safe question to ask is, "Who lives at your house?"), whether they and their parents go to church, and what their interests and hobbies are. This will be useful to you all week, but also when it comes to time to do follow-up after camp.

  The first discussion is also a good opportunity to tell them about the purpose of the devotion time, explaining why you want to tell them about God's word and the place it has in your life. Let them know why the Bible is so important to you, and why you are bringing out this book as your authority in life.[121] You could also let them get to know you by giving your testimony. Again, focus on some passage of the Bible as you give your testimony, such as a passage that has especially been used of God in your life.

- *Through the week.* Cabin devotions are a good time to talk about whatever the speaker has been talking about, or to discuss questions brought up by campers. This is also a great opportunity to communicate the gospel to the unbelievers in your cabin, and to disciple your new or maturing Christian campers (going over basic truths such as the Bible, prayer, resisting temptation, going to church, knowing you are a Christian, sharing your faith, etc.). Remember to focus on a passage of Scripture!

- *Last Day.* This is an occasion for feed-back and reflection. Get them sharing about what they have learned, and decisions they have made. Maybe have a cabin appreciation time, with the group focusing on one person at a time to tell him what they appreciate about that person. Teach them from God's word something that they can take home as a challenge.

4. Study the passage yourself.

Once you have chosen a Bible passage, ask God to speak to *you* through it before you attempt to communicate it to your campers. When I am preparing a Bible discussion, I often find myself being taught the same lesson in my daily life, and God can be a strict teacher! Don't try to teach something unless you are willing to pay attention to it yourself.[122]

Study the passage just as you would for your own personal Bible study. In fact, often what you teach others *will* come directly out of your personal study of the word of God.

- *Read it, and come to understand what it* says. Read it as if it were the first time. Pay attention to what is going on before and after your passage.

- *Think about it, study it, and come to conclusions about what it* means. What is the one main idea that comes out in this passage? What questions come to mind about these verses?

- *Decide what you will do about it.* How will this passage affect your life personally? To what changes will you commit yourself? How can you be an example of this to your campers?

If you take notes while you are doing this, half the job of preparing your discussion will be done. The other half is putting it in a form that will invite your campers to study God's word with you. You want to help them

202 PART THREE - COUNSELING SKILLS

think through the teaching of the passage, contribute their thoughts and opinions, and decide what to do about it all.

5. Prepare discussion questions and activities.

Your devotional will be your own wild and wonderful creation, but it should generally contain these three components (with headings you should find easy to remember):

- *Ready.* You need some way of getting your campers ready to move in the direction you want them to go, something that will draw your campers into studying the Bible with you. It may be anything from a question like, "If you were to write a book about yourself, what title would you give to it?" to an activity such as acting out the parable of the Sower and the Seed, with your campers as seeds. It should be something fun and interesting that will draw them into discussion.

- *Set.* Your job is to get them to firmly set in their minds and understand one or maybe two main ideas that are communicated in that passage—without simply *telling* them what those ideas are. Why? Because they will forget 90% of what you tell them, but retain 90% of what they discover for themselves.[123] Good discussion questions will enable campers to discover for themselves what the passage says and what it means.

- *Go.* Without this part your devotional is a waste of time. As James says,[124] we need to be doers of the word and not hearers only. This "application" part of your discussion is what will motivate your campers to go and do something in response to the word of God. It needs, then, to be motivational, interesting and perhaps even a hands-on experience of applying what they have learned.

The Bible discussion workshop in Resource Section "F" is full of ideas and suggestions for pulling these three parts together, and will give you a hands-on, step-by-step experience of preparing a Bible discussion (hey—maybe one you can use this summer!). The more experience you gain with this kind of preparation, the more comfortable and proficient you will become in leading Bible discussions. If possible, seek an opportunity to lead a discussion in your church or care group at home to help you prepare for what will become a daily activity at camp.

6. Evaluate your discussion questions and activities.

Before you carry your devotion excitedly off to the cabin, run it through a few checks first:

- *Are my questions too general?* For example, which of these two sets of questions (based on Hebrews 4:12-13) would you be more willing to answer if you were a camper and it was 11:00 p.m.?

    - What does the writer of Hebrews mean here? And how should we apply this to our lives?
  or - Think of one thing in your life that you would not want your mom to see. Are you trying to hide this from God too? Is it working?

    Now notice: the second set of questions may be easier to answer, but they look as if they were also more difficult to think up. If your campers don't seem to have much interest in discussing your questions, it is probably because you have not put enough time and thought into *forming* your questions.

    A very general question like those in the first set above could apply to practically any topic in the whole Bible. Asking it of your campers is like asking your computer to repaginate your 500 page document. It is going take some time and energy to process, and your computer (and your campers) may decide to crash instead. Ask questions that are *specific* to the passage you are studying together, like the second set above. They take more work on your part, but hey, you *are* the counselor! Specific questions will hold your campers' interest immeasurably better.

- *Are my questions easy to understand?* A good way to tell if your questions are too deep is to show them to another counselor. If he has any difficulty knowing what you are asking, it is time to re-word the question. Keep it simple while keeping it interesting.

- *Is there a possibility my question will be answered by a simple yes or no?* Yes and No questions will not lead to discussion (unless you consider one word to be a discussion). For example, rather than ask, "Can you trust God to answer your prayers?", ask the same question this way, "Can you tell me about a time when you were not sure you could trust God to answer your prayer?" Your questions should usually ask for an opinion rather than just an answer (e.g., instead of "What should you do when you are tempted..." ask "What *do you think* you should do when you are tempted...?" or possibly, "What *would your friends at school say* you should do when you are tempted...?").

• *Have I asked a leading question?* I am personally bad at this. Do you think I have ever asked a question that forced the campers to answer the way I wanted them to? There, I just did it! Take for example the question, "Would James really be saying that we should be *happy* about the problems we face in life?" Even the camper who thinks James *is* saying we should be happy is not going to answer the question with a "yes," because the question told him you are looking for a "no" answer. Avoid questions that people will answer quickly but not honestly. Avoid giving your campers the idea that there is a certain answer you are looking for and that you consider to be the right answer. Devotions are not an exam, but a discussion.

• *Do my questions converge to lead them to the main idea the passage is teaching?* Discussion is not an end in itself. We can have a great discussion but totally miss the point of the Bible passage we are discussing. Look through your questions and pull out those that would easily lead the group off track and on to some new topic. Wrap things up with a question that will let you know if they have caught the point of the passage.

• *Do my questions challenge the campers to think and search for answers?* Could a camper sit through your discussion without having to push his brain past first gear? Are your questions so obvious that no one will want to answer? Will your questions make them struggle with the passage a bit? On the other hand, have you made your questions so deep that they will likely never come to solid conclusions?

• *Do my questions cover the whole passage?* Have you only focused on a verse or two, or have you managed to get them to look at the whole context? Will they notice what is going on in the passage before and after those special verses you want them to discuss?

• *Am I ready to be flexible?* If the Holy Spirit began guiding the discussion in some other way, will you be hanging on to your discussion sheet for all you are worth? Are you willing to be taught by your campers? Are you ready to cut out some questions if the discussion seems to be stalling?

- *Did I remember to ask about this?* You are about to use God's stuff, and he wants you to ask first. Take time to pray over your preparation, so he will be at work through you. Talk with other staff members and ask them to remember you in prayer during the time of your discussion. There are usually non-counseling staff who love to be included in this way. Be sure to let them know how it went!

THE SETTING OF A GROUP DISCUSSION

The emotional state of your campers, the location of your discussion and the way your group is physically arranged can have a huge affect on the outcome of your time together:

1. Emotional setting.

When you are on your way to the cabin to start cabin devotions, try to read and anticipate the situation you are approaching. For example, let's say that a big issue has erupted among your campers because someone is stealing the candy they have hidden away in their bags (probably a mouse, but try to tell them that). And your topic for your devotions tonight is, "God loves you and has a wonderful plan for your life." You need to realize that this is going to be a hard sell. Pray that God would so direct your day as a cabin that each of you will be in the right space for God to do his work that night. "Do not let the sun go down" on issues like anger and other things that need resolution and forgiveness.[125] Try to go into cabin devotions with tempers soothed, apologies made, and forgiveness in place.

Your relationship with your campers communicates much better than your words. Be a servant all day. If things have not gone well between you and your campers, or if you have been physically or emotionally unavailable to them all day, this will affect what happens in the cabin at night. Take up the example of the Apostle Paul who said to those he served, "We loved you so much that we were delighted to share with you not only the gospel of God but our lives as well, because you had become so dear to us." Not just the gospel at night, but your life all day, is what God will use to reach campers' hearts.

I THESSALONIANS 2:8

Sometimes you will think to yourself (or tired campers will moan), "Can't we just skip it tonight?" Except in extreme cases, don't give in to the temptation! A week of camp is so short! Make the most of every opportunity to draw their attention to the word of God, and cabin devotions may be your best opportunity in the entire day.

2. Location.

A particular setting can sometimes speak volumes more than mere words, as the Psalmist discovered:

> *The heavens declare the glory of God; the skies proclaim the work of his hands. Day after day they pour forth speech; night after night they display knowledge. There is no speech or language where their voice is not heard. Their voice goes out into all the earth, their words to the ends of the world."*

PSALM 19:1-4

It is true. I remember a night on a canoe trip with a group of youth, camped out under an incredible array of stars. No lights anywhere, not even a moon. After singing together, we all laid on our backs looking up at the brilliant night sky to pray. No one prayed—out loud anyway—and we lay there for fifteen minutes not speaking a word. Many in the group said it was one of the most significant experiences of their lives. One of them said it was the first time he had taken God seriously, and not long after this he came to faith in Christ. And no one had said a thing—except the stars.

If you have opportunity, choose the location of your discussion carefully. Often when cabin groups are sent off to meet for a discussion, valuable time can be wasted rounding up your campers. Make sure they know beforehand where to meet, and that you expect them there promptly. Locate your group far enough from other groups that you will not mutually disturb one another. Don't plan to meet so far from the others that you use up your time getting there, or miss the signal when the discussion time is over. The cabin is a sensible place to meet for evening cabin devotions, but occasionally meet in a special place, such as the dock, a lookout, the middle of a field, or in the hot tub!

3. Seating arrangement.

If the cabin is the place you meet for your devotional time, realize that if everyone just lies on their bunks they will likely fall asleep or be disruptive rather than focus and participate in the discussion. If you are meeting outside the cabin and your campers are spread all over the room or field or beach, don't expect them to pay much attention to you or one another.

The general rule of thumb is this: sit as tightly together as you comfortably can. Sit rather than lie around or stand because sitting is comfortable but not too comfortable, and your campers can stay alert. Sit tightly together—in a circle or on one bunk or in one corner of the room—so that you can easily hear one another and so you will stay focused and have good eye contact. Only a small percentage of communication is verbal, so it is important to arrange your group so you can see one another during the discussion.

Mind you, "General Rules of Thumb" always have their exceptions—I gave you one above. Sometimes darkness enables people to speak up who have not been brave enough before. Occasionally a standing huddle might be the best way to focus your group for a short discussion. Do what is needed to help the group pay attention to one another and feel comfortable enough to speak up.

LEADING A DISCUSSION [126]

1. Open the time in prayer.

You might ask a confident Christian in your group to pray that God will teach all of you and help you understand his word. This will train your campers to look to God as their Teacher and rely on him for understanding.

2. Create and maintain an atmosphere of acceptance.

Let them know that you are not looking for the "right" answer, but *their* answers, whatever they may be. Use the words, "What do you think...?" so they know you are looking for opinions. If their answers are off track or sheer heresy, be careful not to put them down, but use them as an opportunity to explore the truth. The word of God will stand such scrutiny. You don't want them to accept everything without question anyway.

3. Use good listening skills.

Eye contact with one another is essential; encourage them to voice their opinions to one another, not just back to you. Insist that they listen to one another and not interrupt with their own experiences or opinions. Try to get more talk out of them than they initially offer by asking them questions like, "What do you mean by that?" or "Give me an example."

4. If appropriate, determine some ground rules for the discussion.

Let the group decide the guidelines for your discussion. For example, when one talks, everyone else stops and listens. If you don't agree with someone, hear him out anyway.

5. Don't be intimidated by silence.

Sometimes your group won't say a word. Try to understand why. Your question may be too hard to answer, or the answer may be so obvious no one wants to give it. Ask the group what the silence means. At the same time be willing to wait out a few seconds of silence rather than jump back in to answer your own question. If no one answers, re-word or simplify the question, or ask someone specifically.

6. Be "askable."

Instead of barging along with your morning sermon, communicate openness and your willingness to stop and listen to their questions and concerns. If they bring up other topics that are important, but not directly related to the discussion at hand, this can serve as great material for later discussions (e.g., at the end if you have extra time) or a private talk between you and the questioner. Write down their questions so you will remember to address them later.

7. Don't give away answers to the questions too easily.

The purpose of discussion is not to get a string of answers but to encourage campers to discuss the issues. The ideal is for the counselor's voice to be heard only when asking or answering a question, and otherwise that there be only *campers* talking. Resist the urge to spoon-feed your campers. It is those who are hungry who will feed themselves, those who realize their illness who will want to be healed, and those who are confused who will try to understand. Give them time to struggle with ideas and discover the truth for themselves.

8. Never finish early.

When you finish your discussion, don't let your group go before the allotted time is up. When other groups see your group wandering off, it will end the discussion for them immediately. Use the time to discuss other things. There should never be a reason to "finish early."

DEALING WITH DISTRACTIONS AND PROBLEMS

As described at the beginning of this chapter, small group Bible discussions with campers can be difficult and sometimes seem impossible. Have no doubt, you will run into hazards and obstacles in this game. Be prepared for problems, and practice maintaining interest and control. It gets easier with experience, and often a cabin that is unmanageable at the beginning of the week soon settles down as your expectations and boundaries become established, tested and proven. Pray for the patience to persevere, because the rewards can be great!

Here are some problems you may expect to encounter:

1. Ants in their pants.

Children and some junior high youth are just not able to sit still for ten to twenty minutes. How will you keep them from dancing around with nervous energy? The best way is to do it *positively*—by holding their attention—rather than by negatively forcing them to sit still and pay attention. Use fun and interesting activities to start and end your time, with discussion sandwiched in-between.

2. Totally distracted.

Unless you have a sound-proof room to meet in (which wouldn't be any fun), expect distractions. Campers will throw grass at one another, members of another group might call out to yours and people will walk by. Kids who are easily distracted may focus their attention better if you *give* them a distraction: a simple craft to work on; a piece of paper to fold or doodle; or a bug to supervise.

3. Gotta go.

Prevention is the best cure here. Make sure they know they have to go to the bathroom *before* the discussion starts. Don't let them go unless it is an emergency, and only one at a time.

4. The monopoly game.

What can you do when one camper answers all the questions and the others can't get a word in edgewise? Direct your questions at other people in your group, or encourage the others to challenge that camper's opinions ("What do you think? Is what Joe is saying always the case?").

5. Too shy.

Some campers' personalities just don't lend themselves to discussion. Don't let quiet kids go unnoticed in the group. Give them a way to get involved that they can handle: holding your Bible open for you; looking up a reference for someone who can't find it; or maybe reading a verse or two.

6. Boorrrriiinnnggg...

What does a kid mean when he says he is bored? Generally he doesn't mean that the discussion is not exciting enough, but that the camper feels neglected or insignificant and needs some attention. Make your time a discussion where everyone is contributing and participating; this is much more effective against boredom than "entertaining" them.

7. No time to prepare.

This will happen, as long as camp is camp. If you have opportunity, *prepare*, and thoroughly! But if it should happen that you find yourself sitting in a ring of campers and your mind is a blank page, remember that the real Teacher is, of course, the Holy Spirit. He is the one who will challenge your campers, convict them and enlighten them. He may do it through you, but be ready for him to teach your campers through one other too. Pray a "Nehemiah Prayer,"[127] clear your throat, speak up and dive in, trusting God to give you everything you need to do his will.

---

[118]Wayne Rice, *Great Ideas For Small Youth Groups*, ©1986 Youth Specialties, pp. 55ff

[119]Gladys Hunt, "How To Lead Small Group Bible Studies With Campers", *CCI Focus Series #9*, ©1983 Christian Camping International

[120]II Timothy 3:14 - Timothy had become "convinced" of the truth by the life of Paul, who had taught him

[121]Possible Bible references might include: II Timothy 3:14-17; Romans 15:4; Hebrews 4:12-13; Joshua 1:8; Psalm 102:18; Ephesians 6:17

[122]James 3:1

[123]Gladys Hunt, "How To Lead Small Group Bible Studies With Campers", *CCI Focus Series #9*, ©1983 Christian Camping International

[124]See James 1:22-25

[125]Ephesians 4:26-27

[126]I appreciate the insights of Steve Sundby reflected in this section

[127]Nehemiah 2:4-5 - how much time did Nehemiah take to pray when the king of most of the known world asked him a question? It was one of those wordless "Help me!" prayers! But what would have happened if Nehemiah had *not* prayed before he spoke?

CAMP PREP #10:
MAKE-YOUR-OWN CABIN DEVOTIONS

Suggestions on how to prepare for your counseling experience.

There is no better way of becoming familiar and comfortable with Bible discussion preparation and leading than by doing it.

• In Resource Section "F" there is a workshop that will take you through preparation for a Bible discussion step by step. I highly recommend that you go through this workshop several times before you arrive at camp and find yourself without sufficient time to prepare.

• See Resource Section "G" for a long list of ideas for getting campers interested in the topic you want to discuss with them.

• When you have put together a Bible discussion plan, find an opportunity to use it before you counsel at camp. Perhaps your Bible study leader or youth leader would allow you to lead a group in your discussion, or you could just ask a group of friends to humor you and help you get ready for counseling. To make it fun, get them to act as if they were junior campers!

15. Communicating Your Faith: Leading a Camper to Christ

It was a disturbing article. The director read it to us at staff meeting in the middle of summer at a Christian camp. It came from the commentary section of a local newspaper, and we all wondered, "Could this ever be about us?" The writer described her own experience at a Christian camp over several summers as a child, and called it a nightmare. She wrote accurately about the basis of a Christian camp's ministry: a philosophy centered on asking Jesus into your heart and receiving eternal life. But she also wrote about a counselor who demonstrated the alternative route by roasting a live slug in the campfire before several hundred horrified eyes.

She was told that her God was not good enough, that she was a helpless and worthless creature, and that she could reduce the beautiful journey of faith to saying a prayer that would transform her and enable her to think correctly. You could feel her anger about being deceived into thinking that God condemned all faiths but this rigid form of Christianity. She came home each summer full of guilt and fear and bad dreams, because she did not believe. She wanted to know why children had to have these intolerant ideas forced on them, and be told that their best friends and parents are on the road to hell. She conceded that the leaders of the camp were kind and well-meaning, but their ignorance enraged her.

The article rocked me on my foundations. I had to think about it for a long while, and I worried about the effect it would have on our ministry the rest of the summer. Was she right? I knew that my ultimate purpose for being involved in camp ministry was exactly along the lines of what she was talking about: kids coming to know Jesus Christ and being *saved*. Was the whole basis of Christian camping off the mark? Were we doing something that is wrong?

IS IT OKAY TO LEAD A CHILD TO CHRIST?

The term we usually apply to those who have not yet put their faith in Christ is "non-Christian." Unfortunately, the term can convey the idea that being a Christian is merely a matter of personal preference—some prefer Christianity, some prefer Buddhism. They are non-Christians, we are non-Hindu's.

COMMUNICATING THE GOSPEL 213

In the Bible what we call "non-Christians" are called "unbelievers," "the ungodly" (meaning disobedient to God), "pagans" and "the heathen" (that is, a people group without faith in God). The Bible considers people who have not yet responded to the gospel to be in a state of unbelief and rebellion against God, no matter what religion they profess.

Why is that so important to understand? In a day when people are almost paranoid about issues like intolerance and human rights, some people would challenge our right to take a ten year old child and convince her that she should give up whatever beliefs she came with—and some come from homes that are connected with the eastern religions or the cults, or denominations other than our own—and take on our beliefs, our practices, our "religion." It would seem to some people like the height of presumption and the depth of bigotry to do that. To attempt to convert someone from one religion to your religion is a violation of her religious freedom.

However, the New Testament describes an unbeliever as a rebel, someone who has been exposed to the message of the gospel in some way and has willfully rebelled against it. God has revealed himself, in his creation and especially in the person of the Lord Jesus Christ whom he raised from the dead. When people are exposed to that revelation and refuse to believe, they are "unbelievers." If they continue to rebel, there is no hope for them, and they will go to hell. Not my words, but those of the Bible. [128]

Compare unbelief in Christ with the practice of smoking. Some people have a preference to smoke, some don't. Yet because we know that smoking ruins people's health and eventually kills them, as a society we don't treat smoking as a "preference." We run big ad campaigns and raise taxes on cigarettes and limit where people can smoke in an attempt to persuade them to take on *our* way of life, which is smoke-free.

That is how we should think about unbelief in Christ. Is it right for us to share the gospel with children and pray for them in the hope that they will come to Christ and escape hell? If we don't, they will someday turn and accuse us of our failure to love them enough to tell them about Jesus. Smoking is only fatal; unbelief in Christ is *eternally* fatal.

The great evangelist Paul put it this way, "For Christ's love compels us, because we are convinced that one died for all..." In other words, the love of Christ pulls us along to share the gospel

II CORINTHIANS 5:14

with everyone who will listen. If Jesus so loved a child that he died for him to rescue him from an empty life and hell later, how dare I not love that child enough to share this good news with him? We are doing no wrong thing at Christian camps by sharing the gospel of Christ with children and youth, and if this is wrong, then there is no right thing in this world.

RESPECT FOR THE UNBELIEVER

At the same time, we need to show respect toward campers, and whatever belief or religion or church background with which they arrive. Roasting slugs to depict hell is not a good idea. Neither are any of the other scare tactics and pressure strategies that may have been employed in the past. When Jesus was out preaching the gospel, he was much more concerned that someone might hear and profess faith in him before he was *ready* to take up his cross and follow him.[129] Rather than push Christianity on campers as if it was some cheap product, hold it out to the world with dignity—and with compassion—and challenge campers to count the cost of this life-long change of direction.

Be careful not to criticize or put down your campers' religious heritages, but ask honest questions about what they believe. Practically everyone has some form of religious background, perhaps a grandmother who is a believer, or Sunday school attendance when they were younger. Sometimes there are bad experiences in their religious backgrounds, such as misconceptions or someone who has offended or hurt them, which act as a barrier keeping them from faith in Christ. Take this as an excellent opportunity to clear up the problems and misconceptions they have and give them a better impression of Christians. Focus on a personal relationship with Jesus rather than the differences between your "religion" and theirs.

Depend on the word of God and your prayers and the Holy Spirit to bring about the needed change in your campers' lives. Paul was able to boast to the once-heathen Thessalonians, "For the appeal we make does not spring from error or impure motives, nor are we trying to trick you. On the contrary, we speak as men approved by God to be entrusted with the gospel."[130] To their neighbors, the Corinthians, he was able to say, "My message and my preaching were not with wise and persuasive words, but with a demonstration of the Spirit's power, so that your faith might not rest on men's wisdom, but on God's power." There is no need for a camper to look back on her experience at camp and feel bitter about being manipulated and deceived.

I CORINTHIANS 3:7

WHAT IS THE GOSPEL?

What exactly is the gospel that we as God's people hold out to the world? Without a firm grasp of the gospel, a counselor is likely to leave wrong impressions with a camper and perhaps do more damage than good.

1. The gospel is the "good news" of Jesus.

How does a story about a man who lived and died 2000 years ago bring us into fellowship with the God who created us? It is no ordinary story, but "the power of God for the salvation of all who believe."[131] When people hear about Jesus Christ and put their faith in him alone, God forgives their sins and begins transforming them into the image of his Son.

2. The gospel is also your story.

The Apostle John wrote about the gospel as a first-hand witness, and he still bubbled over with the experience sixty years later: "That which we have seen from the beginning, which we have heard, which we have seen with our eyes, which we have looked at and our hands have touched—this we proclaim concerning the Word of life." The story of Jesus was also the story of John, because John had a personal encounter with him that changed his life. If you are a Christian, you also are part of the gospel story, because Jesus has come and made himself known to you, and you have responded. Resource Section "H" includes help in putting together your story—or "testimony"—in an effective way.

I JOHN 1:1

3. The gospel is communicated by relationship.

Why did God choose you and me to be the vehicle for his message? "We have this treasure in jars of clay to show that this all-surpassing power is from God and not from us." When God wanted to communicate this message to the world, he sent his Son. When Jesus had completed his work, he sent his followers to carry the message to the ends of the earth. The gospel is communicated *relationally*, and it is very rare for anyone to come to faith in Christ apart from some connection with a Christian. The way God will reach the hearts of your campers is through you, when the story of Jesus in your life is communicated to the lives of your campers.

II CORINTHIANS 4:7

CAMP IS A PLACE OF HARVEST

One of Jesus' favorite ways of describing how a person comes to faith in him was agricultural. Perhaps he used this analogy to relate to the farming communities where he spent most of his time, but it is a very good analogy. You prepare some soil, you plant a seed and care for it, and by some miracle a plant grows and can be harvested. Some plants grow almost overnight; others take years to mature and produce fruit. There is much to learn from the farmer about leading campers to Christ.

So imagine yourself as an apprentice farmer, just arrived on the job. "Open your eyes and look at the fields!" says Jesus, your boss. "They are ripe for harvest! Even now the reaper draws his wages, even now he harvests the crop for eternal life, so that the sower and reaper may be glad together. Thus the saying, 'One sows and another reaps' is true. I have sent you to reap what you have not worked for. Others have done the hard work, and you have reaped the benefits of their labor."

JOHN 4:35-38

That is a good description of what happens at a Christian camp. You arrive there and find fields golden and glistening, ready for harvest. Kids come to faith in Christ even in the first days of camp, when the speaker hasn't talked about the gospel yet. How did it happen, this waist-high crop that nearly reaps itself? The truth is that a great deal of work has gone into this harvest before you ever saw it. God has employed someone in campers' lives to cultivate the soil, others to sow the seed and still others to water and weed the emerging plant. Some of this takes place at camp as kids return year after year; most of it takes place in their homes, communities and churches. Camp, however, has traditionally been a place of harvest.

LIFESTYLE EVANGELISM

Since the 1970's, the Christian church has become more aware of the *process* involved in people coming to faith in Christ. One of the terms given to this process is "lifestyle evangelism."[132] This is a more relational and sensitive approach to evangelism than the "soul-winning" method, which was effective with the generation before the baby boomers. The emphasis of lifestyle evangelism is that presenting Christ involves more than talk; people need to see Christ displayed in the lifestyle of Christians before they will respond. In recent years the church has also recognized that becoming a Christian is more than a momentary event in people's lives, but a process that takes people from their position of hostility or apathy towards Christ to becoming disciples of Christ and following him daily.

This is a very important idea to understand as we talk about bringing kids to Christ at camp. Unfortunately, perhaps due to the shortness of time we have with campers, some camps hold on to the old model of "soul-winning." They are satisfied if at the end of the week a number of hands have gone up to indicate that there are new believers in the crowd. Often those who don't get their names on that list receive little spiritual attention, and often the ones who come to new birth in Christ are left to flounder on their own after camp. Camps need to find their place in the process of evangelism and become part of the program, rather than a side show.

My suggestion is that the camp counselor should make a *commitment* to the spiritual progress of your campers, not for just one week, but for a minimum of one year. This is a commitment not only to the ones who respond while they are at camp, but even those who remain cold to the gospel right through to the end of the week. You will not be the only one or even the primary one involved in their spiritual lives when they are at home, but it is important for you to be *one* of the people involved for at least that period of time. In this way you will become part of the process—one of the farm hands if you like—as the camper responds to the claims of Jesus Christ step by step.

THE PROCESS OF COMING TO FAITH IN CHRIST

A person's salvation is something that occurs by God's *grace*. "For it is by grace you have been saved, through faith—and this is not from yourselves, it is the gift of God—not by works, so that no one can boast."[133] In other words, God does it. "Neither he who plants nor he who waters is anything, but only God, who makes things grow."[134] The person who makes personal choices in Christ's direction could not do so without being called and drawn by God. He places the unbeliever in the vicinity of Christians so that when the gospel is planted, it is encouraged to grow by the lives, prayers and words of the believers around them.

The process can happen quickly—as in the case of the criminal on the cross next to Jesus—or it may take place over a long period of time. When does a person actually become a Christian? Can we nail it down to the moment she put her hand up at fireside, or the night she prayed with a counselor? Sometimes becoming a Christian is a specific event that alters the course of a person's life, as in the case of Saul becoming Paul, or the Philippian jailer and his family coming to faith in one night. However, sometimes you just can't pin-point the event, even though clearly the person once did not believe in Christ and now he does. This is often the case of those who have grown up in Christian homes. An example is Timothy, whose mother and grandmother were Christians before him, and who went through a process of becoming *convinced* of what he had been taught all his life, mainly through the example of Paul.[135]

"There's a mystery to it," as Billy Graham says, and salvation never takes place exactly the same way each time. Jesus said, "The wind blows wherever it pleases. You hear its sound, but you cannot tell where it comes from or where it is going. So it is with everyone born of the Spirit."[136] The most unlikely people become believers—along with the likely—and in the most unlikely ways. A girl in my youth group discovered that she had become a Christian after her family and friends started commenting on how much she was changing in her attitudes and actions.

A SERIES OF MINI-DECISIONS

On his journey to faith in Christ, whether it be jet plane fast or a slow boat to China, a person makes a series of mini-decisions that lead him to the cross of Christ. These decisions might run like this:[137]

- "He's okay" (a decision about us).
- "I'd like to get to know him better."
- "I'm going to find out why he's so different."
- "It seems that he gets his outlook on things from the Bible."
- "He's a Christian, but he's okay."
- "Being a Christian sure has its advantages."
- "I like his friends. I envy their confidence."
- "It might be interesting to look at the Bible someday."
- "The Bible isn't impossible to understand after all."
- "The Bible says some important things."
- "What the Bible says about life fits my experience."
- "Jesus seems to be the key. I wonder who He really was."
- "Jesus is God."
- "I need to do what He says."

Notice that the unbeliever begins with a decision about the Christians in his life, and progresses to a decision about Christ. Observe your campers and try to determine at what point they are in this process during the week they are with you. Are your campers still making decisions about *you?* These campers need to see Christ displayed in your life. They are soil that is still being cultivated, and may not be ready to respond to the gospel. This is a critical time to pray for these campers, but don't be disappointed if by the end of the week there is no evidence of progress. As you keep in touch over the year and they see your sincere interest in their lives, they may begin to respond.

When campers start to make the connection that what they like about you is related to the Bible, they may have a greater interest in what the speaker is talking about, and start making contributions during cabin devotions. The example of the staff and their love and encouragement of one another confirms to them that you are not an exception. They begin to realize that those who pay attention to the teachings of the Bible seem to have more to offer than the average person. This is the time when the gospel may be sown in their hearts. They have not accepted Christ at this point, but they are positively moving in that direction. Prayer is needed here too, because as Jesus noted in his parable of The Sower and the Seed, this is a precarious time.[138] Even a sprouted and growing interest in the things of Christ can be snatched away, prove to be too shallow or become choked by the pleasures and cares of the world.

Hopefully, though, the time will come when a camper shows that he is being convicted by the Holy Spirit and is struggling with the claim of Christ on his life. One evidence of this is when he expresses frustration about dealing with personal sin and guilt. He feels that he can't be good enough, or he doesn't know what to do about his guilty feelings. Often God uses crisis experiences to draw people to himself. A camper facing major trauma of some kind will often be open to the things of God. It is the camper who questions and challenges you who is probably closer to faith than the one who yawns and falls asleep every time you open your Bible.

When you notice signs like these, how should you respond? Your relationship with the camper is still the main catalyst God will use to draw your campers to himself. Remember what the evangelist Paul said, "We loved you so much that we were delighted to share with you not only the gospel of God but our lives as well, because you had become so dear to us."[139] Jesus said, "I am with you always," as the explanation of how to "make disciples."[140] Sharing our faith is just extending our relationship with Jesus to include a growing relationship with our campers. If there is no relationship, there is nothing to share. But hopefully at some point the camper will indicate that he is ready to talk with someone about putting his faith in Christ.

220 PART THREE – COUNSELING SKILLS

WHAT IT MEANS TO BELIEVE

Many camps continue the tradition of having an "altar call" or raising of hands so that campers who are at this point of decision can let someone know it. No one has ever become a Christian simply by raising her hand in a meeting, and we can't assume that every child who does raise her hand is ready to believe. But many are, and it is a way of connecting them with their counselors so they can talk about faith.

During his ministry, Jesus preached the simple message, "The time has come. The kingdom of God is near. Repent and believe the Good News!"[141] Another way he put it was, "Come, follow me, and I will make you fishers of men."[142] To become a follower of Jesus means to *leave* our past way of sin behind ("repentance") and *believe* in Jesus. Repentance gets left out of too many presentations of the gospel. Saying "yes" to Jesus means also saying "no" to sin. Jesus will not enter a heart that he has not swept clean.

What does it mean to *believe* in Jesus? This story is a classic for explaining the kind of "believing" that Jesus meant:

> *Charles Blondin stretched an eleven-hundred foot tightrope across Niagara Falls on June 30, 1859. About twenty-five thousand spectators gathered to watch the incredible stunt. Charles stood in front of the crowd and asked, "How many believe I can walk across Niagara Falls?"*
>
> *"We believe!" the crowd roared. And so Charles walked safely across Niagara Falls, one hundred sixty feet in the air.*
>
> *Five days later he asked, "How many believe I can walk across Niagara Falls blindfolded and pushing a wheelbarrow?"*
>
> *The crowd cheered. And Charles did it again.*
>
> *Two weeks later, the crowds gathered again. "How many of you believe that I can walk across with a person on my back?" he asked.*
>
> *The crowd screamed: "Of course! We believe!"*
>
> *Charles looked straight at a person in the front. "You, sir. Climb on!" The man refused.*[143]

Did the man really believe in Charles Blondin? If he did, he would have climbed on the performer's back. I hardly blame him for not doing so, but it would have been a good demonstration of the true nature of believing in Christ. It is putting the full weight of our future lives and destiny on Jesus, trusting in him alone. Believing is not a passive thing that we do only with our minds. It must be an active thing that moves our mind and body in a new direction, that changes the way we think and what we say and do. It is not just acknowledging that there is someone named Jesus, but obeying him too.

Can faith in Jesus be just a private matter, something we keep to ourselves? "For it is with your heart that you believe and are justified, and it is with your mouth that you confess and are saved."[144] Believing in Jesus includes *telling* people that you believe in Jesus, by your life and by your words. If we claim to have faith in Christ, but our claim is not supported by the way we live, the writer James tells us that our "faith" is dead and useless. Even demons believe better than that.[145]

THE GOSPEL: WHAT A CAMPER NEEDS TO HEAR

It is very important that the camp counselor becomes so familiar with the essential points of the gospel that it is second nature to share them with an interested camper. I would suggest that you memorize a simple outline of the gospel and several Bible verses as the basis of your explanation. The simplest outline is this: *you've got a problem, God has a solution, and you need to accept it.*[146] The most famous explanation is the Campus Crusade booklet entitled, "The Four Spiritual Laws." It does seem that the main teachings of the gospel can be stated clearly in four points (given here in ordinary kid-friendly English):

1. God made us to be his friends now and forever.

This is a good place to begin because not all kids realize or believe that they are created by God or that there is a purpose to their lives. Evolution is assumed these days. Talk with campers about why God made them—so that he could have a wonderful relationship with them during the course of this life and forever.

2. But all of us do bad things God can't stand, and deserve punishment.

Many kids don't think of themselves as being "sinful"—just average, like their friends. Show them that the bad things we do every day—such as telling lies, speaking unkind words and disobeying parents—are just as offensive to God as any other kind of sin. All sin is against God, and it distances us from him and keeps us from having a friendship with him. We all deserve to be punished and separated from him forever.

3. God sent his Son Jesus to teach us about God and to take our punishment on the cross.

The idea that Jesus is more than a man, but God the Son, is probably new to many kids. Jesus didn't die by accident. He came to earth first of all to help us know who God is, and to tell us about our need to turn away from our sin and trust in him. His main reason for coming was to die on the cross, taking all of our sin on himself as he hung there. He made it possible for people to become God's friends again and not be punished for their sins.

4. When we trust Jesus to take away our sin and change our hearts and lives, we become God's friend now and forever.

Our word "believe" can mean simply accepting something as true; the word "trust" communicates to a camper a bit more of what we mean by faith in action. It is important that the camper understands that this decision is life-changing. It is a decision to turn away from their sins and follow Jesus.

THE WORD OF GOD AS YOUR AUTHORITY

When sharing these points of the gospel with a camper, take them to the word of God as your authority on the subject. The gospel is not something you made up; it runs like a red line from Genesis to Revelation, and is clearly outlined in several passages. Show the camper one or more of these verses in your Bible, though it is good to also know them by memory in case you don't have your Bible with you. One of the passages used by camp counselors and others for years is the classic "Roman's Road" (quoted here from the New Century Version, which states it very simply):

* *Romans 3:23.* "All have sinned and are not good enough for God's glory."

* *Romans 6:23.* "When people sin, they earn what sin pays—death. But God gives us a free gift—life forever in Christ Jesus our Lord."

* *Romans 5:8.* "But God shows his great love for us in this way: Christ died for us while we were still sinners."

* *Romans 8:1.* "So now, those who are in Christ Jesus are not judged guilty."

- *Romans 10:9,10.* "If you use your mouth to say, 'Jesus is Lord,' and if you believe in your heart that God raised Jesus from the dead, you will be saved. We believe with our hearts, and so we are made right with God. And we use our mouths to say that we believe, and so we are saved."

Other passages are found in the first four books of the New Testament, appropriately named, "The Gospels." Some of these contain the whole message of Christ in just one verse. For example:

- *John 3:16.* "For God loved the world so much that he gave his one and only Son so that whoever believes in him may not be lost, but have eternal life."

- *John 5:24.* "I tell you the truth, whoever hears what I say and believes in the One who sent me has eternal life. That person will not be judged guilty but has already left death and entered life."[147]

MAKING THE GOSPEL CLEAR

There are several ways you can make these Scriptures clear and relevant to a camper's needs.

1. Personalize a verse.

For example, you could take John 3:16 and place the camper's name in it. "For God loved Jeremy so much that if Jeremy believes in him he will not be lost, but Jeremy will have eternal life."

2. Use an illustration.

For example, not even the best swimmer can swim across the Pacific Ocean. The strongest man cannot climb a ladder to the moon. And not even Billy Graham or Mother Teresa could reach God's standard of goodness by their own effort, as Romans 3:23 shows us.

3. Tell a story.

For example, Romans 5:8 brings to mind a story of a hero pushing an enemy out of the path of a train and losing his own life in the process.

4. Draw a picture.

For example, Romans 6:23 can be made into simple diagram, which shows that sin separates us from God but that Jesus is the Bridge:[148]

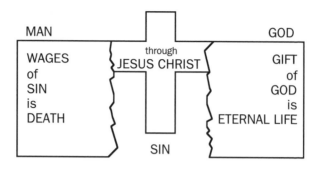

LEADING A CAMPER TO FAITH IN CHRIST

When you meet with a camper who has indicated that he wants to talk with you about faith in Christ, remember that you are just part of a process, a harvester who is picking up from the hard work of those before him. God has led the camper to himself in a unique way. Therefore, we need to be ready to respond to a camper's needs individually, not mechanically taking him through a number of steps. Be praying silently, and if possible, have others pray for you and the camper as you talk together.

1. Find out what he came to talk with you about.

What does he want God to do for him? This lets you know what is going on in the camper's mind, and helps him sort it out too. You want to know if he has a *felt need* for salvation, or if he is still simply curious or just following the crowd.

2. Use his response as a bridge to the gospel message.

For example, if his response is that he wants to become a Christian, talk with him about what it means to be a Christian. You might want to share your testimony as an example. If he said he wants to ask God to forgive him, discuss with him why God is willing to forgive: he sent his Son to die for us so that we could be forgiven.

3. Prayerfully bring out the main points of the gospel.

With your Bible and the gospel outline you will have in your head, show him his need and how it can be met by faith in Christ. Use his questions and responses to focus back on the main issues.

4. Ask him if this is what he wants Jesus to do for him.

Clear up anything he is not sure about. Don't pressure him if he is hesitant, but tell him you are always ready to talk about this. Make sure the camper "counts the cost" of being a Christian. Some things he enjoys doing now will lose their appeal, friends may change, and parents may disagree.

5. Pray with him.

The usual way a person expresses faith in Jesus is in personal prayer. Be careful that the child or youth understands that prayer is no "magic formula" that will make him a Christian. You can give him a prayer to pray, but it is far better that he prays in his own words. If the camper prays and shows by his prayer that he hasn't understood the essentials of the gospel, go back over what he has missed and (gently and tactfully) ask if he would like to add those things to his prayer.

This doesn't have to be an emotional event, though often it is. Let him be emotional, or if he is not, don't for that reason doubt his experience. Remember that it is God who is responsible for bringing a child to faith in himself. If you have presented the gospel well and the child decides against Jesus, don't feel guilty. And if he believes, give the glory to God. Celebrate like the angels of heaven![149]

WHAT TO DO AT CAMP WHEN A CAMPER HAS MADE A DECISION

The following chapter will go into more detail about discipling campers and teaching them how to follow Jesus. Here are some things you can do to help campers confirm the decisions they have made, and give them the encouragement that it was the right thing to do:

1. Help them tell people about it at camp.

When campers who have put their faith in Christ begin to tell people about their decision right away, it helps confirm to them what they have done, and it is encouraging to those they tell. Ask your campers questions to coach them on what to say (but be careful not to put words in their mouth). Encourage them to go *with* you on a "proclamation tour"—to the speaker, the head counselor, your cabin group, a maintenance person, camp grandma and grandpa and anyone else who will listen with interest and encouragement. This is a way of "confessing with their mouth" their new faith and making it public.

2. Bring their decision up in casual conversation often during the rest of the week.

One of the biggest mistakes a counselor can make is to help campers put their faith in Jesus and then not mention it again the rest of the week. It gives campers the impression that their decision was no big deal and that it has nothing to do with his daily life. Ask them questions, answer their questions, and talk about how you handle different aspects of Christian living. Help them understand in what ways they can expect believing in Jesus to alter their attitudes and lifestyle. Show them what it means to obey Jesus during the course of the day. Begin their discipleship, as outlined further in the next chapter.

RE-DEDICATIONS

Another type of spiritual decision made by campers is some form of re-commitment or "rededication." Perhaps they became Christians at some point in their lives, but because of their experiences at camp and God's work in their hearts they sense a need to make a fresh commitment to him. As with a salvation decision, campers should be encouraged to tell other people about their decisions, either personally or publicly, such as at a fireside. Here are some of the types of decisions campers might make:

1. Personalizing their heritage of faith.

Especially when camper have grown up in a Christian home, it may be at camp that they first realize that faith in Christ needs to be a personal commitment of their own. Campers who are coming into their own faith in Christ need to be challenged to live what they believe, and may need to do some "spiritual house-cleaning." Older campers should also be encouraged to get involved in serving God in their churches.

2. Repentance from a lifestyle of sin.

Christian campers who realize that sin is defeating them, or that their commitment is lacking, need a time of reconciliation with God. This begins with confession and repentance, and a discussion of how they will get back on track and begin walking with God again.

3. Response to a call to Christian service and ministry.

This is more likely to happen with older campers, but it can happen at junior high or even juniors camp. Be careful not to down-play the campers' seriousness about committing their lives to Christ's service. I was about 11 or 12 when I first sensed God's call on my life. Take them seriously, and talk and pray with them about their commitment. Offer help in finding opportunities to serve now in their churches or on a missions trip. There are opportunities for even junior campers to get involved in ministry.

Those who make a re-commitment to Christ will also benefit greatly from discipleship. Get them connected with discipleship in their own communities, so that the process of God transforming them into the image of Christ can continue consistently.

---

[128] For example, Revelation 21:7-8

[129] Matthew 8: 18-22 and Mark 8: 34

[130] I Thessalonians 2:3-4

[131] Romans 1:16

[132] Rebecca M. Pippert, *Out Of The Saltshaker & Into The World*, ©1979 Inter-Varsity Christian Fellowship; and Joe Aldrich, *Life-Style Evangelism*, Multnomah Press, 1983

[133] Ephesians 2:8-9

[134] I Corinthians 3:7

[135] II Timothy 3:10-15

[136] John 3:8

[137] K.C. Hinckley, *A Compact Guide To The Christian Life*, ©1989 NavPress. Used by permission of NavPress. For copies call 1-800-366-7788

[138] Mark 4:1-20

[139] I Thessalonians 2:8. Hmmm... might be a good verse to memorize

[140] Matthew 28:19-20

[141] Mark 1:15

[142] Matthew 4:19

[143] *The Youth Bible*, ©1991 Word, Inc., Dallas, Texas. All rights reserved

[144] Romans 10:10

[145] James 2:14-19. Note: if the new believer will be threatened if their faith is made known, care is needed (e.g., if they are from a strongly opposed family)

[146] My thanks to my friend David Lee for putting it so frankly

[147] New Century Version (NCV)

[148] See the booklet, "Knowing God Personally," Sonlife Ministries, 1-800-770-4769

[149] Luke 15:7, 10

CAMP PREP #11:
BE PREPARED TO SHARE YOUR FAITH

Suggestions on how to prepare for your counseling experience.

You should "always be prepared to give an answer to everyone who asks you to give the reason for the hope that you have." Are you ready? Here are some ways to make sure:

- Resource Section "H" includes instructions and ideas for putting together the story of you and Jesus—or your "testimony"—in an effective way. Take the time to write out your testimony, and find an opportunity to share it in a small group before you begin your counseling experience.

- Memorize an outline of the gospel (such as the ones suggested above), and a number of related Bible verses, so that you will always have them with you.

- Ask a Christian friend to allow you to share the gospel with him, and get his feedback on how well you covered the essentials. Ask God for an opportunity to share your faith with an unbelieving friend before camp begins.

16. Discipleship & Follow-up: Direction For The Christian Camper

"Then Jesus came to them and said, 'All authority in heaven and on earth has been given to me. Therefore go and make disciples of all nations, baptizing them in the name of the Father and of the Son and of the Holy Spirit, and teaching them to obey everything I have commanded you. And surely I am with you always, to the very end of the age.'"

 MATTHEW 28:18-20

Catch the immensity of this. Someone has been given all the authority in the world and beyond, and on his way out the door he gives you a task to fulfill before he comes back: Make disciples. Do you think you had better sit up and take notice? Don't be satisfied with making *converts* at camp; that was not what Jesus had in mind. The goal of the counselor is to have his campers become *disciples* of Jesus, not simply to get the kids to say a prayer so he can mark another notch on his Bible.

What is a disciple? Literally, a disciple is a student, but Jesus' disciples were much more than that. Jesus wanted these twelve men to be *with* him so they would become *like* him. Peter, James and John and the others were devoted to their Teacher, not just to his teaching. A disciple of Jesus is someone who is getting to know him in daily life, and is beginning to display his nature and character.

Unfortunately, in the past many camps have not been very concerned about camper discipleship and follow-up. The reasoning is that usually we are responsible for them only for a week or two; that there are problems with making contact with campers when they get back home; and besides, it is the churches' job to make sure campers grow spiritually in their own communities.

Ultimately it *is* the churches' job, but the camp can become an important part of the process as an extension of the church, and work to ensure that the process continues. I challenge you to commit yourself to the process of making disciples of your campers for a minimum of one year of their lives.

DISCIPLESHIP AT CAMP

How can you disciple your campers at camp when so often they wait until the end of the week to make a commitment to Christ? Be involved in discipleship all week, even *before* they make a commitment. Each of your campers is at some specific point in his pilgrimage: hostile and angry, mildly disappointed, apathetic, curious, interested, searching, ready to accept, new baby, toddler, maturing, backsliding, victorious, serving or exemplary. Discipleship is encouraging him to move from where he is towards becoming more like Christ. It is something you can do all week, no matter at what point he makes that milestone commitment.

1. Teach the basics.

What are the basic teachings and skills your campers will need in order to continue searching or growing spiritually? Equip them during the week by including the basic topics of discipleship in your conversation and discussions. Take time in your evening devotions, during a snack, activity time, down time, every opportunity you get to discuss these things. Check it out during the week: have you covered everything at some point? What topics do you still need to bring up?

- *Salvation.* Your personal testimony can be part of your discipleship of your campers. It is an opportunity to share with them things such as the meaning of salvation, your assurance that you are a believer, and how God helps you deal with temptation and sin. Encourage some of the Christians in your cabin to share their testimonies as well, to strengthen their faith.

- *The Bible.* This is a whole new book to many kids. Take them on a tour of your Bible. Show them where everything is. Explain that the Old Testament looks ahead to Jesus and the New Testament looks back at him. Read them a few favorite Bible stories. Share with them the verses that have helped you most. Show them how to mark their favorite verses in their Bibles or memorize them. Have a "sword drill."[150] Most of all, encourage them to begin reading and applying God's word daily on their own.

- *Prayer.* Your own example is most important, so pray often with your campers. Make it personal, pray in everyday language, and be visible and available when you pray on your own. Answer their questions about prayer, and encourage the ones who never pray out loud to get started. Explain the basics, like whether a person needs to fold his hands and close his eyes when he prays, and how to start and stop.

- *Lifestyle.* Part of discipline is teaching your campers better behavior. Take it further by encouraging them to live a holy life, develop the fruits of the Spirit[151] and conquer bad habits. Talk about how you resist temptation, and how you handle influences such as friends and TV. Teach them how to confess their sins to God when they mess up and how to deal with guilty feelings.

- *Witness.* Many kids from unbelieving homes will be concerned for their families and friends. Explain to them the importance of sharing Christ by the example of their lives, and prepare them to gently, simply and tactfully share the gospel with their words. Help them memorize one of the verses discussed in the previous chapter and give them a simple method of explaining its meaning to someone.

- *Church.* In our very independent and individualistic world, faith in Christ is often viewed as a decision we make autonomously and that we maintain on our own. God never intended it that way. Believers are to be believers together. Who gives birth to a baby and then sends it off to find a job and home of its own? It won't survive, and neither will a new Christian mature without other believers.

Talk about your own experience in church in a *positive* light, even if your church isn't everything you would like it to be. Challenge campers who are already connected to a church to pay better attention and gain a greater appreciation for what they have. Find out if they are connected with children's or youth ministries in their churches. Often these kids will complain that their churches are not as exciting as camp; discuss with them the purpose of the church in God's plan. Encourage older campers to get involved in service and ministry at their churches.

Show the non-church kids that church involvement is what will enable them to continue learning about God and growing in their new faith. Give each one information about churches in his community; if possible, find out about the children's or youth ministries available in his area. There may be campers without a church in your cabin or at the camp who live in the same communities as your campers who attend regularly. Do what you can to connect them, and have them talk together about the church and what it is like. Encourage campers who go to church to invite along campers who do not have one. If it seems unlikely that the parents will allow them to get involved in a church, offer to stay in touch with them regularly to talk further about their Christian walk.

2. Be an example.

The most effective method of discipleship is your own example. Jesus taught his disciples, but he also lived in such a way that one of them later declared, "This is how we can be sure that we are living in God: Whoever says he lives in God must live as Jesus did."[152] Are you excited about the idea that your campers could become like you? Would they do well to imitate your devotional life, your love for others, your prayer habits and your commitment to your church? They are watching you constantly, and the main reason they will apply what you teach them is because they see it in you.

I remember one of those incredibly busy weeks of camp when—I am afraid—I did a less than adequate job of cabin devotions. But I built good relationships with my kids, and I was amazed to see how much the week affected them and how several grew spiritually that fall. I know that the reason for their growth had to be more than my words or the words of our speaker. They were watching me and the rest of the staff, and later decided they wanted to be like us. When I read the reasons people apply for our Counselor-in-Training program, they very often say that they want to be like the counselors they had at camp. Be the person whose example you would want campers to follow.

3. Challenge them to apply it.

You can often discern when your campers are starting to understand a new biblical concept, or seem convicted to make some change in their lives. Don't leave it at that; instead, help them think through how they can put into practice the things they have learned. Talk with them about what they plan to do when they get home, but also (if possible) get them started on practical application while they are still at camp.

For example, let's say you have a camper who has a habit of exaggerating to impress other people. Through your devotions together, he has discovered that there is an alternative to lying, which is "speaking the truth in love."[153] How will he put that into practice? Perhaps you could give him an object such as a bracelet or a stone to carry in his pocket. It can be a reminder to him to think before he speaks, and decide if love or pride is motivating what he is about to say.

FOLLOW-UP OF CAMPERS

At times you just won't want your campers to go home. If you could, you would adopt them all and take them home with you. Some of them are going back to great homes and have every opportunity for church involvement and discipleship. There are others whose parents are cold and defensive when they come to pick up their kids, or who scream at them all the way to the car for spending too much at the camp store. Some of your campers may have no meaningful contact with Christians from now until they return to camp next summer. You think of their joy in discovering a relationship with Christ this past week and sigh.

Should a camp be involved in the business of follow-up, helping campers make a connection with a church in their community and maintaining contact with them over the year? Some camps have firmly decided not to do follow-up, saying that it is not their territory and that the potential for confidentiality problems are too great. Other camps determine that the risk is worth it, and some even have full-time staff working in that area. Check out your camp's policies and procedures on follow-up, but take a look at what a camp and its counselors can do to continue the process of camper discipleship.

WHAT THE CAMP ADMINISTRATION MIGHT DO FOR CAMPER FOLLOW-UP

1. Camper reports or profiles.

Counselors are often given a form to fill out at the end of the week, including information on the campers' family background, church involvement, interests and spiritual development. This information is then used by the camp to connect campers who do not have a church with a church in their community. This report is probably the only transfer of the counselor's experience with the camper to the office staff, and so it is essential that it is done carefully and accurately.

The more seriously you take this process the more helpful the information will be, not only to the camp office, but to you as well. After a summer of counseling, you will not be able to remember who made what decision, nor anything to write or call them about in the winter. This record is for you as much as anyone, and after the summer it will matter to you how well you filled it out. Camps usually have a deadline for getting these reports in. If at all possible, fill them out while you are still at camp and the memory is fresh, rather than letting them gather dust at home.

You should not fill out the report in the presence of your campers. Hopefully, you will have gathered all the information you need by the end of the week through your camper survey and conversations. It will be helpful to take notes all week about your campers so you can later transfer that information over to the report. For the purposes of follow-up, the critical points of information are the campers' church involvement (name of church and nature of involvement) and the campers' spiritual progress and commitments. Remember that pastors and other church workers will take seriously everything you submit in the report.

2. Permanent camp records.

How was it done before the age of computers? Many camps now have a computer database containing regularly updated information on every camper who passes their gate. Basic information is entered into the computer when campers register, and records are added from the reports or profiles submitted by counselors at the end of each week. The advent of video input or inexpensive digital cameras has made it possible to include a photo of each camper in the database, taken as part of the registration process. This makes it easier for staff to remember who is who, and also encourages those involved in follow-up to remember that these are real kids and not just a name on a page.

3. Reports to churches.

The other advantage of using a computer database is the ease of forming reports on campers who need follow-up, which can be sent to churches and also returned to the counselors. This is where confidentiality becomes an issue, and there is no doubt some risk involved in passing camper information on to a third party. The risk can be reduced by contact with the churches on the use of the material, and by being up-front with the camp's intentions when parents submit the information at registration.

One of the primary goals of follow-up is to connect campers with a church. The pastor or other church leaders are encouraged to make a call or a visit to each of the campers on their list. Because campers will rarely attend a church or church program solely because of an invitation from someone they don't know, there is no better person to make that initial contact than someone the camper met at camp—perhaps you! Campers from Christian homes who make a decision will best be helped if their Christian parents are aware of the decision. A camp might do this directly, or encourage the pastor to contact the parents.

4. Reports to counselors.

Many camps also send a similar report to counselors so they can carry on follow-up of their own. This eliminates the problem of getting campers' addresses down correctly each week, and provides counselors with enough information to write intelligently to every camper. Counselors need to be aware that this is confidential information, and that they must not pass it on to anyone. Other staff who want access to information on a camper should do so through the camp office. Some camps also provide help such as envelopes and stationary for letter-writing, stamps, cabin photos and resources such as lists of churches, Christian bookstores and Christian organizations in the campers' various communities.

5. Camp testimony book.

A tradition of some camps is to have a large book available for campers to record their spiritual decisions themselves. This helps affirm the camper in their decision, and gives them something to look back on as they return to camp year after year. Staff are encouraged by glancing in it, and may discover spiritual decisions not otherwise observed.

6. Materials given or sent to campers.

Camps vary greatly on this, but some give discipleship and promotional materials to campers at the end of camp and/or throughout the next year by mail. Several Christian organizations provide camps with Bibles or with samples or whole courses of devotional and discipleship programs to be passed on to campers. A few camps still operate a correspondence course with campers, but find that most campers will return the answered material only once or twice before giving it up. Other camps have regular newsletters, which include articles, information and interaction to help campers stay in touch and grow spiritually. Others will give you postcards or stationary to write notes to your campers during the summer, which are mailed for you later in the year. Find out what your camp offers.

7. The Internet.

An increasing number of campers have access to the Internet at home or through their schools. Camps who launch their own web sites have gained access to an immense potential audience, and can provide services of great benefit to their own campers. Possibilities include information on every aspect of the camp; interactive programs for discipleship or just for fun; downloadable pictures, videos and sound clips; bulletin boards where campers can leave messages for each other and staff; a weekly chat-line for live interaction with a staff member; access to staff through e-mail;

electronic camp post cards to send to friends; electronic registration accessible to people all over the world; links to other Christian resources such as music, magazines and organizations; and the list goes on and on. Encourage your camp to get on-line! If you have expertise in this area, let your camp know of your willingness to be involved.

8. Post-summer camps and weekend retreats.

More and more camps offer programs year-round, providing more points of contact with campers throughout the post-summer months. Volunteer to attend one or more of these, and check to see if any of your campers will be attending. Also, check with the office to see if any of the campers you will be counseling at the retreat recently made a commitment at the camp. Connect with these campers over the weekend so you can encourage them and carry on the discipleship process.

9. Off-site camp events.

Camp comes to the city! Many camps bring special events to the communities of their campers; some make this a regular occurrence right through the year. These gatherings often include lots of music, drama and memories, and either a speaker or small group discussion. Some camps run or sponsor sports events such as tournaments or races or ski days, or bring in a music group for a concert.

These can be great points of contact between staff and campers; stay informed about such events and get involved if you are able. Often you can invite an otherwise-reluctant camper to come with your church's youth group to an event because it is sponsored by "his" camp, thus helping him to get to know people in the group. However, camps should be careful to not take the place of the local churches or compete with them. The whole idea of camp follow-up is to get campers connected with their own churches.

The camp's promotional program is another point of contact that can broaden the follow-up of a camper to include his family. Many camps have a slide or video show they take around to churches and schools to promote the camp. When campers and their families are invited to come to the camp presentation at a church and catch a possible glimpse of themselves in the pictures, it gives the church the opportunity to meet them.

THE COUNSELOR IS THE KEY PLAYER IN CAMPER FOLLOW-UP

The counselor is the key person for the follow-up of campers because of the relationship they share after a week of camp. Your encouragement to the camper to get connected with a church, continue with devotions or get involved in ministry will carry much weight. You can extend the opportunity to be part of the process of your campers' spiritual growth right through to the next summer. You don't want to overwhelm campers with personal contact, but here are some practical ways of continuing discipleship with your campers. Further ideas are to be found in Resource Section "I."

1. Pray for your campers.

If you decide to do just one thing by way of following up your campers, do this: pray for them regularly. Keep cabin photos in your Bible to remind you, or keep a prayer list or calendar to help you pray for them in rotation. If you know of prayer warriors in your church, ask if they will pray for one or several of your campers regularly. Invite campers to send their prayer requests to you, and promise to remember them in prayer. God will work in ways you may never know this side of heaven.

2. Write letters!

Some counselors maintain correspondence with dozens of campers after the summer, which is a big commitment from a big heart. Plan to write a minimum of two letters to your campers if possible, perhaps one in the fall and one in spring. As a bare minimum, write to those who accepted Christ or made significant decisions or who are close to making a decision, or to campers with whom you were especially close. The letter can be brief, but make it as personal as possible, using your camper reports to help you recall their interests, memorable moments and decisions. Birthday cards, bookmarks and other fun stuff can help show the campers that you have a lasting interest in them and in their spiritual and personal growth.

3. Help your campers connect with a church.

You will have some campers who have made a commitment to Christ but are not yet attending a church or youth group. In an open, friendly way, call or write to these campers and offer to help them find a church. If you know of other staff members who live in their area, you may be able to arrange to have your campers go to church with them. Again, be sensitive to resistant parents and respect their decision to not allow a camper to attend.

4. Keep a personal follow-up record.

Use a notebook, calendar, or the camper report the camp gave you to keep a record of each time that you call or write a camper, or discover a prayer need he has. Keep it in a prominent spot. This will help you keep track of what you have done, and may motivate you to keep consistent about staying in touch with your campers and maintaining your role in their discipleship.

There is no one in the world who can accomplish what a counselor can in the life of a camper by staying in touch. It may seem a small thing to you, but it can mean the world to a camper. Often, by the grace of God, your letter arrives at a camper's door just at the time she needs the encouragement or challenge. Your faithful prayers may affect the course of her life. Show you care in Jesus' name, over the long haul.

---

[150] A race to see who can look up a Bible verse the fastest

[151] Galatians 5:22-23

[152] I John 2:5-6, NCV

[153] Ephesians 4:15, 25

> ### CAMP PREP #12: PLAN YOUR LONG-TERM COMMITMENT TO CAMPERS
> *Suggestions on how to prepare for your counseling experience.*
>
> What's your plan for following up your campers after this summer? Plan and commit yourself now to a full year of counseling. Camp lasts a week or two; what will you do to ensure your campers are getting the encouragement and teaching they need for the other weeks of the year?
>
> • Find out what your camp offers and expects regarding a follow-up program, and what policies they have concerning your ongoing contact with campers.
>
> • Get your plan down on paper, so that when the summer is over and you pick up your busy schedule again, you will have already decided how you will stay in touch with your campers. Check out the many ideas for follow-up offered in Resource Section "I."

THE LAST QUESTION

Well, do you feel ready to counsel? I hope not!

Counseling is like learning to waterski. It can't be done simply by reading a book; you have to get in the water and try it. Fine time to tell you that! My hope is that this book has helped you with your preparation and given you a better idea of what to expect at camp this summer. I know that you are going to learn it all over again as you counsel this summer, and the next summer after that. I will be satisfied if you occasionally say to yourself, "Hey, that's just what the guy said in the book!" Then I will know I have not left you totally unprepared.

One day, maybe when he was walking by a ring of rocks and bush that formed the enclosure where a flock of sheep were kept, Jesus said this:

> *I am the good shepherd. The good shepherd lays down his life for the sheep. The hired hand is not the shepherd who owns the sheep. So when he sees the wolf coming, he abandons the sheep and runs away. Then the wolf attacks the flock and scatters it. The man runs away because he is a hired hand and cares nothing for the sheep. I am the good shepherd; I know my sheep and my sheep know me—just as the Father knows me and I know the Father—and I lay down my life for the sheep.*

JOHN 10:11-15

Shepherding was considered a noble profession if you owned the flock. Because the shepherd owned the sheep, he would genuinely care for them, and treat them accordingly. Like David, he would fight off wild animals to protect them. Like Jesus, a shepherd would even die for his sheep.

Another kind of shepherd often looked after sheep. These were hired hands, usually outcasts or criminals who couldn't let their faces be seen in town. The hired hand was there for the money, and would do just enough to get by. He would not look out for the best interests of the flock, because they were not his. At the first sign of risk or danger, he was gone.

Here's the question: This summer, will you be a shepherd, or just a hired hand? Will you care for campers as if they were your own, or do just enough to get by, since they are not "your" sheep? These lambs belong to Jesus. My prayer is that you will be the same kind of shepherd to them that he is to you. God bless as you serve him this summer.

RESOURCE
SECTION

*A big bag of goodies to prepare
you for summer, and to keep
handy as you counsel at camp.*

A. A STORY: CHRIST AT HOME IN MY HEART

This story, adapted (by permission[154]) from a tract by Robert Lloyd Munger, is primarily for use with **CAMP PREP** #1, *to help you consider how God might search your heart and make the necessary changes there that would prepare you for camp counseling. This analogy would also be a good resource for introducing a cabin Bible discussion, as a bedtime story, or for a staff devotional. Read and consider...*

One evening, while my camp counselor was praying, I invited Jesus Christ into my heart. It was incredible! No big, emotional entrance, but I knew that things were going to be different from then on. Something happened at the very center of my life. Jesus walked right in and pulled back the heavy drapes. He turned on every light in the house. He built a blazing fire in the fireplace and took away the chill. The music he cranked up made me want to dance for joy, and he filled every empty, hollow corner of my life with his warm and wonderful self. I have never regretted inviting him in, and I never will.

Breathlessly, I said to Jesus, "Lord, make yourself at home. Everything I have is yours. Let me show you around the place."

I first took him to the den, the place where I studied. It was a small room but very important, because it was the control center of the rest of the house. Jesus took time to look at everything. He crouched down to read the titles of my books and magazines; he studied the pictures and posters on the walls. He checked out my video collection, listened to a few CD's on the stereo, and even tried out a video game on the computer. But as I followed his searching eyes I became increasingly uncomfortable.

Funny, but I had never felt so self-conscious about all this stuff. With Jesus looking at the room of my mind I became embarrassed. There were images there that his eyes were too pure to behold. I had trash and garbage on the floor that I was afraid would dirty his feet. The TV and stereo were blaring at the same time, and I quickly turned them both off. As for the pictures on the walls, I tried in vain to stand in front of them all at once to block his view. He could see everything.

I turned to him and said, "Jesus, obviously this room needs some renovations—radical ones. Will you help me get rid of the things that shame me, and bring all my thoughts under your control? I don't even know where to start!"

His frown turned into a smile. "I was hoping you would say that. Here, let's throw away this garbage, and everything else that isn't pure or beautiful or respectable. And the empty shelves we will fill with the books of the Bible and everything else that is true and right. As for the pictures on the wall..." He and I were able to tear down many of them, but a few stubbornly remained. Then he placed a large portrait of himself there, and I have found many times that when my attention is focused on him, those old images are forgotten all together.

From there we went into the kitchen, the place where I concocted all kinds of foods to satisfy my hunger and desire. "So, what will you have?" I asked him. Opening the fridge I listed what was on the menu that day—old bones, corn husks, stale Coke, moldy bread—the kind of stuff I enjoyed most days. It didn't seem so appealing now. Jesus was not at all impressed. He ate nothing I placed before him, and I could hardly blame him. Finally I sat down and admitted I had nothing to offer him. "How about you?" I asked him. "Do you cook?" His eyes lit up, and in a moment he was dashing about the room, filling the garbage can with most of what I had offered him, and coming up with new dishes from who knows where.

"What is it?" I asked, sampling a bit of what he was making. It was delicious.

"As you can see, I have food you could hardly imagine," he explained. "My food is to do the will of God. When you try to satisfy your own pleasure and desires, you will never get enough. But if you seek to please me and my Father, I promise you that you will never go hungry." He was right. By the time I pushed back my chair from the table a half hour later, I was contented and happy.

I suggested that we go into the living room after supper. This was the one room that he seemed to like at once. It had a fireplace, comfortable chairs, and a view that couldn't be beat. "This is a wonderful room," he said. "Let's meet here often. It is quiet here, and we can talk together without interruption."

Well I must say, I was excited about that. Imagine meeting each day, just Jesus and me, talking about anything and everything. "I will be here early every morning," he promised. "Meet me here, and we will start each day together." So, early the next morning I joined him in the living room. He took a book of the Bible from the shelf and we read it together, and since he was the Author he pointed out things I had never noticed before. What he said there stayed with me all day, and molded my thoughts and actions to what they should be. I promised myself to never miss a morning with Jesus.

And then I got unexpectedly busy. You know how it is—a homework assignment I forgot to do the evening before, a late night that made me sleep in. Sometimes I would sit with Jesus just long enough to hear him read, and then I would be out the door. Once I even grabbed the book out of his hands and read it myself. He read so slowly and intently, it seemed. Soon, I was just poking my head in the door to say good morning. And then I stopped coming to the living room all together.

I remember one morning, as I was rushing out of the house, I happened to glance in the living room and there was Jesus, sitting on the floor by the fireplace. He had a good blaze going, for it was a chilly morning, and English muffins and orange juice were laid out on the coffee table—for two. I stopped, and with my head hanging entered the room. "Oh Jesus," I said, "have you been here like this every morning?"

"Yes," he said, "just as I promised. Remember, I love you. You can't imagine what it cost me to win you back into my friendship. My one desire is to be with you. If you cannot keep this time for your own sake, please do it for mine." I dropped everything and sat beside him on the floor. He forgave me entirely, and we spent half the morning there, talking and laughing. I had never realized how much he valued my friendship, and that one thought has kept me returning to that room more consistently than ever.

One day Jesus asked, "You have a workshop here, don't you? May I see it?" Now to be honest, I had an excellent workshop, and knew it. But I spent very little time there. Occasionally I would go down when I had nothing better to do, and there were a few pet projects I fiddled with. I wasn't producing anything substantial.

I led him down there. He picked up one of the toys I had made—a rather flimsy thing I had thrown together one day—and it fell apart in his hands. "Is this all you are producing for my kingdom?" he asked. "You have such wonderful tools here, supplied to you by my Father. Surely you can accomplish more than this!"

"I know it isn't much, Lord," I admitted, "but I don't seem to have the skill or strength to do more. And I never have the time."

"Well, you are a bit clumsy at times," he said with a twinkle in his eye, "but I know a Master Craftsman who will help you. If you make your hands and heart and time available to him, He will work through you to produce things that will last forever. Ask for anything (and be sure to mention my name) and he will do it." From that day on I began to produce more than flimsy toys, or rather the Craftsman did through me.

One evening I planned to go out with my friends. I found it hard to look Jesus in the eye as he watched me get ready, because I knew that he would not approve of where I was going and what I was likely to end up doing there. To my surprise, as I grabbed my coat and headed for the door, he started to follow.

"Jesus, you wouldn't want to come. My friends and I—well, we like to have fun sometimes, and..."

"I like fun." he said, "You hardly take me anywhere."

"Tomorrow, Jesus," I stammered, looking at my watch. "We'll go to a park or something, or maybe the Christian book store. You would like that. Come on, let me close the door, would you? I gotta go!" I was starting to get angry.

He didn't say anything. He just looked me in the eye and stood his ground. When I started to leave, he began to follow. Suddenly I lost my temper. I grabbed his arm, pushed him back inside the house, and slammed the door. As I got into the car, I looked up and saw him with his face glued to the window, arms stretched out wide... It was the most miserable moment of my life because I knew what I was doing to him, and I did it anyway. I spent an awful night with my friends, and in the morning I didn't want to pull the covers off my head. I heard a sound and peeked out. Jesus was there, breakfast tray in hand. He put it down as I rushed to his arms, and we wept together.

Things went well after that. I found some new friends, and some of my old ones were getting to know Jesus too. Then one day I found him waiting for me at the door. I could tell something was wrong. "Something smells in this house. A dead thing. I am sure it is in the closet upstairs." As soon as he said it, I knew what he was talking about.

It was just a little closet upstairs that I kept under lock and key. There were a few things there I didn't want Jesus or anyone else to see. He led me upstairs and pointed. "In there," he said, with a look of disgust on his face. "Some dead thing." I could smell it now. It was pretty bad, but I was angry that he should point it out. I had given him access to everything in the house. Now he was asking me about a little closet. It was too much. I wasn't going to give in.

It was as if he had read my thoughts. He said, "If you think I'm going to stay up here on the second floor with that smelly thing, you had better think again." And with that he started down the stairs. I panicked. "Jesus, wait!" He stopped and gave me a questioning look. "I'll give you the key, okay? But I don't have the heart or strength to clean out the closet. Could you...?"

"I can," he said, "and I will. But yes, you must give up the key to me." With shaking hands I drew it out of my pocket and gave it to him. It was over in a minute. He grabbed the rotting pile in the closet and carried it out back. I heard the sound of digging. Then he returned with cleaning supplies, and it was done. I was surprised that his clothes showed no signs of his work—they were as clean and white as ever. And the smell was gone.

I made up my mind right there. "Jesus, obviously you are a much better manager of my home than I will ever be. So far I thought you would only be my guest, but now I see that you must be my Master, and I your willing servant. Will you take over my life and my home?" I signed the deed over to him that very day.

Things have been very different around here since Jesus made himself at home in my heart.

---

[154]Adapted from *My Heart -- Christ's Home*, by Robert Lloyd Munger. Revised edition ©1986 by InterVarsity Christian Fellowship/USA. Used by permission of InterVarsity Press, P.O. Box 1400, Downers Grove, IL 60515

B.   RESOURCES FOR LISTENING INTELLIGENTLY TO CAMPERS' PROBLEMS

This is a very limited list of issues you might encounter among campers this summer. Your camp may offer more resources in its staff manual, or books and pamphlets may be available from the head counselor or director (see the ones listed in Resource Section "J"). Remember, it is not your role to solve campers' problems or offer them professional counsel. But the following notes may help you listen to campers with care and understanding, and know when to seek further help for them.

RELATIONSHIP ISSUES

The most common problems campers will bring to you will be about their relationships: friends with whom they can't get along; battles with mom and dad; or the desire to do right but pressure from friends to do wrong. Remember to listen, encourage them to talk, and then listen more. These issues will often resolve themselves as campers talk. You also have a huge resource in God's word for dealing with relationships—this is what Christ's kingdom is all about. Healing in relationships comes through forgiveness, and we can forgive because we have been forgiven by a loving God.

You may discover that a camper is involved in some unhealthy relationships. He may have a parent who is overprotective or negligent, or who has become dependent on his or her child because of an addiction or mental disorder or an inability to cope with stress. A youth may be involved in a sexual relationship with another youth or even an adult. In some of these situations, the camper will need more assistance than you can offer, and you will need to talk with the head counselor about getting him further help.

SELF-ESTEEM AND INSECURITY PROBLEMS

Emotional problems arising from a camper's view of himself may be expressed in a variety of ways, from extreme shyness to dishonesty to overly-aggressive behavior. The unfamiliar experience of camp can produce these emotions in a child who doesn't usually experience them in his sheltered home. You will not change a camper's personality in one week at camp. However, you can offer him understanding, and you can give the camper a better picture of himself to go home with. Equip him with skills for dealing with his feelings, such as turning his focus outward when he feels bad about himself.[155] Of course, campers with these feelings will find it difficult to talk about them, but if you can just get them talking about themselves this may be enough.

GRIEF AND LOSS ISSUES (INCLUDING HOMESICKNESS)

Some campers have recently experienced the death of a friend or family member, or some other loss such as a pet that died or a move to a new city. Even two or three years after such an occurrence they may still be carrying difficult emotions and suffering from confusion. Camp is a place where their pent-up emotions are sometimes finally released, resulting in crying or depression or anger. If campers do not have a satisfactory means of expressing these emotions—such as talking with their counselor—their feelings will probably come out in their behavior instead.

1. Expect that a wide range of feelings could be expressed.

These may include fear, rage, guilt, helplessness or isolation. Do not offer answers or explanations, which are not what they are looking for. Just listen, and spend time grieving and questioning and wondering with them. Do not be afraid to ask questions: "How did it happen? How did you hear about it? What was the funeral like?" Avoid sympathy or pity or other responses that will highlight their loss and make them feel worse. Use appropriate physical touch—a hug they aren't expecting, or an invitation to sit with you—to let them know you are there for them. Try to get them involved in activities, but realize that they may have difficulty with basic decision-making and participation. If necessary, help them make some short-term goals, such as hiking to the summit on Thursday.

2. Homesickness is also grief.

How does homesickness fit here? The feelings associated with being separated from family and everything familiar is similar to the grief we associate with death, on a lesser scale (though in some cases not much less!). The signs to watch for are tears, lack of enthusiasm, isolation, and stress indicators such as stomach aches, as any grieving child might experience. Treat homesickness as grief. Spend time listening, ask questions, let them know their feelings are normal and help them with short-term goals (for example, waiting until Wednesday to phone home). Involve them in activities they enjoy the most, and involve them with other staff, such as a camp grandma and grandpa or camp pastor. If they do need to go home, don't give them the impression that they have failed or that you are disappointed; talk about "next summer."

SIN OR HABITUAL PROBLEMS

Sometimes a camper will voluntarily come to talk about and deal with sin or bad habits in his life. This will include the more usual offenses such as dishonesty or swearing or impure thoughts. But you may also meet youth who are involved with more conspicuous habits such as sexual sin or substance abuse. If you do not feel competent or comfortable discussing these problems with a camper, or if you feel that a camper is in serious trouble, talk with the head counselor about it.

Sin is sin; take it seriously any time a camper wants to talk about these problems, even if you think they are not significant. Gently help him understand God's viewpoint on his actions or thoughts, not in a condemning way, but so that he can *confess* his sin to God (remembering that confession is simply telling on ourselves to God, and agreeing with him on his view of our sin).

Confession must always include *repentance*, or turning away from sin in our actions and attitudes. You can help a camper think through what it will mean for him to turn from his sin and come up with a plan of action to gain victory over a nagging habit. Of course, some sins are more enslaving and will take more serious measures. If a camper is dealing with serious substance abuse or deviant sexual behavior, it is time to suggest meeting with the head counselor and/or camp pastor.

CRISIS OR TRAGEDY WHILE AT CAMP

Occasionally a camper will come to camp still dealing with the shock of a tragedy or crisis at home, or even receive bad news while at camp. This camper will need special time and attention while she is at camp, and may not be able to stay. A special staff member may be needed to give her the time and attention she will need. Be prepared to help her through the simple daily decisions and tasks that will be more difficult for her because of the numbness she feels. You will also need ample time to simply be with her—she should not be left alone—and to listen to her with love and compassion. If this cannot be done for her at camp, she may be better off at home.

Sometimes the hedge God places around his people is—for his own unimaginable purposes—removed,[156] and tragedy strikes at camp. Campers will suddenly become very serious and cling to you, while you are still trying to deal with your own trauma. Some campers will respond in ways that may seem strange to you, such as over-excitement, withdrawal, loud voices or hysteria. Your responsibility is to help bring things back to normal while not denying the reality of what has happened and the emotions involved.

Always, God takes what is evil and turns it into good for those who love him, and you will find that hurting campers will open their hearts as they would not have done otherwise. Tragedy at camp is a time to lead the way in turning your hearts to God in faith and trust. Counselors should deal with the tragedy as a cabin group, letting campers support one another and pray together. Avoid speculation and gossip and laying blame, and focus on dealing with the hurt and stress that has resulted.

PROBLEMS FOR WHICH YOU WILL NEED SPECIAL AND IMMEDIATE HELP

In the following situations, do not attempt counseling the individual camper. Stay with him if necessary, but get help as soon as possible:

1. Threat of suicide.

Never leave someone who is threatening to commit suicide. Even if you suspect he may be doing it for attention, take it seriously. Stay with him or take him with you, but get help immediately. Also watch for signs that suicide is being contemplated: conversations about death; giving away of possessions; severe changes in emotions or behavior; risk-taking or suicide notes. Don't ever take chances. Get help if you suspect a camper is a threat to himself.

2. Mental or emotional illness.

If it seems to you that a camper is responding abnormally (for example, has extreme shifts in mood or personality, talks about hearing voices, or has inexplicable behavior) talk with the head counselor. There is a possibility that there is a mental disorder involved that was not included on the camper's medical form, such as ADD (Attention Deficit Disorder), FAS (Fetal Alcohol Syndrome), manic depression or schizophrenia (less common). You may also encounter eating disorders—usually among teen girls—such as anorexia nervosa and bulimia. If a camper's eating habits are extremely irregular, or if a camper excuses herself to the bathroom during every meal, talk with your head counselor about your observations. Even if you have some experience with any of these disorders, you should not try to deal with them entirely on your own. Get help for your campers.

3. Severe depression.

Depression is relatively common among adolescents who are groping to make sense of their world and are getting discouraged. Often they just need someone to talk with in order to relieve their feelings and get them back involved with the program. But more severe depression can affect all their usual daily habits—eating, sleeping, regularity and physical activity—and then they will need more help than you can offer. If your efforts to listen and understand are having no effect, talk with the head counselor.

4. Problems that hit close to home.

Sometimes a camper will want to talk with you about a problem with which you are also struggling and not yet finding victory. The Bible cautions that "if someone is caught in a sin, you who are spiritual should restore him gently. But watch yourself, or you also may be tempted." If a camper comes with a problem (for example, with pornography) and you are struggling with it yourself, talk to the head counselor and have him deal with the camper. You should also talk with someone about your own problem, so that you can be a clean and sanctified instrument for God's use.[157]

FAMILY BREAK-UP

As many as one quarter of the children in our countries are from single-parent homes. These are often hurting and angry kids. What can you do for them?

1. Be aware of their home situations.

Find out early in the week the home situation of each camper. On the first night of camp, do a survey of your cabin. Along with asking fun questions like what they would do with one million dollars, ask campers the simple, non-threatening question, "Who lives at your house?" Knowing their home situations will help you understand their emotions and responses right from the beginning.

2. Expect strong emotions.

Campers from broken homes, especially if it was a recent occurrence, are struggling with strong emotions children shouldn't have to face, such as anger and hatred, shame and embarrassment, rejection, depression, guilt (blaming themselves for the break-up), hostility, aggression and confusion. Maybe you have never experienced strong emotions such as these yourself, so how can you help these kids? What they need from you more than anything is your care and attention. Lend them your ears.

3. Expect unusual behavior.

Campers from this home setting are looking for attention from someone who will take time to listen to their feelings. If we fail to meet this cry for attention their emotions will likely come out in unusual and distracting behavior. Remember to give them *all* of your attention *part* of the time. When it comes time to discipline their behavior, be firm but have compassion for the huge emotions that are causing it.

4. Be a friend, not a therapist.

Get the child involved in the program, and watch for the slow times when his thoughts go back to the problems at home. Encourage him to avoid spending lots of time alone. A caring ear is the best gift you can offer.

ABUSE AND NEGLECT

Child and youth abuse is a frequent topic in the news, perhaps because more abuse is taking place but certainly because those who are abused are reporting it to a greater extent than ever before. A camp counselor needs to be ready to respond to the child who gives any indication that he or she has experienced abuse, and to know what steps to follow from there.

In a home where abuse or other serious problems are taking place, children live from crisis to crisis by "martial law" as if their family is at war. The unwritten rules in their house are:[158]

1. Don't talk.   2. Don't trust.   3. Don't feel.

These are the three things they *need* to do if they are going to find relief and help while they are away from home at camp. The best gift you can offer them is a listening ear, genuine care, and the opportunity to release their suppressed emotions.

1. What you should do when someone indicates he or she has been abused.

Children and youth who have been abused have usually been warned or threatened about telling anyone. They may tell you directly if they have gained enough trust in you, but you should also be aware of indicators that may show that abuse has taken place. Usually it is a *combination* of these signs that will indicate abuse, rather than a single bruise or comment. Other resources will offer more extensive lists,[159] but some common combinations to watch for are:

- *Sexual abuse.* Unusual sexual knowledge or behavior; unusual modesty or immodesty; complaints about private parts; withdrawal or promiscuity.

- *Physical abuse.* Wariness; unexplained injuries or bruises (especially under clothing); extremely aggressive or extremely withdrawn; avoids physical contact; fearful of discipline.

- *Emotional abuse.* Poor self-image; extremes in behavior and habits; bed-wetting; exhaustion; excessive crying or whining.

- *Neglect.* Lack of personal disciplines; stealing; endangers self; extremely clingy; extremely independent; stories about being left alone.

If you suspect abuse, or if campers tell you they been abused, encourage them to talk about what happened, but be careful not to interrogate them. It is not your responsibility to find out exactly what has taken place. Be careful not to ask leading questions that may cause them to invent incidents or exaggerate. Even if their stories are hard to imagine, believe them and let them know that you believe them.

You will need to bring other people into this situation, but tell the child that you will inform only those people who need to know and no one else. Show compassion, but keep control of your emotions so the child will be encouraged to keep talking, which is what will help and comfort him the most. Let him know that you have heard him, and that you understand and care. Pray for guidance and wisdom.

When a child has talked with you about abuse he has experienced, it will be traumatic for you, and you will be responsible to take some action. Give yourself time alone to think it through. You will probably find that your time with the child was about 95% emotion and only about 5% information. A social worker will ask some very basic facts besides the event itself—do you know the answers? Pray for wisdom, courage, strength and patience.

2. What you must do when someone indicates he or she has been abused.

Every province and state in the western world has laws that make you responsible to report any suspected child abuse. For example, the law in my home province of British Columbia states, *"Any person who has reasonable grounds to believe that a child is in need of protection must report the circumstances to a Ministry of Social Services social worker."* If it is found that a person has been negligent and has failed to report abuse, he is considered to have indirectly assisted in the abuse and may face fines or even imprisonment.

When a child indicates that he or she has been abused, you may be unsure if the matter is serious enough, or you may not want to cause trouble for the family. It is true that when you report abuse, things are set in motion that will be traumatic for the family. But you must report it, even if you only have reasonable suspicions and not hard facts. It is for the child's good, as it will stop the abuse and keep him from further harm in the future. You may be afraid that the child will be removed from the home and the parents will blame you. In most cases these days it is the offender, not the child, who is removed. In any case, it is better to have this kind of disruption in the home than for a child to suffer all through his childhood. By doing this, you tip the balance of power that the offender has over the victim.

Start by telling the child that you will be telling someone about what he has told you. Assure him that it is for the sake of his own safety, and that no one will know except those who have to know. From there, talk with someone who has more experience than you, probably your head counselor. He or she will know what to do from that point, and will then be able to offer you the emotional support you need. Be sure to know your camp's policies and procedures.

Most child protection services move only to protect a child and do little or nothing to bring healing into his life. Reassure the child that he has done the right thing, and that now healing can begin. Give him time to talk with you further during the rest of the week. Assure him that he is not to blame for what has happened, and talk with him about his anxiety for his family in the future. After he has left, keep in contact with the child if possible, as you would for a camper who has made a spiritual commitment.

[155]This is the suggestion of the Apostle John in I John 3:18-20. We can overcome our bad feelings about ourselves by actively loving those around us

[156]A biblical example is in Job 1:6-12; thankfully, camp examples are few and far between

[157]II Timothy 2:20-21

[158]Danna McClintock, "Role of a Leader at Camp with Kids from Troubled Families", *Training For Camp Counselors*, ©1990 Young Life

[159]See Dr. Becca C. Johnson, "Seven Keys To Understanding Child Abuse", *CCI Focus Series #21*, ©1996 Christian Camping International, which is a summary of her book, *For Their Sake: Recognizing, Reporting and Responding to Child Abuse*, ©1992, American Camping Association. Information for this section was also dependent on Dr. Gary Grams, "What to Do With a Disclosure of Sexual Abuse: The Camp Counselor's Guide," ©1994 Gary Grams

C. HOW TO DEAL WITH SOME SPECIFIC DISCIPLINE ISSUES

It would be impossible to cover every problem you might come across as a summer camp counselor. Many times you will simply need to ask God for wisdom and common sense to decide how to approach and handle a specific situation. Remember that there are others at the camp who likely have more experience than you. If in doubt, ask your head counselor or director for advice and further resources. Here are a few pointers from those who have been there:

DISHONESTY

1. Lying.

Why do people tell lies? Lying is an attempt to regain control in a situation where we are losing it. For example, a camper is afraid he will not be accepted by his fellow campers, so to gain acceptance he invents or exaggerates a story about some amazing thing he did. Often other campers won't believe him and he feels his control of the situation slipping again, so he lies some more. With younger campers it is sometimes a case of speaking without knowing, until even the speaker believes it to be true.

Lying is not a personality trait, and can be disciplined. Lying is a response to insecurity, so the camper needs to find better ways to deal with situations in which he feels insecure. If other campers start labeling him as a liar (which they probably will, a good occasion to mention Jesus' words about throwing stones[160]), it would be appropriate to take the time to talk with him, explore the problem together and come up with some solutions. For example, if a camper has been telling tall tales, you could discuss whether these were things that actually happened or only things that he wished would happen. Perhaps you could help him channel his imagination into the real world; for example, you could encourage him to tell fictional stories for fun rather than acceptance.

Some campers have learned to use lies to deceive and manipulate others. This is a little more rare, but when it happens you will need to take a firm hand to maintain control of the situation. Let the camper know that you understand what he is doing, and don't permit him to use his fellow campers' naiveté to get his own way. If manipulation is a way of life for a camper, you will not change his habit in one week. However, you can help him see his need for integrity and reliability, and his need for a Savior.

2. Cheating.

Younger campers may cheat in games because of a basic self-centeredness. They get very upset if anyone else cheats, but prefer holding the edge they themselves get from cheating. Older campers will cheat out of laziness or lack of interest in a game, or simply out of rebellion. Beyond the fact that cheating spoils the game for other campers, you want the one who is cheating to learn the value of honesty.

The primary way of doing this is to be an example of honesty yourself. Avoid all appearance of cheating (which can be tough if other counselors are cheating or if the game seems unfair). During the game, hang out with campers who have a tendency to cheat. It is not hard to convince younger campers that it is cool to be able to say, "I don't need to cheat to win." It may be more of a hard sell to older campers. Your own example of integrity is still the best influence, and every game presents many teachable moments that relate to everyday life. Using a game as a learning opportunity will be more effective than penalizing them or making them sit out the game, which just teaches them to not get caught next time.

3. Stealing.

A case of theft in the cabin can be very upsetting to campers. Beyond the feelings of loss to the one who has been robbed, theft makes everyone feel vulnerable and at risk. Emotions can elevate, and accusations will soon follow. Even a fight among campers will do less to bring chaos and disunity to a cabin, and so theft needs to be dealt with quickly.

The best thing to do, of course, is to prevent theft in the first place. As campers arrive, observe or ask about valuables they have brought with them. You should not agree to hold valuable items for safe-keeping (which would then make you liable for them if something happened) but the camp office will probably be willing to put them in a secure place. Most camps will at least keep campers' money in account for them. Avoid keeping your own valuable property in the cabin—you are not immune to theft. If an item goes missing, don't let your campers assume it has been stolen. Have everyone check their stuff to "see if it got into the wrong bag." This might give the one who stole the item an easy way out of his predicament, but it solves the problem.

If an item can't be found, and especially if more things disappear, it is time for a cabin conference. Tell the group that if someone has taken the item, he must come and see you, that you will straighten it out, and that it won't mean doom for him when he does so. If someone comes to you to admit to a theft, deal with the matter as sin that needs forgiveness and restitution. You will need to judge whether it is necessary for him to go and admit his theft to the one robbed or to the cabin group. All unresolved thefts should be reported to your head counselor. If you discover a camper who steals compulsively or on a broad scale at home, you will need to take time to talk with him about it, and perhaps seek additional help for him.

AGGRESSIVENESS

1. Disputes and fighting.

Basic first action when there is a dispute and especially when there is a fight is this: Don't let it continue. Stop the conflict as soon as you can safely do so. When a dispute involves arguing or behind-the-scenes nastiness, step in, let those involved know you are aware of what is going on, and begin to resolve it as soon as possible. A week is a short period of time, and conflict between campers can rob them of much of it. At juniors camp, you can expect a dispute or fight to be between just two campers; at youth camps, it is more likely that several people are involved. Unfortunately, it is no longer considered cowardly for a group to gang up on one person to beat him up.

If there is a fight and you feel you can step in without endangering yourself or getting more campers involved, do so immediately. Don't stand and watch to see what will happen (this is not the National Hockey League). If you are not sure you can stop the fight, or if any weapons are involved, immediately get or send for help. Cold water is used to separate fighting dogs, and it works well on people too. The main thing is to reduce the possibility of injury. If the campers are angry enough, they may try to go after one another even after you separate them. So it is best for staff to get them far apart as quickly as possible and begin dealing with the issues involved.

When those involved in a fight or dispute have been taken aside by staff and have calmed down enough, one staff member (often the head counselor) should talk with each of them separately, getting all sides of the story. Make forgiveness and reconciliation your goal. When there is evidence that the individuals at fault are ready to apologize, bring them together. If another outbreak seems likely, warn the instigators that it will be dealt with strongly and immediately. They should come under close supervision and be kept busy. It is not unusual for someone who has taken a beating to want to call home; unless it is against your camp's policy, you should allow him to do so, but be sure a staff member talks with the parents first.

2. The picked-on camper.

If a camper is being picked on by other campers and a warning doesn't immediately stop it, tell the head counselor right away. Don't wait for a camper's whole week to be spoiled by aggressive, angry and insecure people. Avoid leaving the picked-on camper alone without supervision; if necessary, let him hang out with you.

Remember that those who are doing the bullying also need help and discipline. Why are they acting aggressively? Is the one being picked on at fault (e.g., teasing others or being obnoxious)? Who is the instigator among them? Let them know that you will not permit their behavior to continue, but don't allow them to get you uptight—which may be their whole purpose. Try to get at the reasons for their aggressiveness and then deal with them. Work towards an agreement to finish the week with no more aggressive incidents.

3. Cabin take-over.

Occasionally you will get a camper who is aggressive enough to challenge your leadership of the cabin group. He will talk loudly, try to get you uptight, and draw the other campers to side against you. A counselor's natural reaction will be authoritarian: to take control. You will be more effective if you balance control with love and support. Try to get behind the aggressiveness of the camper and see why it is there. Don't ignore or override the camper, but befriend him. However, be careful not to reward his acting out. Often his aggressiveness is a learned way of gaining attention and acceptance, so show him that you are ready to offer these unconditionally.

DESTRUCTION OF PROPERTY

1. Practical jokes.

Practical jokes can be fun. I know, because I have been involved in many, on both sides of the joke. Among my favorites was the time my CIT's tied me to a chair in front of the whole camp for a "Great Houdini" spoof (so they told me) and then proceeded to decorate my bald head with felt markers and shaving cream.

But practical jokes can also be thoughtless and destructive. Some of this can be prevented by establishing a "Practical Joker's Code Of Ethics" at the start of the week if your group seems inclined that way (e.g., no one's stuff can be taken or ruined, it has to be fun for everyone involved, etc.). When someone has played a tasteless practical joke, forget about the joke part of it (especially if the joke was on you) and deal with the damage done to things or people's feelings. Let your campers have fun, but not at the material or emotional expense of others.

2. Raids.

Most camps no longer permit any invasion of other people's cabins, but "raids" still occasionally happen. If you overhear campers talking about "raids," let them know you are aware of their conversation and warn them of the serious consequences of their plans. Many younger campers seem to almost *want* to be raided, and may report a raid to you the first time someone rumples their sleeping bags. Sometimes they even mess up their own cabin so they can say they have been "raided." If your cabin is messed up by another group, talk with the head counselor about it and do your best to calm the anger, accusations and threats of retaliation.

3. Damaged property.

Campers who purposely or carelessly destroy another camper's property (or the camp's property) should be held liable if there is no doubt about what they have done. If possible, this should be taken care of at camp (for example, a camper replacing a ruined flashlight with one bought from the camp store). If not, the camper's parents should be contacted. Unless it is very minor, it is not good discipline to let purposeful damage go unpunished by simply saying it is too bad and that the camper shouldn't have done it. Teach them the costly consequences of failing to respect another person's property.

PROBLEMS OF THE TONGUE

1. Swearing.

There are three basic forms of swearing: obscenity (using socially unacceptable words that describe body parts and functions), profanity (using God's name or God's stuff improperly), and cursing (verbally abusing or controlling another person). This language goes against the standards of a Christian camp, and as guests in our place campers must uphold the house rules. Don't ignore swearing, but keep on top of it right through the week if necessary. Talk with campers about their offensive language and why it is a problem (many kids do not even know it is a problem), and offer help in overcoming it. Bad language should be considered verbal abuse and dealt with seriously.

2. Inappropriate stories.

When campers are hanging out together it is natural for them to pass on their personal repertoire of jokes and stories to one another; unfortunately, there seem to be more bad ones than good ones out there these days. It is appropriate to set higher standards for jokes and stories than campers are used to; it is only right that they live by the house rules. When a joke is starting to go past the boundaries of decency, don't hesitate to step in and stop it. If the person persists, talk with him personally and decide on consequences. There will be some fairly sheltered kids in your cabin who don't need to go home with seared consciences. Talk about why the stories are inappropriate.[161] Provide them with some good and hilarious examples of clean jokes from your own wealthy collection!

3. Put-downs.

In spite of our nations' attempts to promote "tolerance," it is still human nature to elevate ourselves by putting others down. There may be a place for put-downs in a joking manner, but even a joke can unintentionally do damage. "Like a madman shooting firebrands or deadly arrows is a man who deceives his neighbor and says, 'I was only joking!'"[162]

Make it a standard in your cabin group to be *constructive* in your language with one another. "Do not let any unwholesome talk come out of your mouths, but only what is helpful for building others up according to their needs."[163] Constructive language could possibly include the competitive kind of fun that stands for "intimacy" among guys as they slam one another. What you should avoid in your group is the negative and destructive language that the world uses every day out of insecurity and pride. Help those who have developed this habit to see why it is inappropriate, and to develop more positive language.

ATTITUDE PROBLEMS

1. Uncooperative campers.

The reasons for an uncooperative spirit in a camper may range from shyness to rebellion, but will always put a drain on your time and energy, and cause problems for your cabin group. As soon as you detect this attitude, take the time to talk with the person and explore the reasons for his uncooperativeness. You may discover he is angry about being dumped at camp or getting stuck in a cabin where he has no friends. He may be homesick or feeling insecure. It is better to deal with an attitude as a counseling problem first than to have it as a discipline issue all week.

Some campers seem to never be where they are supposed to be, because of their attitudes or lack of self-discipline. Make regular head counts of your campers at meals and other events where they are to be together. Anticipate the uncooperative campers' habits so you can remind and motivate them to go where they are expected. Check occasionally to make sure they have been at their activities when you were not scheduled to be with them.

2. Prejudice.

Thankfully, many children and youth pay little attention anymore to differences in race, culture and ability. But prejudice (or "pre-judging") will always be with us, and is likely to show up at camp. This attitude is defeated when people take the time and effort to get to know one another and discover what they have in common. Don't tolerate labeling and name-calling and exclusion of the "different" camper. Instead of lecturing the prejudiced camper, help him see that he is judging before he has given someone a chance, and encourage him to get involved with those he is judging.

3. Big mouth.

Some kids are just loud and obnoxious. This may be part of their personalities, which shouldn't be disciplined. However, you can help the obnoxious child learn to be more aware of people around him, and to think before he acts or speaks. Be firm, but be ever loving and accepting. Don't let him get away with doing damage to other campers' dignity or self-esteem, and encourage him to take up his responsibility to put the needs of others ahead of his own.

4. No respect for authority.

When you feel threatened by a camper's lack of respect for you, your natural reaction might be to *demand* respect. The place to begin with a disrespectful child is with your own attitude: Do you really need to defend yourself or your authority with this person? Get it in perspective. This child is hurting, angry or untrained. Perhaps she is only testing you, and you have an opportunity to become one of the few people she has learned to respect. Don't allow campers to back-talk you or speak to you disrespectfully. Tell them you will only listen if they talk in a normal tone and manner. Some campers have learned to use a disrespectful tone or pretended ignorance to manipulate adults into becoming flustered; don't play their game. Let them know who is boss, but also let them know you love them and have chosen to spend a whole week with them. Whether or not you finally win their respect, be ever deserving of it.

SUBSTANCE ABUSE

1. Smoking.

Researchers agree that nicotine is a drug equally addictive to hard drugs such as cocaine. Most smokers begin their addiction as children or young youth and within a year are almost incapable of quitting. Camps have varying policies concerning smoking; some provide a place for smoking, while other camps send smokers home. You will be expected to follow the camp's policy and not simply ignore infractions.

You can help the child or youth who is addicted to nicotine. Encourage him to make this the week that he begins to overcome the habit that controls him. Some camps provide help such as nicotine gum as a substitute, though some kids will be too embarrassed to use it. They *can* go for a week without the drug, but you should expect that this will affect their moods and emotions.

2. Drugs and alcohol.

Alcohol and illicit drugs are not part of any children's or youth camp. In the Christian camp, this should apply to all staff as well. Any use or sale of drugs or alcohol by campers or staff must be reported to the camp leaders, who will likely advise the counselor how they are to proceed with discipline.

When a child or youth shows signs of suffering from an addiction—mood swings, physical discomfort, sweating, anxiety—or wants to talk about his addiction, gently help him think through the extent of his problem. An addicted person usually denies having a problem and can be manipulative. You could discuss with him questions such as this: "Do you ever find yourself using more of your drug than you or your friends think you should?"[164] This question alone would identify a drug addiction about 90% of the time.

It is likely that after an initial discussion about his problem, you will need to refer the camper to other help, starting with the head counselor. You can continue to be a firm support to him. Be sure to keep his problem as confidential as possible.

GUY /GIRL PROBLEMS

1. Camper to camper.

Your camp will have a standard of conduct between the sexes, and you will be expected to enforce—and exemplify—its policies. If you observe inappropriate behavior between a guy and girl, don't ignore it. Talk with their counselors, and if one of your campers is involved, talk privately with him or her yourself. The camp's standard may be a new idea to some campers, and this will give you a good opportunity to discuss with them God's view and purpose for sexual behavior.

If you know that one of your campers has developed a relationship with another camper, you will need to be more aware of where they are at all times, and will need to keep them involved in the program and not just with one another. Show them respect, but make sure they also respect one another and those around them.

2. Infatuation with staff.

It happens every summer: staff get little notes passed on to them from some secret admirer. It may seem cute, but remember that to the camper it is no joke. He or she feels something for the staff member that has been interpreted as true love. Emotions are involved here, and they can be damaged or encouraged easily. If you receive such attention and you know its source, go to the camper, thank him or her and say that you are glad to be a *friend* (yes, you can gently and tactfully put stress on that last word).

Watch yourself. It feels good to have that kind of attention from someone who may be only several years younger than you. Never take advantage of such attention. Allow no physical contact or time alone with this camper. Some children or youth who have been abused or sexually active at an early age become seductive and promiscuous, particularly with people older than themselves. If the problem persists, talk with that camper's counselors, who should gently help their camper return to reality and deal with his or her emotions.

CONTROL PROBLEMS

1. Disruptions at firesides, chapel and other meetings.

At the beginning of every fireside, chapel session or other meeting, locate all your campers. Younger campers will usually sit with you, but older ones could be anywhere. Make sure that they are all there, and do what is necessary to locate yourself strategically in among campers, especially those who might cause a disturbance. If they haven't left space for you, move yourself in among them in a friendly way. It is better to move campers around to prevent a disturbance before everything starts than to move them because of a disturbance later.

If there is a disruption (e.g., campers talking during the speaker's time, or bothering people around them, etc.), the best method of dealing with it is to trade places with one of the trouble-makers. Don't remove someone out of the meeting except as a last resort. Generally this makes a bigger disturbance than the one caused by the camper. Campers who are not participating (e.g., not singing or not standing with everyone) are not necessarily being disruptive and should not to be forced to participate. Instead encourage them by your own example and enthusiasm.

2. Problems at meals.

Mealtimes are very important at camp because they are one of the few meeting-points in the busy daily schedule. Make them fun times, but don't allow campers to spoil the fun of others around them. The smallest food fight will escalate into chaos in no time. A camper who spoils another person's plate of food will also destroy his appetite. Meals are a time when conversation flows easily, but it will be up to you to keep the topics positive and constructive. Maintain firm but friendly control at meals, and direct potentially disturbing energy into fun stuff—like straight-face contests to see who is going to scrape the plates—so that, as with all discipline, the result is a better relationship with your campers.

3. Campers out-of-control.

Pray that it will not happen, but on rare occasions (sometimes on the last night of the week), campers will go wild, imagining that if everyone gets involved no one is going to get sent home. It can be very unnerving to counselors and staff to realize that control is slipping from their grasp, and it can cause them to do some very unwise things such as scream and yell and start grabbing kids.

You want the campers to calm down, so remain calm yourself. Work together to get the more mature campers back on-side, and from there get to the real instigators of the "riot." These are the ones who will need discipline—there is not much purpose in disciplining everyone. The head counselors will be involved from this point with the instigators, but it will be left to you to deal with the physical and emotional damages in your own cabin.

[160]John 8:7

[161]Ephesians 5:3-14 is a good basis for this

[162]Proverbs 26:18-19

[163]Ephesians 4:29

[164]Josh McDowell and Bob Hostetler, *Handbook on Counseling Youth*, ©1996 Word Publishing, p. 408

D.   ROLE PLAYS AND SCENARIOS TO HELP YOU WITH DISCIPLINE ISSUES

This section goes along with CAMP PREP #6, *which suggests that you get together with a few others and have fun (seriously!) role-playing these scenarios. To make it more fun and challenging, try using the rules of Theater Sports games, such as the right to yell "freeze" and take over the part of someone you think is doing a bad job of it, or acting it out in a certain style such as country and western or opera. If this is beyond your personal inhibitions, at least read these scenarios. Choose a few and write an ending to the story, describing how you as the counselor would handle the situation and how you imagine it might work out. Resource Section "C" will help you with your decisions.*

#1   As you enter the cabin, ten year old Stephannie is sitting with the other girls on one bunk, looking at a teen magazine. She is doing most of the talking and is so absorbed that she doesn't seem to notice you. Stephannie is telling the girls quite a number of things that don't sound true, such as talking about people pictured in the magazine whom she has met personally, places she has been and opportunities she had to be in photo shoots herself. Some of the girls seem skeptical, but most are taking it all in with wide eyes. Will you intervene? What kind of help does Stephannie need?

#2   It has been a very frustrating wide game, invented by a fellow staff member on the spur of the moment. You haven't seen the guys in your cabin for at least half an hour and wonder what they are up to. Finally you discover them holed up in the bush; they are counting a huge pile of ribbons and film canisters to see how many points they are accumulating. You ask Brandon, their natural leader, where they got all those points, and he excitedly tells you about a loop-hole in the rules that they have been exploiting for most of the game. When you start to tell them that what they are doing is cheating, Brandon says, "Hey, it was a counselor who told us how to do it!" How will you respond?

#3   He shouldn't have brought it to camp, but that's not the point now. Aaron's expensive CD player is missing from his backpack. He is furious, and he has already accused two other campers in the cabin of stealing it, though they deny touching the disc player. Aaron found a CD in one of their bags. However, CD's have been lying around the cabin all week. If you don't do something soon, there is going to be a fight. What could have prevented this from happening, and what are you going to do about it now?

#4   It started with one bigger camper pushing his way into the line-up at the camp store. He had done it before, but this time a camper about his size took exception. In no time they were going at it with fists and feet, with the whole line-up crowded around to watch. By the time you arrive, they have already hurt one another—there is blood on their clothes. Suddenly someone in the crowd tosses in a baseball bat, which the two youth start fighting over desperately. You know this has to end now. No other staff have come to the scene yet. What should you do—and not do—to end the fight and deal with the issues?

#5   Among your campers is a very little girl named Tara whom you can hardly believe is 12 years old. The other 12 and 13 year olds in your cabin are much more mature physically and emotionally. You suspect that two of them are picking on Tara when you are not around. You have twice come into the cabin to find her crying by herself, but she won't tell you what happened. The second time she had a big bruise on her upper leg. When you ask the other girls later, no one seems to know anything about it. What will you do to protect Tara without adding to her problem, and how will you deal with those who are doing this?

#6   You have a very large and loud camper named Megan. You have never known such a domineering girl in your life. All the campers in your cabin feel intimidated by her, though they laugh when she makes rude remarks and acts up. This morning she had the nerve to take the rest of the girls to the waterfront—which was closed—while you thought they were doing cabin clean-up on their own. Right now she is sitting across from you on her bunk, looking defiant and defensive. You are pretty angry yourself, especially after the waterfront director bawled *you* out for this incident. How are you going to handle this one? What does she really need from you?

#7   It should have been funny. It was the old joke where you put a full bucket of water above a door so it spills on the next person who walks in. Trouble is that no one told your campers that they have to tie the bucket up so only the water—not the full bucket—falls on the person's head. Now you have a camper in the hospital with a concussion, angry parents on the phone to the director, and a crew of very sheepish and silent junior campers sitting in front of you. One of them starts to cry. Now what?

#8   Don't you hate it when you overhear a conversation you would rather not have heard? You have a few campers this week who decided from the start that they don't like you. Arriving at the cabin in the mid-afternoon, you are surprised to hear voices there, since all of your campers are supposed to be at the waterfront. You stop to listen, and discover that they are planning to stick a sock (a dirty one) in your mouth and duct-tape you to your bunk during the night. Very funny. But then they start laughing and you realize they are into your suitcase. With what attitude are you going to enter the cabin now?

#9   There has been a big improvement in Jason's language this week. When he first arrived in the cabin, the 11 year old used every foul word in the book, plus a few you hadn't heard before. You kept on top of it, however, and Jason was responsive enough to eventually curb his tongue—except for using the Lord's name inappropriately. Jason is getting frustrated because he thinks he has done very well to change most of his vocabulary in less than one week. You wonder if it is worth it to keep commenting every time he says "Jesus" or "Oh God." What's your call? How will you back up your decision on this?

#10   Jillian is not having a good time. Not only that, but she is keeping the rest of your cabin from having a good time. She takes up so much of your day with her whining and refusal to participate that the other girls are suffering a lack of attention. The result is that they resent her even more, and let her know it, so that she clings to you all the time. She is not sleeping well (and keeps you up too) and hardly eats a thing. She has trouble making the smallest decision and spends much of the day crying. How can you help her without neglecting your other campers?

#11   It seems that Ryan thinks he is immortal. He walked right through the archery range, and if you had not grabbed Dave's bow at the last moment, Ryan would likely be lying there with an arrow through him right now. Instead, when you yelled at him in anger and disbelief, Ryan leaned back to spit at you with a look of utter disdain on his face. You can feel the anger surging in you now, and lots of words rising to the surface about ingratitude and stupidity. The thought even crossed your mind that you wished you hadn't stopped that arrow... Regain some perspective and decide what words are going to come out of your mouth.

#12   Walking along the path, an unmistakable scent of cigarette smoke drifts by your nose. You feel like ignoring it, because you know that the camp's policy is that anyone caught smoking will be sent home immediately. You don't want to be the cause of kids getting sent home. But at the same time, you are responsible to enforce the camp's standards. It makes sense—the woods are bone dry this time of year, and one neglected cigarette butte could result in disaster. Are you going to spring a surprise on these smokers or not? By their whispered voices, you know they have spotted you already.

#13   You have returned to the cabin to collect a camper's Bible for chapel, and are surprised to hear voices in the cabin as you approach—especially since one voice is of the opposite sex. Opening the door, a guy and girl madly scramble to move apart and adjust their clothing. There is an awkward silence as they stare at you with a combination of fear, embarrassment and defiance. Chapel has started, and you will be needed in a few minutes to lead a discussion with your campers. What will you say? What steps must be taken?

#14   You have a cabin full of junior high campers and it is the first night of camp. Devotions were over long ago, but your campers are still talking, yelling over to other cabins, and occasionally getting up out of bed. You tried telling jokes to help them wind down, but it only encouraged them to start up some rude ones of their own. Two other counselors have come to ask you to keep your cabin quiet, but they may as well have asked you to calm a raging sea. How will you enable everyone to get some sleep tonight?

#15   There has been a rumor going around all day that this last night of camp is going to be the wildest on record. In spite of warnings from the director, it seems the rumors were accurate. It is midnight and kids are running everywhere; only a few are staying in their cabins as they were told. Some of the other counselors are starting to lose their tempers, yelling at kids and trying to chase them down. You are surprised at some of the kids who are out running around, and when they see you, they look embarrassed at what they are doing. A few others are much more deliberate and defiant about it. What can you do to help bring order and peace back to this situation? Kids are going to get hurt if someone doesn't stop them soon.

#16   As soon as you saw the little group gathered in the back row at fireside, you could tell they would likely be disruptive, and so you sat close to them. Most of the group took this as a warning and resigned themselves to paying attention. But two other campers have taken it as a challenge. They keep glancing at you as they ride the edge of what is acceptable and what is disruptive, and several times they have gone over the edge, causing other campers to turn their heads. Finally, you tell one of them that you will be trading seats with him. He says, flatly, "No." Now what?

#17   You hate to admit it, but you probably started this food fight when you flicked a pea at a fellow counselor. Now your whole table is into it, sending food projectiles everywhere. One counselor has yelled out a warning to stop, but the campers are not stopping. Oh, oh—here comes the cook, normally a nice guy until he sees the food he prepared being wasted. The lecture begins, everyone stops, silence prevails—and one of your campers says, "But my counselor started it!" Now all eyes are on you. What little speech are you prepared to give now?

#18   One of your youngest campers is not at her assigned activity. After searching for ten minutes, you find her back at the cabin. She has evidently been crying, and is not yet ready to tell you what it is about. She just keeps saying that she wants her mom. Nothing you say makes any difference at all. This could be a long afternoon. How will you start helping this camper?

#19   It is 3:00 a.m. and something has awakened you. Sitting up, you see the dim outline of one of your campers doing something with her bed. Getting up and walking over, your nose tells you the problem before you get there. The camper is extremely embarrassed about having wet the bed and begins to cry softly. How might you have prevented this problem, and how are you going to deal with it tonight?

#20   A camper with whom you sat on the bus seems to be everywhere you are. He has taken to jumping on your back when you least expect it, and sitting on your lap every time you sit down. It might be okay if you could have a decent conversation with him, but he talks non-stop about every bit of nonsense you can imagine. At this rate you are going to be exhausted in a very short time. How can you retain your sanity without hurting his feelings or turning him against you?

E.   RAINY DAY IDEAS TO KEEP YOUR CAMPERS HAPPY

A little rain can change the atmosphere at camp in more than one way. Here are 30 ideas to create happy campers in those times when activities are canceled, rest time is declared or rain keeps you all under one small roof. In addition, many of the ideas for Bible discussions in Resource Section "G" can also overcome the gray sky blues. See also the books listed in Resource Section "J."

• **Have a lazy morning.** Sleep in, bring your campers breakfast in bed (arranged the night before or earlier in the morning with the cook) and stay in your pajamas all morning. But if you choose this route, be ready to later expend the energy they are saving up!

• **Have a pity party.** Give each person five small stones, pennies or candies. Have each person in the circle say one thing he or she has never had opportunity to do (e.g., ride a horse, go to Disneyland). Everyone who *has* done that activity must give one stone, etc. to that person. See who ends up the richest in "pity" after several rounds.

• **Do cabin Olympics.** As a cabin, make up a list of crazy Olympic events, such as the straw javelin toss, the pebble shot-put, the little bug marathon and the one-legged long jump. Enter each person in several events, and perhaps invite another cabin over to compete with you.

• **Make a cabin family tree.** It is unlikely that the people in your cabin are closely related, but you never know! Plus, you can fill in the gaps with imaginary ancestors who make you one big happy family. Chart it out on a big piece of paper. Can you "prove" that you were all descended from Cinderella and her prince?

• **Tell a cabin story.** Start a story about your cabin off the top of your head, and after a sentence or two, point to a camper to carry on the story. When he has contributed ten seconds worth, point to someone else. Occasionally, let each camper contribute just a word or two. See where the story leads, but steer it clear of offensive topics.

• **Untie a cabin knot.** Begin by gathering your campers in close huddle in the middle of the cabin. Hold one hand up in the air and with the other grab the hand of a camper across the group from you, who grabs the hand of another camper, and so on. Have the last person grab your free hand. Now, try to untie the "knot" you have formed of yourselves without anyone letting go!

• **Play human tic-tac-toe.** Half of your cabin are "X's" (arms crossed above heads) and half are "O's" (arms in circle above heads). Make a tic-tac-toe grid on the floor with string or branches, line up on opposite sides of room, and on the word "Go!" each team tries to get three of themselves in a row, without pushing or shoving anyone.

• **Secret rock / paper / scissors.** Each person chooses one article of the famous trio, writes it on a piece of paper and puts it in his pocket without showing anyone. Everyone mingles in the room, stopping occasionally to whisper in each other's ear whether they are Rock, Paper or Scissors. Whoever loses each whispered confrontation (Scissors beats Paper, Paper beats Rock, Rock beats Scissors), dies dramatically on the floor. When no one is losing anymore, see which of the three articles has come out on top, and how many chose that one.

• **Spell my fingers.** Form two teams. Have each team write as many of the letters of the alphabet on the ends of their fingers as they can (i.e., four campers can get 40 letters on their fingers, or one and a half alphabets). Think of a word in which each letter is used only once (e.g., "rainbucket") and have the teams contest to be the first to spell it with their fingers.

• **Quick math.** Make this a tournament. Two campers face each other and on the word "Go!" hold out from zero to ten fingers. The first one to mentally add up the total fingers between them and shout out the number is the winner.

• **Interrogation.** Give your campers five minutes to ask any question about *you* that they can think of, and give them quick answers. Then ask them a list of questions you made up ahead of time (for example, "What is the name of my dog?" or "What is my birthday?" or "What is my favorite color?"). Have them write down the answers to see who was paying attention the best.

• **Play "spin the bottle" (with a twist).** Rather than kiss anyone (yuck!), the one who has the bottle pointing to him or her must take out a rolled up piece of paper with instructions on it and do what it says (e.g., "Tell us your most embarrassing moment" or "Go to the nearest person wearing something green and give him a back massage").

• **Colored values.** Take several sheets of paper of various (preferably bright) colors and cut them into hundreds of small pieces. Toss them all over the cabin (don't worry, it will be okay!). Then have everyone gather up as many as they can, telling them that the various colors are each worth points. Then have them trade with each other for the colors they think are worth the most points. When they are all satisfied, tell them the (pre-determined) value of each color and have them add up their points to determine the winner. This can lead to a discussion about what is really valuable in life, and what only *seems* valuable.

• **Silent line-ups.** Challenge the campers to line up, *without talking*, in order of the month they were born, or alphabetically according to last names, or according to the first digit of their phone numbers. A good team-building activity.

• **Toe tilting.** Have each one find a partner, face one another and grab each other's shoulders. On the word "Go" they try to step on one another's toe. Have winners face winners, and losers face losers, until a champ is found.

• **Cabin investigation.** Give every camper a slip of paper with a category of information that they have to find out about every other cabin member (e.g., middle name, favorite kind of ice cream, name of school, town of birth, favorite TV show). They must talk with one another and try to get the info on as many campers as possible, while not giving away what category they are after (e.g., don't ask, "So, what's your middle name?"). After a certain time period, everyone tries to guess what each person's category was. Then each person divulges the information he has gathered.

• **Ya ya, no no.** Like with the old game "hot and cold," an object is hid somewhere in the cabin, and a camper tries to find it. He is guided by the rest of the cabin, who say, "Ya ya ya!" louder and louder as he moves toward the object, and "No no no!" louder and louder as he moves away from it.

• **Play a cabin version board game.** Choose a familiar board game (e.g., Monopoly) and create a cabin version of it, using only items found in and around the cabin and using names and categories that have to do with the camp.

• **Two truths and a big fib.** Have each person say two things about himself that are true and one that may sound true but isn't. The rest of the group tries to decide which is not true.

• **Hot 'tator.** The old game "hot potato" is fun, but try tossing back and forth something that winds up and makes a noise when the time is up, such as an alarm clock or toy, or one of the commercial toys made for this sort of game.

• **I went to camp.** Have each person in turn finish the sentence, "I came to camp and I brought..." Start the game yourself, naming an item that corresponds to the initials of your first and last name (e.g., if your name was "Jo Schmoe" you could say that you brought "Jelly Salad"). For each camper who doesn't catch on, tell him that he is "not ready" for camp, until after several rounds he finally names something that corresponds to his initials.

• **De-sock 'em.** Have everyone put on socks and sit in a circle. Call out two to four names and say, "De-sock 'em!" Those campers try to pull off each other's socks without losing their own.

• **Bang! Bang! Who did I shoot?** Use your finger to "shoot" anybody and everyone you like. Then ask, "Who did I shoot?" and let them guess. They will not get it right even after you do it several times, because the person you "shot" was the first person to *speak* after you said, "Who did I shoot?"

• **Play reverse charades.** There are multiple versions of the old game of charades, from acting to drawing to writing with your bum the word or phrase to be guessed. Try this one: everyone but the person doing the drawing knows the word or phrase, and they tell him what lines to draw and where, until he guesses what he is drawing.

• **Dictionary.** Another oldie but goodie. Each camper chooses a difficult word out of a dictionary (like "quixotic") and writes down several definitions for it. One is correct and the rest only *sound* correct. As each camper in turn reads his or her word and definitions, the other campers decide which is the right definition, receiving points for getting it right.

• **I like everyone.** Have everyone except one cabin member sit in a circle on the floor, and mark each of their spots with a pillow or stuffed animal to sit on. The remaining cabin member stands in the middle of the circle of campers and says, "I like everyone except..." then names a characteristic such as "people who know how to waterski" or "those who are wearing boxers." Everyone with that characteristic has to switch places, while the one in the middle tries to find a seat. The one left without a seat then goes into the middle.

• **Who, what, where.** Sit in a circle, and have everyone whisper in the ear of the person to their right a new identity of *who* they are (e.g., Wayne Gretzky, or a TV star). Then they turn to the person on their left and whisper what they are *wearing*. Mix up the circle, and conclude with (to the right) what they are *doing* and (to the left) *where* they are. Then have everyone reveal the four parts of their "new identity" to the group (e.g., "I am Luke Skywalker wearing a potato sack while sun-tanning on the subway"). Insist on keeping it clean and kind!

• **Bag biter.** Stand a large brown paper bag in the center of the room and challenge your campers to pick it up with their teeth, hands behind their back. Then cut off the top inch or two of the bag and let them try again. See who can pick up the bag at its lowest level as you keep trimming it away.

• **I can, can you?** Each camper in turn makes a claim to be able to do some unusual thing (anything from a one-arm chin-up to quoting twenty Bible verses) and challenges anyone in the cabin to match it. Of course, they have to be able to prove their claim!

• **Become a percussion band.** The neighboring cabins may never forgive me for this—unless you make it sound *good*! Experiment with different sounds that can be made by campers within the cabin and orchestrate it into a cool rhythm. Practice quietly at first, and when it is perfected, let the whole camp hear it! Decide on a signal to stop and leave the camp in dead silence.

F. A WORKSHOP TO HELP YOU PREPARE YOUR OWN BIBLE DISCUSSIONS

Yes, it is time to go to work! There is no better way of becoming familiar and comfortable with cabin devotion preparation than doing it. You might be tempted to just read this chapter and "pretend" you are writing things down, but I implore you not to yield to temptation! Your campers will suffer for it! Put the book down and grab a pen, about three pieces of paper and a Bible, and any Bible study resources you might have about you. You will be very glad you did (honest!).

Got everything? Okay, here we go. What we are about to do might take half an hour or more, which is probably more time than you will have when you are counseling a cabin of kids. But it will give you a better idea of how to prepare and next time it won't take nearly so long.

DETERMINE THE NEEDS OF YOUR CAMPERS

Hmmm... if you are doing this at home or as part of a training seminar, you don't *have* any campers. So you will have to create your own (if you *do* have campers, where did you find the time to read this book? You are incredible and probably don't need me at all!). Anyway, make a list of your "virtual campers" on a piece of paper (see the example below), and give them any names you like.

Then for each name, jot down (using rich imagination, and the first thing that comes to mind):

• *Their home situations.* Who lives there (M for mom, D for dad, C for cat, etc.), whether their families have any church involvement, and if the camper shows any spiritual interest. Include any special problems or situations you are "aware" of.

• *Their learning styles.* From your "observation" of them, where would you place these kids on the continuum between being very analytical in their learning style (kids who like details and things with steps to them) or very intuitive (kids who like to just do things, not plan them)? By the way, I am a very intuitive person using an analytical method to teach you, so I hope in this way to cover everyone's style.

- *Their needs and interests.* Imagine some questions they have asked you recently, topics of conversations you have overheard, and other indications of their concerns, fears, interests and curiosities. What things have happened this week in your cabin group that has had a significant effect on each one? By the way, the camp speaker is talking about *honesty* this week.

My list looks like this (and I made mine to be all ten year old boys). I hope you are more creative than I am, and that you will copy me only if desperately short of time:

Billy	M/D/B/2S/Gerbils. Attends church with family regularly. Knows everything. Analytical. Wants to know why God lets people suffer. Pet dog died recently.
Joe	M/Boyfriend. No church. Mildly curious about God. Intutive. Talks about girls all the time (already!). Hardly ever sits still.
Sam	D/Step mom. Attends church seldom. Intuitive. Seems bored and lethargic all the time. Would rather be on the skateboard ramp. Fight with another camper this week. Still talking about getting even.
Hermy	M/D/2B/1S. Attends church regularly. Analytical. Challenges everything I say about God. Nearly uncontrollable behavior this week. Scared of dark.
Frederick	M/D/Dog. Home schooled. Attends church regularly. Intuitive. Always comes up with the right answer. Gets picked on by other campers, and finds this hard to understand.
Dan	M/D/S/Horses. No church. Intuitive. Outdoorsy guy—would rather be sleeping in the woods. Christianity is all new to him, doesn't seem very interested. Homesick for horses.
Ryan	M. Attends church occasionally. Analytical. Very hurt emotionally, I think. Usually calm but has a violent temper. Turns his face away when we talk about God.
Jonathan	M/D/B. Can't remember name of church. Intuitive. Has reading and comprehension difficulty. Everyone likes him. Swims like a fish. Always concerned about doing the right thing, and gets upset if someone is dishonest.

Assessing my list above, I see that:

- *All the boys live with moms, but I can't assume more than that. Some have experienced the pain of a broken home, particularly Ryan. A few may be from fairly "sheltered" Christian homes and need to be challenged about what they claim to know. But I also need to bring in the gospel clearly. Some have never heard, and I can't assume they have understood.*

- *I have a wide range of learning styles to deal with, and Jonathan has learning disabilities. I won't go "around the circle" to have them read. I will have to use quite a variety of methods in my discussion to hold each one's attention.*

- *Several of them seem to be dealing with "fairness" issues this week (typical of this age group). Is God being fair with me? What do I do when people don't treat me fairly? Do people think of me as a fair person? These questions fit in well with the "honesty" theme of the Speaker. I think that "fairness" is at least one topic we will address this week.*

Get the idea? Now try it with your list. Take a look at your created crew and think about their *needs.* What are some spiritual concerns that they might want to discuss? Come up with two or three topics you could address.

Now think about what you have been studying in your personal devotions lately. What themes and concepts has God been pointing out to you? What issues have been on your mind? Write down passages and themes you have considered recently that your campers would relate to and benefit from. Add these to the topics you have determined by looking at the needs of your campers, and you will have a plethora of good ideas to discuss in your cabin devotions this week! Good job! Let's keep going...

ACCESS THE WORD OF GOD

1. Choose a Bible passage to discuss.

You may already have a Bible passage in mind. If not, take one of the topics you have chosen and think about the Bible passages that would address the topic. A Bible concordance (a list of words and the places in the Bible where they can be found) will help you; many Bibles have a concordance in the back. If you know of one verse on the topic, use the cross-references in the margin of your Bible to help you find related verses in other parts of the Bible.

What passages has the speaker been using in his talks? Were the campers challenged to memorize any verses this week? If you can't find an appropriate Bible passage on your own, ask a more experienced counselor to help you. Perhaps the camp will have other resources you can use.

In my case, I have decided to talk about fairness, and to base our discussion on Luke 6:27–36, which includes their memory verse for today, "Do to others what you would want them to do to you." How convenient!

2. Study the passage for yourself.

This is a good time to pray and ask God to teach you from his word so you can teach others. He won't mind that this is just a practice run. Besides, you may really use this discussion someday. Remember that when you want to use God's stuff, you need to ask first.

Once you have prayed, write the reference of your passage at the top of a piece of paper, and take notes as you briefly and prayerfully study the passage with the intention of applying it to *yourself*.

- *What does it say?* Read the passage a few times (try reading it out loud!), and read the passages before and after it. What ideas and phrases stand out to you, and what have you never noticed when reading this before? What seems to be the purpose of the writer, and to whom is he writing? Are there any words you don't understand? Jot down your observations—they will be useful to you in a moment.

In my passage I noticed that Jesus is speaking to ordinary people like me. He isn't focusing on how people treat us, but on how we need to deal with others. We need to treat people fairly, and more than fairly. I think it is cool that his own heavenly Father is the example he offers of how to treat people fairly.

- *What does it mean?* What is the main point or idea in this passage? How does it compare with other passages in the Bible on this topic? What is the real issue here? Keep jotting notes.

In Luke 6:27–36, the main idea is summed up in the memory verse: "Do to others what you would want them to do to you." I discovered by means of a cross-reference that this is also quoted in Matthew 7:12, where Jesus says that this rule sums up the whole Old Testament. In another place Jesus said that the law to love God and love people also sums up the Old Testament. Putting two and two together, it seems to me that "Do to others what you would want them to do to you" is just a very practical description of love.

- *What will I do about this?* Is there an action I should take? A promise I should claim? An attitude to change? An example to follow or a warning to heed? If I expect my campers to do something about this, what am I willing to do about it myself? What is there that I should pray about? Jot down your commitment, and go to it!

Hmmm... this passage strikes home! Will I treat my campers as I would want to be treated? Will I be fair—and more than fair—with them? I need to apologize to my friend Tom for blowing up at him before I had heard the whole story. I will need to listen to my campers better than that.

CREATE A DISCUSSION

Now that you have done your research and applied it to yourself, you are ready to lead your campers to the same discoveries you have made. Grab another piece of paper and work out your plan for the three parts of your discussion. If you are hungry, you could think of your devotional as a sub sandwich! The "Ready" and "Go" sections are the easy-to-chew parts that form the bun, and the "Set" part—the discussion—is the "meat" sandwiched in-between!

1. Ready.

How will you get your campers *ready* to think and move in the direction you want to take them on this adventure? How will you motivate them to explore this Bible passage with you? You need to choose a starter question, or an activity like a game or object lesson or role play to get them interested and get them talking—and have a bit of fun! This part of your "sandwich" needs to be tasty and easy to bite into. Check out Resource Section "G" to get an idea of the kinds of activities you could use.

Once you have chosen an idea to get started, how will your activity or question lead into the discussion of your Bible passage? What questions can you ask that will help them catch the point of what they have just done or discussed, without just giving it away? What will be the transition from your activity or question to opening up your Bibles together?

By a bit of quick initiative I managed to book the fire pit after the singing as the site for our cabin devotions. It will help keep Joe, Sam and Hermy occupied with sticks in the flames while we talk. I have decided to gross out my campers by suggesting that we play spin the bottle together, but of course by new rules: "Whoever the bottle points to takes out a piece of paper that gives him a question to answer." The questions I will put in the bottle relate to their feelings about being treated fairly or unfairly (e.g., "How do you feel when your parents get something for your brother or sister but not you?"). My transition to the Bible is simple: "Wouldn't it be cool if everybody treated you like they expect you to treat them? Let's take a look at what Jesus said..."

2. Set.

Here is where your campers will bite into the "meat" of God's word. What questions will you ask of the passage to get them interacting with it and with one another so that the main idea will be *set* in their minds? Some of your questions need to help them take a good look at the passage and notice what it really *says*. Ask other questions to lead them to the real issue—the main idea—and help them firmly understand what the passage *means*. Using your notes from your own study of the passage as a guide, jot down eight to ten questions, in any order.

This is a good time to evaluate your questions and make sure they will promote good discussion in your cabin group. Are your questions:

* *Specific to the Bible passage?* Or are they so general that they could apply to anything?

* *Easy to understand?* Or are they so deep that no one will understand what you are getting at?

* *Made for discussion?* Or will campers give a one-word answer (like yes or no)?

* *Asking for an opinion?* Or for "the answer"? Remember to avoid "leading" questions that force a certain answer.

* *Focused on the passage and leading to the main idea?* Or going off in various directions, never to be seen again?

* *Designed to challenge your campers to think and struggle with the issues?* Or so obvious that no one will want to look stupid by giving an answer?

- *Comprehensive enough to help them explore the whole passage?* Or based on just one phrase or verse?

- *Flexible, so that you can address your campers' needs as they come up, and so you can follow the leading of the Holy Spirit?* Or something you will be forced to march through without a break?

Here are my discussion questions, which I invite you to evaluate—not because they are perfect—because exactly one half of them are badly constructed! Can you pick out which ones fail the test? Also, can you pick out which ones are observation questions (about what the passage says), and which ones are interpretation questions (about what the passage means)?

1. *What are the reasons we should be kind to people who are unfair with us, according to Jesus?*
2. *You probably know what it means to be cursed by someone. How would you "bless" someone in return?*
3. *How can we apply what Jesus says to our lives?*
4. *What is the symbolic meaning of turning the other cheek, according to the usage and customs of the day in which Jesus gave this instruction?*
5. *What are some things that Jesus says we should do that sound like they are even more than fair?*
6. *Could Jesus possibly mean that we should keep on giving away our possessions to people until we have nothing left?*
7. *Who should we love besides people who love us and treat us fairly?*
8. *What would your friends think of you if you started treating them exactly like you would like them to treat you?*[165]

Once you have jotted down your discussion questions and weeded out or changed the bad ones, put them in a logical order. These questions should leave your campers with an understanding of the main idea of the passage. They should be ready to make some decisions about what they will do in response to what God is saying to them.

This is my corrected and re-ordered list of questions:

1. *What are the reasons we should be kind to people who are unfair with us, according to Jesus?*
2. *You probably know what it means to be cursed by someone. How would you "bless" someone in return?*

3. What do you think is the difference between following what Jesus says to do here and being a wimp?

4. How far do you think you should you take Jesus' instructions: until you get beat up; or until you have no possessions left; or what? Should you ever defend yourself or your property?

5. What are some things that Jesus says we should do that sound like they are even more than fair?

6. What does Jesus say you can expect to get out of loving your enemies and not just your friends?

7. How does God treat his enemies, who are ungrateful and wicked?

8. What would your friends think of you if you started treating them exactly as you would like them to treat you?

3. Go.

This last bite of your "discussion sandwich" should be as tasty and easy to chew as the first. How will you help your campers decide to *go* and do what they have learned? Will you use an activity, such as self-expression (e.g., a letter to God), or plan something (e.g., a surprise for someone who needs encouragement)? You might decide to simply use more discussion questions, as you did in the "Set" part of your devotional. These can be just as effective if they bring the campers to a point of decision. The lists given in Resource Section "G" contain many activities and questions that can help your campers apply the truth of God's word.

This is not an easy part of your discussion preparation, and you will be tempted to rush through it, wing it, or skip it all together. Remember, if you decide not to help your campers come to some conclusions about doing what God's word says, your Bible discussion (everything you have done above) was a waste of time. It would be the equivalent to looking in the mirror, seeing how you look and then walking away without having done anything about it.[166] Try *that* some morning!

Activities can be a great way to drive home the point and application of your Bible passage, especially for the more "intuitive" learners in your group. The important thing is to make sure the activity underlines the Bible passage and doesn't detract from it. Remember that younger campers will have greater difficulty with symbolism and metaphor and will need to have more things explained to them. Don't assume that campers have made all the connections you intended between the Bible concept and the activity. When you *observe* them making the connections, then you know they have caught it. For example, "Oh, I get it—praying to God is kind of like calling someone on the phone."

If you decide to use discussion questions for this section, make your questions very specific to the real-life situations of your campers at camp and/or at home. Obviously you will not ask, "So, how can we apply this to our lives?" or you will put the last of them to sleep and accomplish nothing. Ask questions that will help them think about what would change if they decided to obey God on the issue you have discussed. In your discussion, give campers the opportunity to make a personal commitment to doing what God's word says. For example, "Thinking about what Jesus said about love, how do you want to treat your own brothers or sisters differently when you get home?"

Prayer is another essential part of application. We tell God what we intend to do, by his grace, about what we have learned. Ask your more confident Christian campers to pray about a simple but specific part of your study; for example, that we would remember next time to ask God first instead of worrying first. You might have your campers express themselves to God in another way, such as a letter to him, or silent prayer as you look up at the stars. Encourage campers to think about their commitments during the day (that is, meditate on it), and to come to you with any questions they may have.

Write down your plan for making your campers aware that their discussion of God's word needs to affect the way they live.

I decided to ask my campers to make two columns on a piece of paper. On the one side they will write the names of their friends and on the other the names of their enemies, or people they don't like or can't forgive or who have been mean to them. Then I will ask them to choose two people on the "enemy" side who they want to move over to the friend side. A bit of discussion takes place here: what would it take to move them from the enemy side to the friend side? What would you have to do to make that happen? What might it cost you? How will the things that Jesus told us about loving our enemies help? We will finish off by sending our lists up in smoke to God as a sign of our commitment to love our enemies, and then I will pray out loud for each of my campers.

Well, there you go! How does your "discussion sandwich" look? Are you satisfied that you have these three components in place?

- **Ready.** Something to make your campers ready to explore God's word with you in an enjoyable way.

- **Set.** Discussion questions that will set the main truth of the passage in their minds in a form they can understand.

- **Go.** Something to help them decide what they will go and do in response to what they have learned.

If so, then you are ready to walk into the cabin, prayerfully confident that God will again send out his word and have it accomplish what he intends—through *you!*[167]

---

[165]Hey, you aren't cheating, are you? Remember, the speaker is talking about honesty this week! *After* you have evaluated my questions, check your evaluation against my own opinion: 1. is a good observation question; 2. is an okay interpretation question; 3. is neither - it belongs in the Go section, plus it is far too general; 4. is so deep that I don't even have a clue; 5. is a mixture of observation and interpretation, which is fine; 6. is a bad, bad leading question, and could be answered with one word; 7. is so obvious and brainless it is insulting; and 8. verges on being a Go type question, but would help campers struggle with the real issues, like being considered a geek for your fairness. As a result of being less-than-perfect, my questions also do not cover the whole passage. I will need to change them or cut down on the number of verses I will cover

[166]James 1:22-25

[167]See Isaiah 55:10-11 for a good promise to check out before you go

G. IDEAS FOR CREATIVELY STARTING AND APPLYING BIBLE DISCUSSIONS

Here is a list of ideas to get your campers ready for discussion. Of course, the more practice you have doing Bible discussions the more ideas you will discover or come up with on your own. But this is a good place to get started. Go nuts!

ACTIVITIES:
- Play a game, such as a treasure hunt to find "the most important thing in the world."
- Invite another staff member to visit your cabin dressed a certain way.
- Have them write a Bible verse out in their own words, or in a different style (e.g., poetry, rap).
- Walk to a place that suits the idea (be sure to check with your supervisor!).
- Do an interview like on a talk show.
- Conduct a poll or survey of the group.
- Play a simulation game, like trying to communicate to someone of another language.
- Compose a song, using a TV commercial jingle or a popular tune.
- Make a banner or poster for your cabin.
- Do a simple craft that you can use as an object lesson.
- Have them rate themselves 1 to 10 in terms of a characteristic (e.g., kindness) or ability (good listener) or habit (teasing your brother or sister).
- Do a dramatic presentation or skit or have a guest come and do it with you.
- Find out your campers' opinions by calling out four choices, pointing to a corner of the room for each choice. Campers go to the corner that best suits them.
- Publish a cabin newspaper, with stories of events and things they are learning.
- Surprise them with a multiple-choice quiz, combining fun and serious questions.
- Give them each five candies and have them mingle and talk. Each time they use the word "I" they must give one candy to the person they were talking to.

- Do a role play: you give them a situation and they have to act out what they would do about it.
- Read out loud a chapter of a book such as *The Lion, The Witch and the Wardrobe* (by C.S. Lewis—a wonderful analogy of the sacrifice and resurrection of Christ) or *The Princess and The Goblin* (by George MacDonald—great Christian theology in the story).
- Use a flashlight (or here on the West Coast, the phosphorous in the sea water) to discuss what it means that God is light, or that we are the light of the world.
- Play charades or "Pictionary" (one person draws, the rest try to guess what the drawing represents) using words related to your passage.
- Twenty questions—give the group twenty chances to guess a character, object or animal from the Bible by asking yes or no questions.
- Do a scavenger hunt for objects that describe the idea.
- Have a contest to see who can talk the longest in one breath about a certain topic.
- Go to the beach or into the woods in the dark—a myriad of creepy things are there to use to explain spiritual truth.
- Lie out in the field and look at the stars while you discuss a topic.
- Move your bunks together to make a cozy fort for your discussion.

SELF EXPRESSION IDEAS:
- "10 years from now..."—have them write down what they think will be their height, weight, hair style, location, job, dreams, successes, and best memories in 10 years.
- Theater sports—use classic drama class activities to help campers express feelings, guess some topic you want to discuss, or act out a parable.
- Tell or make up a story—one of Jesus' favorite methods.
- Discuss their feelings about a recent or upcoming event at the camp.
- Write a cabin storybook over the course of the week, with all of you as the characters.
- Have an object (e.g., teddy bear) that is passed to the person who wants to speak. Only the person with the object can speak and everyone else must listen.
- Make up a song or commercial about an idea.
- Draw a picture or sculpt something to express your opinions on something.
- Make a bumper sticker to express your opinion.
- Make "appreciation bookmarks" for one another.
- Ask them to write down questions they have always wanted answered.

STARTER QUESTIONS:

- When do you most hate waiting for your parents?
- What is the hardest thing about being your age?
- What I liked best about today was...
- I feel frustrated when...
- To make life better I would invent...
- When do you feel closest to God?
- What is your favorite name of God?
- What would you do with three wishes?
- What one quality do you look for most in choosing friends?
- What is something that really bugs you?
- What would be the "perfect family"? Would you fit in?
- Describe your best friend.
- If Jesus was sitting on this bunk, what would you ask him?
- What was your most embarrassing moment?
- If you could receive a sixth sense, what would you want it to be?
- Describe the best teacher you ever had.
- Jesus wept (John 11:35). When was the last time you cried?
- If you could give any gift to the world, what would it be?
- If there was an entry on you in an encyclopedia, what would you want written about you?
- What is the best advice you ever received?
- If Jesus was your age and went to your school, who would he hang out with?
- What is the best time you had with your friends in this past year?
- What is one thing you wish you had the courage to say to your parents?
- Would you rather ...be grounded or endure a lecture? ...die in an accident or after a long illness? ...be famous or be loved? ...

H.   HOW TO PREPARE YOUR PERSONAL TESTIMONY

One of the most effective ways of communicating the gospel to your campers is by sharing with them your personal testimony, the story of Jesus and you. This section will guide you through preparing your testimony effectively, and suggestions are given at the end for writing it out. You will be glad you took the time to do your part in getting ready, and you can be confident that God will do his.

Your testimony will include the story of your life up to the time of your initial encounter with Jesus, an account of who he is and how you put your faith in him, and a description of the changes in your life since then to the present. Paul gave us a good example of a personal testimony as he stood before King Agrippa:[168]

1. Where Paul came from.

> *"The Jews all know the way I have lived ever since I was a child, from the beginning of my life in my own country, and also in Jerusalem. They have known me for a long time and can testify, if they are willing, that according to the strictest sect of our religion, I lived as a Pharisee. And now it is because of my hope in what God has promised our fathers that I am on trial today. This is the promise our twelve tribes are hoping to see fulfilled as they earnestly serve God day and night. O king, it is because of this hope that the Jews are accusing me. Why should any of you consider it incredible that God raises the dead?*
>
> *"I too was convinced that I ought to do all that was possible to oppose the name of Jesus of Nazareth. And that is just what I did in Jerusalem. On the authority of the chief priests I put many of the saints in prison, and when they were put to death, I cast my vote against them. Many a time I went from one synagogue to another to have them punished, and I tried to force them to blaspheme. In my obsession against them, I even went to foreign cities to persecute them.*

2. What happened to change Paul's destination.

> *"On one of these journeys I was going to Damascus with the authority and commission of the chief priests. About noon, O king, as I was on the road, I saw a light from heaven, brighter than the sun, blazing around me and my companions. We all fell to the ground, and I heard a voice saying to me in Aramaic, 'Saul, Saul, why do you persecute me? It is hard for you to kick against the goads.'*
>
> *"Then I asked, 'Who are you, Lord?'*
>
> *"'I am Jesus, whom you are persecuting,' the Lord replied. 'Now get up and stand on your feet. I have appeared to you to appoint you as a servant and as a witness of what you have seen of me and what I will show you. I will rescue you from your own people and from the Gentiles. I am sending you to them to open their eyes and turn them from darkness to light, and from the power of Satan to God, so that they may receive forgiveness of sins and a place among those who are sanctified by faith in me.'*

3. Where Paul has been going since then.

> *"So then, King Agrippa, I was not disobedient to the vision from heaven. First to those in Damascus, then to those in Jerusalem and in all Judea, and to the Gentiles also, I preached that they should repent and turn to God and prove their repentance by their deeds. That is why the Jews seized me in the temple courts and tried to kill me. But I have had God's help to this very day, and so I stand here and testify to small and great alike."*

Note that Paul was supposed to be defending himself. Instead, he used the opportunity to share his testimony with the king, who responded, "Do you think that in such a short time you can persuade me to be a Christian?" The king had no idea. Paul would never presume to be able to persuade anyone into the kingdom, but he did know that as he faithfully shared the story of Jesus and Paul, that God himself would persuade hearts.

THE COMPONENTS OF AN EFFECTIVE TESTIMONY

You can develop your own testimony around the same outline Paul used:

1. Where I came from.

This is an account of your life up to the point of the first life-changing encounter you had with Jesus Christ. Are you concerned that your testimony will be less than effective because you can't talk about your life as a "Hell's Angel" before your conversion at the age of nine? No worries—just look at Paul. He went to church in diapers, grew up as a good boy, earned all of his Sunday school pins, and thought he was doing all the right things. Is that your story? Then it can be just as effective as Paul's account. There are many campers who are growing up just as you did, and yet have not realized their need for a personal faith in Christ.

Maybe you were a bad one. If your story is one of trying every door in the world before Jesus caught up with you, your testimony will also be effective, especially among those campers who are currently trying every door. You will need to be careful to keep your description of your life before Jesus appropriate to the age group to which you are speaking. All the gory details about sex, drugs and rock 'n' roll will only promote the fun of sin at a young age, not the need for Christ.

Do what you can to relate your story to the lives of your campers. Here are some suggestions about what to include:

- *Background on your family and yourself before you became a Christian.* If you grew up in a Christian home, talk about what that was like, since it will be a foreign world to some kids, and familiar to others. Otherwise, point to the things that made you realize your need for Christ.

- *Feelings of guilt or emptiness.* Though I became a Christian at an early age myself, I remember feeling guilty about my petty crimes and wondering what to do about it. I also remember feeling confused about this "ask Jesus into your heart" business. Include what you remember and things to which the listener might relate that will show your growing awareness that you needed a Savior.

- *Specific people and circumstances.* Include the names of people and the circumstances that brought you to the place of realizing your need for

Christ. Be specific, including the little details that make it an interesting story.

- *Research what you don't know.* What if you can't remember anything about your life before accepting Christ? Talk with your parents or brothers and sisters or pastor, who may be able to give you details you didn't even know. That would be exciting! You need to have this information for your own assurance of faith as well as for sharing it with others.

- *Re-dedications.* It is fairly common among those who have grown up in Christian homes to hear a testimony like this: "I accepted Christ when I was really young, but it wasn't until I was 14 years old at camp that I realized that Jesus died for *me* personally." Perhaps a re-dedication was the point in your life when you first had an encounter with Christ that was personal and life-changing. Make *that* event the focus of your testimony, with everything else leading up to it.

2. What happened to change my destination.

If there is any part of a testimony that I find to be consistently weak in my experience at camps, it is this one. And this is the most important part. The purpose of your testimony is to be an example that someone could follow to put his own faith in Christ. If you limit this part of your testimony to a brief, "...and then I accepted Jesus Christ as my personal Savior, and ever since then..." how is anyone going to follow your example? Your campers will be saying, "How was that again?" like when an expert demonstrates a complicated knot.

Slow down. Make this part of your testimony very simple and clear. Go through every step, and avoid the "professional jargon" we so often use. Explain in plain language what you did to put your faith in Christ. Here's an example: Like I said, as a child I was very bothered by guilty feelings and did all manner of weird things to cope with them. Once I read my King James Version Bible for the better part of an afternoon (comprehending little), and then tried to talk in its seventeenth century English because I thought it might make God happy with me again.

Then one night as my mom was tucking me into bed (I was about eight years old), I finally got up the nerve to pop the question: How does a person get to be a Christian? I was so surprised by her answer. She said I simply needed to tell God that I knew I had done many bad things (oh, how I knew it!), and that I believed that Jesus had died on a cross to take all my sins away. The light suddenly came on—*Jesus* had done it for me! God would forgive me and be happy with me because I trusted in Jesus, not because I could talk like King James! Mom helped me say all this to God, and I know that very night I was forgiven by him completely. He gave me the desire to turn away from my sins as an eight year old and do the good things he wanted me to instead.

Could you follow that example and know how to become a believer? I hope so. I purposely avoided clichés like, "asked Jesus into my heart" and "received Christ as Lord and Savior" and "became a Christian." There is nothing wrong with these phrases, except that we have come to say them without thinking about what they mean, and so when we use these phrases with campers they don't have a clue what we mean either. Even the word "sin" is a bit foreign to some kids, or may be interpreted as referring to ax murders. Here are some items you could include in this section of your testimony:

- *The realization of your need.* How did you come to understand that there was something missing in your life, or that you needed to be forgiven?

- *What you understood about what Jesus had done for you.* Notice that in my testimony I included only what I understood at the time. There is no word there about the deeper theological concepts I comprehended later. Just the things I needed to understand in order to come to faith in Jesus.

- *What you did (very specifically) to put your faith in Jesus.* Avoid clichés and phrases and say it in plain English! If you don't remember exactly what was said to you or the prayer you prayed, you at least know what must have been included in that event. You had a longing for a relationship with God, you agreed with him that you had sinned and deserved to be punished, you trusted in Jesus' death on your behalf to take way your sins, and you told God of your desire to turn away from your sin and live as he wants you to. Maybe not in those words, so you can word it in a way that suits you. But those are the things you did, and they are far too important to sum up with the phrase, "I asked Jesus into my heart."

- *Bible verses.* Hopefully, the person who led you to Christ took you to God's word at some point. Choose verses that were pointed out to you at the time of your conversion, or that you have since found helpful to understand the event.

3. Where I have been going since then.

The purpose of this part of your testimony is to show how faith in Christ is making a difference in your life. If there is any "salesmanship" in a testimony it is here. You know how you feel about the guy who paints too rosy a picture of the product he is selling, so be realistic about your life since accepting Christ. At the same time, you have much to bubble about. Let your campers know what life with Jesus is like. Here are some things you might include:

* *Things that are present in your life that wouldn't be without Christ.* Give examples of the love, joy, peace, contentment, purpose, hope and compassion you are experiencing.

* *Victories you are experiencing.* Talk about overcoming temptation, experiencing forgiveness, learning obedience and gaining confidence in Christ.

* *Your maturing perspective on things.* Talk about how your faith in Christ affects your daily attitudes, values, priorities and decision-making. Mention people God has used to help you grow, what God is doing in your experience *right now*, and where you think God is leading you for your future.

* *Bible verses.* Read or quote Bible passages that God has been speaking to you about lately, or that have helped you in a special way.

SOME THINGS TO AVOID

* *Roller Coasters.* Avoid sharing things that will give campers the impression that the Christian life is a roller coaster. For example, "Every year I come to camp it's a spiritual high, but a month later I'm right back to where I was. I hope it will be better this year..." That sets up the expectation that the Christian life will be the same for them, and that it is a normal pattern. It is not.

* *Bungy jumps.* If you have recently had a big fall spiritually, don't bring attention to it. For example, "Just before camp I was partying and getting drunk every night with my friends. But ever since coming to camp, things have been great!" If that is your testimony, perhaps you should have come to camp next summer, after a year of more victorious

Christian living. It may remove from the credibility of your testimony to talk about very recent defeats, and possibly raise doubts in campers minds about the quality of the rest of the staff.

- *Shock therapy.* I have heard testimonies that are more about shock than salvation. Stay focused on the purpose of your testimony: to bring glory to God. Avoid sharing things that would be inappropriate to your group, like sharing about your former sex life when speaking to junior campers.

PRESENTING YOUR TESTIMONY

When it comes time to give your testimony, pray and get other staff to pray for you. Share from your heart (not your paper) and don't be too concerned if it doesn't come out just the way you prepared it. God knows what your campers need to hear. You did your part as you prepared, and now he will do his. Offer campers the opportunity to ask questions when you are done. Sometimes campers will want to share their testimonies too (or at least their life stories) which can make for great discussion. Be alert to campers who are asking the serious, searching questions, or who seem to want to talk with you further.

PREPARE YOUR PERSONAL TESTIMONY

This is the point at which you need to pick up pen and paper (or turn on the computer), and start writing. Begin with notes—in any order—about everything you remember about your path to Jesus, your faith encounter with him, and the highlights of your Christian walk. Do whatever research is needed by talking with the people who know you best. Then organize your notes under the three categories we have discussed:

- *Where I came from.*

- *What happened to change my destination.*

- *Where I have been going since then.*

Finally, fill in your outline with the details, forming your work into as skillful a story as you are capable. Write it out just as you would say it to your anticipated age group of campers. Get someone who knows you well to read and critique it constructively, and write it out again. The more you work on it, the better it will get into your head so you can share it naturally and without notes.

You may be tempted to skip this part. Why not just wing it? If it should happen someday that you are compelled to give your testimony and have no opportunity to prepare, I have no doubt (and some biblical confirmation[169]) that God will give you the words to say. But if you have the opportunity to prepare ahead of time, and don't use it, why should he bail you out? There is no better way to get ready to share the story of you and Jesus than to take time to get it down in hard copy. Don't procrastinate! Do it today!

---

[168]See Acts 26:1-29

[169]For example, Matthew 10:17-20

I.   IDEAS FOR STAYING IN TOUCH WITH YOUR CAMPERS

My challenge to you is to make a commitment to stay in touch with your campers and be instrumental in their continuing discipleship for a minimum of one year! Here's some help...

FAITHFUL PRAYER

1. Make a prayer calendar.

Did you know that if you pray for one camper every day, you will pray for 300 campers between summers? Or 30 campers 10 times? Take a calendar, begin writing the names of campers at the bottom of each square, and when you get to the end, start your list over. Keep your calendar in a place where you will be sure to see it every day. Pray for one camper a day, and watch God at work!

2. Get some prayer help.

There are people in your church who have the gift of prayer, and who see prayer as their main ministry. They may be some of the more elderly people who have lots of time on their hands. Your pastor may be able to suggest a few. Go and ask them to pray for a few of your campers regularly. Of course, you shouldn't give out a copy of your whole camper profile, which is confidential. However, it would be okay to give them a camper's first name.

3. Set up a prayer line.

When you write to your campers or call them, give them your phone number, address or e-mail address with the invitation to send you prayer requests and the promise to pray for them. A news release I received recently said that churches in New York have set up prayer tables on the street, inviting people to come and have someone pray for them right there. "One time, volunteers at a booth prayed for 100 people within four hours."[170] People—including kids—are hungry right now to have someone pray for them.

PAINLESS LETTER-WRITING

1. Make a what-to-write-about list.

When you are attempting to write to a number of campers at the same time, make a list of things to write about: events that are happening in your life; memories from the summer; encouragements, challenges and Bible verses you would like to give them; news about the camp or other campers; and things you are learning from the word of God. If you are using a computer, you can "paste" individual ideas into their letters, then add some notes specific to that camper so it is unique and personal.

2. Hold a letter-writing party.

Perhaps you could invite a few other counselors over for a letter-writing party! You could hold one another accountable, share ideas and supplies and pray together for campers.

3. Make up a cabin newsletter.

One way to write many campers at once yet keep it personal is to write a newsletter that is specific to an entire cabin of your campers:

- *Give it a title that has something to do with that week of camp.* Make up a name appropriate for each cabin, like "The Cougar Report" or "Cabin 21 Review." Include funny "advertisements," cartoons and anything else your imagination allows.

- *Include some "news articles."* These can be about yourself and what has been happening with you—some funny, some more serious—and any news you have heard about members of the cabin.

- *Include a small section that is personal to each camper.* It could be a "Dear Abby Column," with the camper's name in the place of "Abby." Or it could be a "Personals" or "Help Wanted" ad directed at each camper. Be sure to sign it or add a comment by hand.

- *A newsletter is easy to do by hand.* Just fill up two pages with writing, doodles and camp memorabilia and photocopy it onto both sides of sheet of paper. Then add on the personal section by hand.

- *A newsletter can also be done on computer.* The personal section can be made by means of the "Print Merge" or "Mail Merge" option of your word processing program. Kids really like to see their names in print.

- *Invite campers to write back.* Include their drawings, photos and notes in your next edition.

4. Create cabin stationary.

Another painless and fun method of letter-writing is to photocopy a page with doodles (e.g., stick drawings of each camper, maybe with dialogue bubbles as in a cartoon), photos and other camp stuff all around the edges, leaving just a little room in the middle for you to write a personal note.

5. Initiate a round-robin cabin letter.

Send a small letter to one camper on a large piece of paper (or a cassette tape, or even video tape if they all have access to a video camera), and ask him to add to it and send the paper to the next camper on the list and so on, until it gets back to you. Then send it around again. Challenge your campers to keep it circulating all winter, letting it get larger and larger like a snowball!

6. Have the campers write to themselves.

Have each camper write something about his camp experience (such as what he learned, the highlights of the week, and decisions he made), collect them and mail them to each camper in six months time. Or do a round-robin encouragement card as described above. You could also have each camper choose another camper's name out of a hat, write a letter to that camper while at camp, and hand it in to you to be mailed out at a later date.

7. Send cabin birthday cards.

Buying cards is much too expensive. Make your own card specific to each cabin (clip art is great for those of you who are not artistic) and photocopy it. Perhaps it could relate to some funny or important event of that week of camp. Get ideas by visiting the card section of a store. Or make a card out of something such as a summer brochure. If you start this, be sure not to miss a birthday! Include them on your calendar and take time once a month to send out cards.

8. Send Christmas cards.

This is a perfect way to remind campers of Jesus and what he came to earth to accomplish. Who knows: maybe your card will be the only thing that will help them consider the true meaning of Christmas! Again, you could make your own cards. Or maybe you thought to pick up some inexpensive bulk cards when they were on sale last January.

9. Send a cabin bookmark.

Make a bookmark specific to each cabin. It can be photocopied on heavier paper called "card stock", which is available at any printer. Write a few words of encouragement on it, and send it with a note suggesting that they stick it in their Bibles at the places where they are reading.

10. Send a stamped, self-addressed postcard.

Are you not hearing from your campers? If you have the ability financially, consider enclosing a stamped, self-addressed postcard in your next letter, asking your campers to write a note and drop it in the mail to you. Most campers will return it, not wanting to waste your stamp.

11. Include an encouragement card.

Christian book stores often have small, inexpensive 2x3 cards that have a picture and a Bible verse or saying on them. I have known campers who have carried cards like these from their counselor in their Bible or wallet for years. A good investment.

12. Watch out for procrastination!

Every day you put off writing to your campers, you increase the possibility that you never will.

NON-AWKWARD PHONE CALLS

1. Identify yourself when you phone.

To avoid coming under the suspicion of a parent, always identify yourself to the person who answers the phone, even if you think it might be the camper: "Hi, I'm Jo Schmoe and I was Chris' counselor at camp this summer. I was wondering if I could say hello to Chris." If the parents are resistant or suspicious of your call, tell them that you respect their privacy and excuse yourself. Most parents will be very impressed that a camp counselor would call and glad you did.

2. Take the opportunity to talk with parents.

Sometimes you will have opportunity to talk with a parent, which can be very encouraging to you and reassuring to them. If a parent has complaints, encourage them to talk directly with your camp's administration office.

3. Think ahead about what to say and ask.

Campers will be surprised and possibly nervous about receiving a call from you. Think ahead about how you will set them at ease and the kind of questions you will ask them. A call does not need to be long to be encouraging.

4. Be careful to not make promises you can't keep.

Sometimes when we are not sure what to say, things might pop out that we later regret, such as "Maybe our whole cabin could go to a hockey game together some time." But it *is* appropriate to talk about opportunities you might have to see one another, such as a retreat or event that you know you will both attend.

5. Give them your "hotline" number to call.

You will have access to your campers' address and phone number, but do they have a way of getting yours? Give campers an address, phone number or e-mail address with which they can contact you, and invite them to call or write.

MEMORABLE GET-TOGETHERS

If a camper lives close by, invite him to get together with you occasionally. It will be best to get together with two or more at a time to make the event less intimidating to the camper and to relieve the possible suspicion of parents. His parents may want to meet you first, which is just more opportunity for you to be the light of your world.

1. Invite non-church campers to come to church with you.

Or volunteer to take them to kids club or youth group, asking the leaders if it is okay for you to come along until the campers feel comfortable.

2. Take campers out for a snack or meal.

Maybe you can't even afford to take yourself out, but if you can swing it, this can be a good venue for conversation.

3. Take them to an event that interests them.

Or go to watch them play their sport or perform their art. This kind of interest is a tangible expression of love, and builds common ground between you. It is also a time commitment, but ask God to open doors of opportunity.

4. Invite them over for a cabin party.

This one you can do even if they live a small distance away. I have known counselors whose campers came long distances to be at a weekend cabin party. Go swimming or bowling, make pizza or cookies, look at camp photo albums or videos, have fun, and spend some time talking about your spiritual lives. Make sure parents understand that you—not the camp—will be responsible for this event, and that it would be appropriate for them to help with the costs.

SOLID CHURCH CONNECTIONS

1. Find out who needs to be connected.

Many of the campers coming to Christian camps do not regularly attend any church. Some of these are not believers and have no interest in attending, and should not be pressured to do so. Many others have made a commitment to Christ but do not attend because they have no encouragement from home. A few are not permitted to go. Check carefully and determine which campers need to get involved in a local church.

2. Divide the responsibility with your junior, senior or co-counselor.

Talk with the ones who counseled with you this summer and divide up the responsibility for making sure non-church campers get connected. This may reduce your responsibility to just a handful of campers.

3. Find out if they have become connected and help them find a church.

This is worth a phone call, if you are able, or at least a personal letter. In an open, friendly way, talk with them about what church, youth group or kids club they are attending, who they go with, and how regularly. If they are not attending anything that will encourage their spiritual growth, offer to help them find a church. Your camp can help you locate one for them.

4. Help them get connected.

If you know of other staff members or campers in an area, contact them and ask if they will bring campers to church and help them get to know people. Check occasionally to see if they are still attending. Be very open and up-front with the unbelieving parents of a camper, and if they resist your efforts respect their decision. In that case, you may be the only Christian contact for the camper that year. Focus on staying in touch with campers in this situation, in a very sensitive way.

---

[170]*Religion News Today*, November 11, 1997

J.   A RESOURCE LIST FOR COUNSELORS

There are so many resources that would be useful to camp counselors these days that this can only be a small representation. Check out your local Christian book store for activity manuals, devotionals, Bible studies, clip art and books on serving children and youth. Your camp may also have many of these available to you.

DEVOTIONALS & STORIES

Jack Canfield and Mark Hansen, *Chicken Soup for the Soul: 101 Stories*, ©1993 J. Canfield & M. Hansen. Published by Health Communications, Inc., Deerfield Beach, IL

David Lynn, *Attention Grabbers for 4th - 6th Graders*, ©1990 Youth Specialties. Published by Zondervan Publishing House, Grand Rapids, MI

David Lynn, *High School Talksheets*, ©1987 Youth Specialties. Published by Zondervan Publishing House, Grand Rapids, MI

David Lynn, *Junior High Talksheets*, ©1988 Youth Specialties. Published by Zondervan Publishing House, Grand Rapids, MI

David and Kathy Lynn, *4th - 6th Grade Talksheets*, ©1993 Youth Specialties. Published by Zondervan Publishing House, Grand Rapids, MI

David and Kathy Lynn, *Zingers: 25 Real Life Character Builders*, ©1990 Youth Specialties. Published by Zondervan Publishing House, Grand Rapids, MI

Robert Lloyd Munger, *My Heart -- Christ's Home*, Revised edition ©1986 InterVarsity Press, Downers Grove, IL

Wayne Rice, *Hot Illustrations for Youth Talks*, ©1994 Youth Specialties. Published by Zondervan Publishing House, Grand Rapids, MI

Helen Turnbull, *Group's Best Discussion Launchers for Youth Ministry*, ©1997 Group Books, Loveland, CO

Jerry D. Jones, *201 Great Questions*, ©1988 NavPress, Colorado Springs, CO

DISCIPLESHIP & ANSWER BOOKS

K.C. Hinckley, *A Compact Guide To The Christian Life*, ©1989 NavPress, Colorado Springs, CO

Paul Little, *Know What You Believe*, ©1987 SP Publications, Wheaton, IL

Paul Little, *Know Why You Believe*, ©1978 InterVarsity Press, Downers Grove, IL

Josh McDowell and Bob Hostetler, *Right From Wrong*, ©1994 Word Publishing, Dallas, TX

Josh McDowell and John Stewart, *Answers to Tough Questions*, ©1980 Campus Crusade for Christ, Inc. Published by Here's Life Publishers, Inc., San Bernardino, CA

Josh McDowell and John Stewart, *Reasons Skeptics Should Consider Christianity*, ©1981 Campus Crusade for Christ, Inc. Published by Here's Life Publishers, Inc., San Bernardino, CA

PEOPLE-HELPER BOOKS

John G. Krus, *Quick Scripture Reference for Counseling*, ©1994 John G. Krus. Published by Baker Books, Grand Rapids, MI

Dr. G. Keith Olson, *Counseling Teenagers*, ©1984 Group Books, Loveland, CO

Joan Sturkie and Siang-Yang Tan, *Advanced Peer Counseling*, ©1993 Youth Specialties. Published by Zondervan Publishing House, Grand Rapids, MI

Josh McDowell and Bob Hostetler, *Handbook on Counseling Youth*, ©1996 Word Publishing, Dallas, TX

GAMES AND IDEAS BOOKS

David Burrow, *The Camp Counselor's Handbook of Over 90 Games and Activities Just for Rainy Days!*, ©1990 by David Burrow, Benjamin Publishing Co., Shirley, MA

Lane Eskew, *Quick Crowdbreakers and Games for Youth Groups*, ©1988 Thom Schultz Publ. Published by Group Books, Loveland, CO

Dan McGill, *No Supplies Required Crowdbreakers and Games*, ©1995 Dan McGill. Published by Group Books, Loveland, CO

Wayne Rice, *Great Ideas For Small Youth Groups*, ©1986 Youth Specialties. Published by Zondervan Publishing House, Grand Rapids, MI

Wayne Rice & Mike Yaconelli, *Play It! Great Games for Groups*, ©1986 Youth Specialties. Published by Zondervan Publishing House, Grand Rapids, MI

Beth Rowland, *Quick Games for Children's Ministry*, ©1992 Group Books, Loveland, CO

CHILDREN AND YOUTH MINISTRY TEXTS

Neil Anderson, *The Seduction of Our Children*, ©1991 Harvest House Publ., Eugene, OR

George Barna, *Generation Next*, ©1995 Regal Books, Ventura, CA

Reginald Bibby and Don Posterski, *Teen Trends*, ©1992 Stoddart Publishing Co., Toronto, ON

Ross Campbell, *How To Really Love Your Child*, ©1979 SP Publications, Wheaton, IL

Ross Campbell, *How To Really Love Your Teenager*, ©1981 SP Publications, Wheaton, IL

James Dobson and Gary Bauer, *Children at Risk*, ©1994 Word Publishing, Dallas, TX

Dr. Becca C. Johnson, *For Their Sake: Recognizing, Reporting and Responding to Child Abuse*, ©1992, American Camping Association, Martinsville, IN

John LaNoue, *A Notebook for the Christian Camp Counselor*, ©1978 Convention Press, Nashville, TN

Joel F. Meier and A. Viola Mitchell, *Camp Counseling: Leadership and Programming for the Organized Camp*, Seventh Ed., ©1993 Wm. C. Brown Communications Inc., Dubuque, IA

Rebecca M. Pippert, *Out Of The Saltshaker & Into The World*, ©1979 Inter-Varsity Christian Fellowship, Downers Grove, IL

Arlo Reichter, *The Group Retreat Book*, ©1983 Thom Schultz Publ. Inc. Published by Group Books, Loveland, CO

H. Norman Wright and Michael J. Anthony, *Help, I'm a Camp Counselor*, ©1986 by H. Norman Wright and Michael J. Anthony. Published by Regal Books, Ventura, CA

Young Life, *Training For Camp Counselors*, ©1990 Young Life, Colorado Springs, CO

JOURNAL ARTICLES

Silvana Clark, "ABC's of Working with Younger Children," *Camping Magazine*, July - August 1997

Robert Drovdahl, "Rethinking Evangelism," *Journal of Christian Camping*, July - August, 1989

Gladys Hunt, "How To Lead Small Group Bible Studies With Campers," *CCI Focus Series #9*, ©1983 Christian Camping International

Dr. Becca C. Johnson, "Seven Keys To Understanding Child Abuse," *CCI Focus Series #21*, ©1996 Christian Camping International

Marlene LeFever, "Adapting Camp Bible Studies To Individual Learning Styles," *Journal of Christian Camping*, January - February 1988

Virginia Patterson, "Age Group Characteristics: Key to Understanding Kids," *CCI Focus Series #12*, ©1996 Christian Camping International

Alison Short, "Kids Want Fun, But Need Help To Have Fun," reprinted in *Journal of Christian Camping*, November - December, 1988

Alison Short, "Preparing Summer Staff for Camp Ministry," *Journal of Christian Camping*, May - June, 1986

Stan White, "The Counselor's Role in Camper Discipline," *Focus Series #5*, Christian Camping International, Colorado Springs, CO